10-3-74

Reform in Graduate and Professional Education

Lewis B. Mayhew
Patrick J. Ford

Foreword by
Winfred L. Godwin

REFORM IN
GRADUATE AND
PROFESSIONAL
EDUCATION

 Jossey-Bass Publishers
San Francisco • Washington • London • 1974

REFORM IN GRADUATE AND PROFESSIONAL EDUCATION
by Lewis B. Mayhew and Patrick J. Ford

Library of Congress Catalogue Card Number LC 73-20968

International Standard Book Number ISBN 0-87589-213-2

Manufactured in the United States of America

JACKET DESIGN BY WILLI BAUM

FIRST EDITION

Code 7407

The Jossey-Bass
Series in Higher Education

Foreword

The comparative adaptability
of a society's institutions is a measure of its capacity for survival.
As one such institution, education, has increased in complexity
however it has also sometimes shown signs of lessened flexibility
and capacity for adaptation to meet changing needs. The Southern
Regional Education Board (SREB) has for over twenty-five years
attempted to remain sensitive to changing demands upon the
educational structure. One area of concern is in the continuing
quest for curricula responsive to the needs of the educational
clienteles which are served.

Lewis Mayhew's research and insights into curriculum
analysis are widely known. Four SREB contributions of Professor
Mayhew dealing with the undergraduate curriculum have already
been updated and given national attention in the volume *Changing
the Curriculum* (Jossey-Bass, 1971), coauthored with Patrick
Ford. These studies of curriculum analysis, innovation, and response
to social change were largely the outcome of Professor Mayhew's
participation in several SREB workshops and seminars.

In coming to grips with curriculum reform at the graduate
and professional levels, Mayhew and Ford have ventured on terri-
tory well known to constituencies of SREB; recognition of regional

gaps in graduate and professional education first stimulated establishment of the southern regional education compact in 1948. Since then, the board has continuously espoused orderly growth of postbaccalaureate education.

In the seventies, SREB concern with the progress of postbaccalaureate education began with two provocative contributions: first, a resounding charge by Lyman Glenny, at the 1970 SREB annual meeting, that graduate education has in many states prospered at the expense of undergraduate education; and, second, publication of two SREB research monographs by Mayhew, one delineating efforts to implement curriculum modifications for continuing relevance of professional training, and a similar excursion into the subject of reform in graduate education.

The board has heeded challenges to the Topsylike growth of advanced degree programs through regulatory activities such as a regional clearinghouse for interstate exchange of information on new and terminated doctoral programs and by publishing periodic reports on comparative productivity of academic programs. It is pursuing development of new procedures for sharing of regional resources through such devices as an academic common market based on waivers of out-of-state tuition.

Because demand for college level manpower in many fields is now standing still or is shrinking, such orderly growth can take place only if individual advanced degree programs remain competitive by taking advantage of all possible organizational and pedagogical improvements and by adapting curriculum content to rapidly changing occupational circumstances. *Reform in Graduate and Professional Education,* a work which draws together and interprets current information on such developments, is a welcome addition to the all too limited body of resources available to higher educational planners today. When a social institution like education is still able to generate the honest self-criticism and constructive insight into procedures for adaptation which are here typified, the outlook for the future is hopeful.

WINFRED L. GODWIN
President
Southern Regional Education Board

Preface

R*eform in Graduate and Pro-*
fessional Education is concerned with changes and innovations in
both professional education and graduate education in the arts and
sciences. We had hoped to present a highly unified volume which
would explore common attempts to change or reform both professional and graduate schools. But it quickly became apparent that
despite continuing criticisms of graduate education in the polemical
literature, actual change, innovation, and efforts to reform were not
nearly so evident in graduate schools or divisions of arts and
sciences as was the case in the professional schools. Hence we have
divided the book so as to consider the issues and practices evolving
in professional education primarily in the earlier chapters and to
treat the problems of graduate education almost exclusively in the
later chapters.

Our effort to perceive common elements in educational
reform in professional fields was first stimulated by casual reading
of several critiques of professional education, where we found that
critics of legal, medical, theological, and engineering education were
dealing with similar deficiencies and searching for equally similar
means of remedial action. Some professional fields have been par-

ticularly active in producing serious and detailed recommendations
for change. Thus, the earlier chapters of *Reform in Graduate and
Professional Education* test in a preliminary and tentative way this
hypothesis: as professional schools and their organizations and
spokesmen attempt curricular reform, they experiment with similar
methods which, in the aggregate, suggest a new and generally
applicable model or pattern.

These chapters on professional education are intended to
stimulate further thought about the nature of professional education, curricular reform, and close cooperation between the various
professional fields. They are also intended to help professional
faculties considering the range of possibilities for reform, and we
hope they will stimulate detailed study of the individual professional
fields so that gradually a truly composite picture may emerge.

Because experimentation in graduate education is difficult
to discover and systematic evaluation of experimentation is virtually
unavailable, the later chapters of this book are considerably more
inferential than the earlier ones dealing with professional education;
and yet, in the aggregate, the criticisms, recommendations, and
beginnings of experimentation present a consistent picture which,
when combined with reforms in undergraduate education and professional education, suggest desirable and likely modifications in
graduate education.

The chapters dealing primarily with graduate education
were also written as an aid to faculty and administrators who must
plan graduate programs in the future, and while we do make
suggestions and recommendations, they are intended chiefly to raise
questions and to suggest ways by which graduate curricula may be
examined and changed. Thus our discussion of graduate education
is not a definitive statement, but a connecting link between the body
of serious but unsystematic criticisms of graduate education of the
past and what may become a thorough analysis of change in
graduate education in the future.

Overall, we have found that there is a great deal of discussion concerning possible reforms; and we have found, especially in
professional schools, a great deal of actual experimentation. But we
have found little systematic evaluation of some of the experiments
which have been undertaken. We hope that our book will prove

useful not only because it suggests possible changes to faculties but also because it underscores the need for systematic evaluation.

In *Reform in Graduate and Professional Education* we have combined materials contained in two works by the senior author for the Southern Regional Education Board, *Changing Practices in Education for the Professions* and *Reform in Graduate Education*, with recently developed information. We are deeply grateful to the Southern Regional Education Board, and we hope that the present volume is a respectable sequel to those earlier reports. We also owe a debt of gratitude to Jane K. White, who so generously assisted in the preparation of the final manuscript.

Stanford, California LEWIS B. MAYHEW
Berkeley, California PATRICK J. FORD
January 1974

Contents

Reform in Graduate and Professional Education

I

The Professions

Not since 1910 when Abraham Flexner published his report on *Medical Education in the United States and Canada,* and thereby brought about drastic reform in the nation's medical schools, has there been as much need and as great an opportunity for reform of professional education. The public, practitioners, and the professoriate, each in response to different spurs, have pointed out weaknesses and malfunctioning of formal education for both the older professions such as law, medicine, and theology, and the emerging professions such as social work, library science, nursing, and business. To clarify the factors forcing curricular reconsideration, we must first delineate the nature of the professions in relation to the traditional purposes of professional education.

Nature of the Professions

Not all vocations can or should be considered professions, nor do all generally accepted professions conform exactly to a

1

theoretical ideal. There are, however, some recognized characteristics of a profession that have a direct bearing on the curricular problems and needs facing formal professional education. There is a systematized body of knowledge related to each profession which entails its recognition as a learned profession. Thus, the professional school must do more than develop technical competencies. However, each profession does use an accepted and unique set of standardized procedures for practice. Hence, the school must develop skill in using these techniques. The claim of the professions to provide unique and specialized services is based ultimately on public acceptance of their authority and integrity. Professional education must, therefore, maintain public acceptance of the professions.

There are two other essential characteristics of a profession. The first is a self-generated and maintained set of ethical principles that direct the profession to serve society and to safeguard the public when it accepts the advice or service offered. The second is that members of a profession constitute a group with an ethos of its own that enables the individual practitioner to feel a deep and lifelong commitment to the practices and life-modes of the profession. Both are exceedingly difficult to bring about within the framework of formal professional education.

Further educational demands occur as various occupational groups seek professional status. Here, a reasonably consistent pattern emerges. One of the hallmarks of a profession is an intellectual detachment that enables the practitioner to remain objective and not too personally involved in an individual case. This detachment derives from universal or theoretical elements as contrasted with the particular or the immediate. As Hughes writes: "Inside most professions there develops a tacit division of labor between the more theoretical and the more practical; once in a while conflict breaks out over issues related to it. The professional schools may be accused of being too academic. The academics accuse other practitioners of failure to be sufficiently intellectual."[1]

This division of professional labor leads inexorably to formal educational requirements. The scope of degrees is increased and the time of preparation before entry into a profession is expanded so that the aspirant can obtain the needed theoretical or universal

[1] Everett C. Hughes, "Professions," *Daedalus,* Fall 1963, 661.

knowledge as well as the practical skills that the public really demands. Greater emphasis is also placed on the academic ability of students, and established as well as aspiring professional groups compete briskly for recruits. Thus, a generally accepted, if not always stated, criterion of an occupation's movement toward professional status is how selective the training institutions can be. Pusey, in a highly critical report on theological education for the Episcopal Church, complained that the ministry was ceasing to be professional, in part because its schools were forced to accept too large a proportion of applicants having a "C" or poorer record in undergraduate work.[2]

Purposes of Professional Education

Two over-arching aims of professional education define the parameters of the curricular problem. Professional education, if it is to justify itself to society, must attract sufficient entrants to insure an adequate supply of practitioners, and must produce graduates able to discharge the duties of the profession with success.

McGlothlin argues that several principles for professional education can be derived from each of these two aims. From the aim of sufficient quantity: Professional schools, in obtaining a monopoly for qualifying entrants for the profession, also assumed the obligation of supplying enough entrants. They must therefore cooperate with members of the profession to insure sufficient numbers of students in the schools. All feasible methods, including reorganization of the ways professional services are provided, should be tried to help offset the shortages that plague the professions and therefore the society they serve. From the aim of quality: Professional education should be directed toward significant objectives, including professional competence, understanding of society, ethical behavior, and scholarly concern. A professional school should periodically review its procedures and programs and make such modifications as are needed to insure that they are contributing fully to movement toward those objectives. Each of the objectives is valid, but professional schools have been more accustomed to emphasizing professional competence

[2] Nathan M. Pusey and Charles L. Taylor, *Ministry for Tomorrow* (New York: Seabury, 1967), p. 71.

than the others. Additional effort should be directed toward the other objectives to increase the overall quality of programs. In conclusion, a program of professional education cannot ignore either the aim of quantity or the aim of quality. It must establish a flexible balance between them, but it cannot allow quality to drop below an essential minimum level.[3]

Persistent Problems in Professional Education

Professional schools must modify their curricula to cope with both long-existent problems as well as recently emerging ones. The present entrenchment of professional education within the national fabric is pointed out by McGlothlin who predicts six developments in the immediate future: (1) The demands of society for professionally educated persons will continue to increase but these demands cannot be met without substantial change in professional educational programs. (2) The professions as now organized will continue with such modification as occurs coming through evolution rather than through cataclysmic change. (3) The knowledge on which practice of the professions is based will continue to expand. (4) The knowledge and skill required for practice of a profession are too complex to be transmitted by apprenticeship. (5) No one can precisely predict the future life of an individual, but his occupation will probably be that for which he obtains professional education. In addition, professional people will be leaders in civic affairs. (6) Professional education can satisfy both occupational and general aims. It can help students to obtain knowledge and skills required by professional practice and to develop appropriate attitudes towards a sense of professional commitment.

McGlothlin's sanguine view assumes the solution of a number of problems both in the professions and in professional education itself. The first problem is finding objectives for a profession that are acceptable to its members and to the society the profession serves. Second, there is the problem of attaining the uniqueness that is so essential for an occupation to qualify as a profession. Uniqueness must come through the educational program that will help those

[3] William J. McGlothlin, *The Professional Schools* (New York: Center for Applied Research, 1964), p. 31.

who follow it render a unique service that is substantive rather than purely formal. Third, the profession must win recognition without which it cannot perform its essential services or select highly qualified potential members. Without recognition, the place of a professional school on a university campus is jeopardized—witness the long struggle of schools of education to be accepted as full academic partners—and financial support is hard to acquire and hold.

As professions and professional schools seek recognition they encounter still another problem—that of standards. Professional service implies service of a special order requiring competence that has been rigorously tested before the professional is admitted to practice. But this raises the question: What connection actually exists between educational standards and professional performance standards? There is increasing evidence of a wide gulf between academic standards maintained by the professional schools and the actual standards of performance in successful practice.

This matter of standards or quality must be considered conjointly with the problem of supply. Professional schools must recruit enough students to meet demands for service, but they must be students who can profit from the programs offered. In the past, it has been estimated that no more than ten percent of the population has the ability to be educated for professional service but, as shall be seen, this estimate fails both to meet increased societal demands for more professional people and to take into account newer notions of the nature of potential talent.

A particularly vexing problem for professional education is the relative importance of theory and skill. The question as to which of these two aspects of professional concern should be emphasized has had an almost pendulum-like quality. Currently there is evidence that a number of professional schools have moved too far in the direction of theory, and some reform now represents attempts to moderate that swing. However, professional schools can and have erred in the direction of overemphasis on practice, resulting in a "how-to-do-it" procedure that limits members in adapting to changed conditions.

A related problem is that of specialization, including the questions of how much and at what point preparation for specialization should be undertaken. Once again a pendulum-like trend becomes apparent, with the tendency in one generation for specialization to come early in the educational career while in other times specialization occurs much later. Frequently the professions collectively reveal a conflicting pattern. Thus, at the same time that some engineering educators are arguing for a four-year curriculum of engineering science with specialization either in graduate school or on the job, medical education, by making the curriculum more flexible, is encouraging students to begin or at least to anticipate specialization within the first year of their medical school career.

The very fact that professional schools are located within universities raises questions of relationships, and these in turn have curricular significance. The definition of a profession as a self-determining collectivity requires considerable autonomy for the professional school. Yet the university has a stake in such things as standards of admissions, qualifications of faculty, and characteristics and expense of the curriculum. The matter of conferral of degrees is illustrative. According to a purist view of the autonomy of professions, the professional schools should be able to set graduation requirements and determine when students have achieved them. Yet the university may wish to impose quality control judgments to avoid inequality of standards between its associated professional schools. The curricular implications are seen in the establishment of proper relationships between the professional schools and the college of liberal arts and its graduate school. The university will generally maintain that a reasonably heavy increment of liberal arts education should be part of the experience of each graduate. Such heavy increments reduce time for purely professional work and are all too frequently judged inappropriate by professional faculty members when this work in the arts and sciences is offered outside the professional school.

Last, the professions and the professional schools must solve problems of relationships with other professions and with the sub-professions. Some professions are frankly competitive for functions. Psychiatry and clinical psychology are illustrative. As complex human problems requiring professional services become more and more interdisciplinary the problem of relationships will become more acute. Then, increasingly, professional practice will require the services of many workers trained somewhat differently from the professional person himself. Engineers, architects, dentists, and teachers all require assistants of various sorts. This raises the question as to who should prepare these assistants and whether some professional assistants should be encouraged ultimately to seek full professional recognition. The problem seems particularly acute in nursing, which now views itself as a profession, although its practitioners are typically used at the discretion of and for the service of the medical profession. Involved in these relationships is the matter of continuing professional education: Who should provide it and how should it be financed? Given the rapid expansion of relevant knowledge for the professions, it seems axiomatic that continuing education is essential, yet few institutions within the university structure have been able to institutionalize continuing education in all professional fields requiring it.[4]

Forces for Change

Assuming that these perennial problems could be solved, there would still be powerful forces for radical change in professional education. First, it has become apparent that a society as complex as that of the United States must establish national goals for at least a decade in advance if it is going to enjoy the quality of life its people want. Consider the sixteen national fields for which various agencies have helped to articulate goals: (1) agriculture, (2) area redevelopment, (3) consumer expenditure, (4) education, (5) health, (6) housing, (7) international aid, (8) manpower retraining, (9) national defense, (10) natural resources, (11) private plant and equipment, (12) research and development, (13) social welfare, (14) space exploration, (15) transportation, (16) urban development. Lecht finds that "not enough manpower will be available in the next decade if the American people and their government try to achieve simultaneously all standards that knowledgeable people regard as desirable and reasonable in the various areas defined as

[4] This discussion of problems is based on G. Lester Anderson, "Professional Status and Continuing Problems," in G. Lester Anderson and others (Eds.), *Education for the Professions,* Sixty-First Yearbook of the National Society for the Study of Education (Chicago: University of Chicago Press, 1962), pp. 14–24.

national goals."[5] But even assuming that the manpower were available, the professional schools seem presently unable to create the requisite educational programs to prepare high level personnel to grapple with these interdisciplinary and interfield problems.

Two of the basic assumptions on which the whole edifice of formal professional education is based is that individuals with potential for professional work can be identified and that the work offered in the professional schools assures successful professional performance. Yet these assumptions have recently come into serious question.

Admission into professional schools has been largely based on intelligence or academic aptitude in the hope that the more intelligent would be the more creative. MacKinnon and others, however, have found little relationship between intelligence and creative achievement. In describing their researches, MacKinnon states: "Among creative architects who have a mean score of 113 on the Terman Concept Mastery Test, individual scores range widely from 39 to 179. Yet scores on this measure of intelligence correlate negatively, a minus .08, with rated creativity. Over the whole range of intelligence and creativity there is, of course, a positive relationship between the two variables. No feeble-minded subjects have shown up in any of our creative groups. It is clear, however, that above a certain required minimum level of intelligence which varies from field to field and in some instances may be surprisingly low, being more intelligent does not guarantee a corresponding increase in creativeness. It just is not true that the more intelligent person is necessarily the more creative one."[6]

Successful performance in colleges, including professional schools, has historically been indicated by grades, on the assumption that success in courses was predictive of successful performance at work. But this also has come into question. Hoyt generalizes after a careful review of most of the available studies of the relationship between college success to post-college accomplishment that "we can

[5] Leonard A. Lecht, *Manpower Needs for National Goals in the 1970s* (New York: Praeger, 1969).

[6] Donald W. MacKinnon, "The Nature and Nurture of Creative Talent," in Dael Wolfle (Ed.), *Discovery of Talent* (Cambridge, Mass.: Harvard University Press, 1969), pp. 192–193.

safely conclude that college grades have no more than a very modest correlation with adult success, no matter how defined. Refinements in experimental methodology are extremely unlikely to alter that generalization. At best they may determine some of the conditions under which a low positive rather than a zero correlation is obtained."[7] Berg reinforces this point in an elaborate study of education and job performance in a number of vocations ranging from unskilled, blue collar to professional and managerial. He finds that by and large relationships are positively minimal or slightly negative between job performance and length and level of education.[8] If such studies are further validated, professional schools, if they are to continue to warrant the support and regard they have obtained in the past, will be forced into radical revision of the entire process of education, beginning with techniques of admissions and extending to organization of courses and requirements for graduation.

The third force pressuring professional education to change is the insistent demand on the part of the black and other culturally deprived minority groups for a fair share of the American society. The overall cultural and health deprivation in which the large minority black population has been reared has not provided the training and experience needed to survive successfully professional curricula as currently presented. Black youth was typically not motivated to seek professional education; hence, for years professional schools did not feel obligated to make specific provisions for students with less than adequate backgrounds. Now, however, with a new social ethos which requires professional schools to increase radically the proportion of black youth admitted, the issue appears poignantly.

Historically, professional schools have evolved in the United States in consonance with Western civilization and indeed frequently even more narrowly in consonance with white Anglo-Saxon Protestant values. The emerging black community, searching for an education, including a professional education that is derivative from

---

[7] Donald P. Hoyt, *The Relationship Between College Grades and Adult Achievement: A Review of the Literature* (Iowa City: American College Testing Program, 1965), p. 45.

[8] Ivor Berg, *Education and Jobs: The Great Training Robbery* (New York: Praeger, 1970).

their own black cultural experience, has placed demands difficult and perhaps impossible to meet during the 1970s. The argument and the challenge is eloquently put by LeMelles who remarks:

> The unprecedented prospect for progressive change in higher education for the black American over the next decade should not obscure the magnitude of the problem. Reorientation of an entire education sub-system cannot be achieved without painful frustration and some agony. To obtain genuine and lasting results, radically creative steps will have to be taken to give new direction and to compensate both quantitatively and qualitatively for past deficiencies. Some leadership and the input of major resources will not suffice to permit the black colleges to attain their true objectives. The tutelary approach to education, which resulted from the worst influences conspiring to miseducate black youth and which has generally characterized a significant segment of traditional Negro educational leadership is no longer tenable and more of the same would undoubtedly be disastrous. The fallacy of the mere application of large sums of money to correct complex problems without fully understanding how such funds should be applied has been lamentably illustrated in the recently lost war on poverty. The kind of leadership that will perform the innovative role that black higher education needs must be distinctively different from that leadership of the past which accepted the limitations placed upon the status of black Americans, and it is for this reason that this book insists that a black educational leadership, distinctively different in its ideals, in its perception of the status of black Americans, and in its willingness to provide new directions, is alone capable of exercising such high responsibility at this crucial juncture in the destiny of black America.[9]

A related force, whose true significance is not yet clear, is the tidal wave of student dissent, protest, and unrest which has characterized American college campuses to a greater and lesser degree since 1964. The student cry for greater relevance in the curriculum would apparently have implications for the professional schools, but

---

[9] Tilden J. LeMelles and Wilburt LeMelles, *The Black College: A Strategy for Relevancy* (New York: Praeger, 1969), pp. 15–16.

this implication is tempered by the frequently observed phenomenon that protesting students typically came from the non-professional schools, especially from the humanities and social sciences, and that the greatest support for existing institutional practices came from such professional fields as medicine, engineering, business, and law. However, students are now included in policy-making bodies of professional as well as liberal arts schools, and since student protest is finally focusing on curricular matters and on university preoccupation with training for a distrusted establishment, it is likely that student opinion will eventually force a reconsideration of professional curricula.

Among the recognized forces driving professional schools to reform is the technological revolution and the exponential increase in knowledge or relevant information. While the manifestation of these are legion, the successful attempts of professional fields to respond are few. Simple expansion of the time required for professional preparation is no solution, as medicine and engineering have discovered. At the rate knowledge is produced today, a student would require a lifetime for even partial coverage. Nor is ever more refined specialization the answer. Both the professions and the society need generalists and specialists who can understand the contributions of other specialties. Professional schools must therefore search for new ways of organizing information so that students can perceive broad dimensions and develop skills to acquire special knowledge when necessary in the future. They must also discover ways of preparing new sorts of generalists such as doctors' assistants or nurses turned general practitioners who can provide service or appropriate referral to patients. Finally, they must tackle the problem of introducing to the curriculum pertinent knowledge previously unknown or considered esoteric.

The technological revolution has produced an array of problems which require both professional attention and technical aids to solve them, and professional students must learn both, in addition to much previously found to be necessary. For example, new areas of professional concern are created by legal questions involving noise from jet aircraft, medical problems arising from pollution of the environment and radioactive fallout, and agricultural problems caused by the use of DDT and other pesticides. Similarly, technical aids for professional practice, only recently available, such as television as an instructional tool, or the computer as a medical diagnostic device, will require detailed training in their use. The curricular demands thus created are large, but the demands from the logical expansion of technology in the future will be predictably much greater.

Technological developments and the related increase in knowledge, as well as other changes in social structure, also call for more extensive professional services which older ways of training people cannot meet. A change in political attitude regarding human welfare results in a drastic increase in need for social workers beyond the capacity of existing schools. Concentration of the majority of people in urban areas attracts professional workers, but leaves other regions undersupplied, but with increasing expectations for professional services. The schools must somehow persuade and prepare people to work in the ghettos, rural areas, and small towns.

Many of these changes invoke criticisms of professional education as it has been practiced during the first half of the twentieth century. Medical schools aided by federal grants are said to have become so preoccupied with research as to contribute seriously to a general decline of medical care in the United States. Law schools have not prepared their students to deal with the revolutionary age of the 1970s. Schools of education have not produced teachers to cope effectively with universal education. Engineering schools, through emphasis on theory and research, are accused of contributing to a general decline in the relative worldwide industrial position of the United States.

Reflecting a basic pragmatism in American character, professional education in the past has been highly practical. Professional schools were created to produce practitioners, and students enrolled in them to prepare for work. There was little in the ethos of professional education to suggest a learned profession of intellectuals. Also uniquely American was the notion of producing a uniform, standardized professional person through a series of required courses presumed to bring about the qualities the profession itself required. These two beliefs brought about a highly prescribed curriculum stressing more application than theory with little or no time in the curriculum for any liberalizing subjects, which faculties usually considered could be provided by a separate faculty in the undergraduate school.

Consistent with the American system, professional schools placed their main emphasis on formally organized courses, which were professor centered and based upon the disciplinary treatment of a textbook. While it has gradually become obvious that specialization was the rule in professional practice, in professional schools the textbook core of required courses seemed to presume a common professional career for all graduates.

The curriculum was compartmentalized in time. Preprofessional and general education courses came first, followed by basic science, theory, and applied courses. When these requirements were out of the way, students were presumed to know enough to undertake practical, working assignments, either in school or on the job. The possibility that these elements of study and experience might be mixed was not a popular idea and in several fields is still not well regarded.

Reforms in professional education, current knowledge of developmental needs of students, and prevailing curricular theory all support a new attitude toward the curricula of professional schools. A psychological rather than a logical structure seems desirable.

Ideally, a new student in the professional field needs some direct guidance as to the nature of the field, some early practice in the field, and the opportunity to select for himself a concentration and a way to achieve it. This does not mean any reduction in essential basic theory or science, but it does suggest a different ordering of such work and in differing proportions. It also dictates a reduction in the sheer amount of material previously held to be essential. Much of the rationale for intensive prescription was the belief that all professional students should first of all be prepared as generalists. Since such a belief is contrary both to reality and to what students perceive as reality, a freer system is appropriate. Once students have accustomed themselves to professional study, their own experience will order an essential structure. This, of course, has been the process established in the successful experimental undergraduate colleges in the past, and it seems realistic for professional schools as well.

If this free elective system is honestly put into effect and the full resources of the university made available to professional students, several results can be expected. A smaller full-time faculty could accommodate a larger number of students by exploiting opportunities throughout the university. The Stanford School of Education enjoys a high reputation and high productivity with a relatively small faculty. Its students are literally forced to do considerable work outside the school, and the newly established freedom of election makes this possible. As students gained insights from different fields a natural approach to interdisciplinary work could evolve which could then bring professors from the various fields into greater concert.

Also, relevancy can be achieved through practice. Many professional schools have drifted away from reality just as the arts and the sciences have become excessively academic. As a general rule the various elements of the curriculum—arts and sciences, professional arts, and application—should focus on actual practice. This clearly means that a change from a preoccupation with basic research in professional schools is necessary and that even those students who will proceed to research careers will first have a grounding in practice.

At times those in professional schools may be forced to confront colleagues in the sciences and arts with a demand to direct their work to meet the needs of professional students. When faculties in the arts and sciences will not yield, the professional schools will be forced to the expensive expedient of offering courses which recognize the validity of application. But the thrust of student and social pressure in the 1970s is such that all elements of the university are likely to become sensitive to real human problems, including the needs of professional schools.

From the two elements of psychological structuring of materials and experiencing of reality comes a third reform: focusing on problems in an eclectic or interdisciplinary way. Thus, the professional curriculum increasingly should insure that real problems in the profession are presented early and that student search for solution is many-faceted.

II

Unresolved Issues

Issues of national and social policy and of relationships in the professions are particularly pressing. First, there is the matter of social need and numbers of professionals. Second, there is the relationship of professional schools to the professions and universities. Both these issues entail curricular considerations.

Problems of Policy and Relationships

A major argument for the great expansion of higher education in the United States since the end of World War II has been the claim that a technological society needed the trained manpower which only education could produce, and the argument is even more impressive with respect to the professions. A society with increasing expectations of health, education, and welfare service requires more and more doctors, nurses, teachers, and social workers, and looks to professional schools to provide them.

But this simple sounding aphorism conceals unanswered

15

questions. We must know how many doctors and nurses we really need. Is there really a shortage in the medical fields or is there widespread misuse or inappropriate deployment of existing professional talent? Further, knowing the needs of the immediate future is not enough. What are the likely needs for people in the several professions ten and twenty years ahead? The professional schools must prepare to meet these requirements. The potentialities for error here, of course, are enormous because of rapidly changing social and economic conditions. Engineers, once in oversupply, became a scarce commodity only to reappear in oversupply, all within two decades. The 1960s began with a presumed critical shortage of teachers while some dozen years later highly qualified Ph.D.'s search for jobs even vaguely related to their training.

Social pressures for an ever-increasing number of professionals also bear on the standards maintained by professional schools. If a serious shortage of professional workers develops due to a change in national policy, as when federal welfare programs increased the demand for social work specialists, should long maintained degree requirements be modified to accelerate the production of needed workers? If more and better professionals are needed, are institutions justified in experimenting with new instructional devices that might make training more efficient? To what extent should the professional schools in the United States concern themselves with the production of or utilization of foreign professionals? And if they should, how should they modify their curricula appropriately? There seems general agreement that more of all sorts of professionals will be needed, but there is very little agreement about questions of standards and training.

A further complicating factor is the changing nature of professional work. Professions are finding it harder to discipline their members because of the wide variety of subspecialties which have emerged, each with its own demands for training in its own esoteric language which shuts each off from the parent profession and other subspecialties. Thus, the professional schools, which once could offer a general core curriculum, must now offer many different curricula during a period of uncertainty as to appropriate content. Also, there is evidence of a steady commercialization of professional practice. Previously, professions maintained an olympian posture of placing the needs of clients ahead of all other considerations. Ethical questions were easily resolved according to that posture. As more and more professionals have descended from Olympus to the marketplace, the professional schools must now consider new and better ways to socialize new members.[1]

The question of the relationship of professional schools to the professions centers on three unsettled issues. First is the question of content. While there is general agreement that the professional school should prepare future practitioners, there is friction over what the content should be. If the school becomes too academic, it alienates the profession, but if it swings too far in the direction of application, it jeopardizes its reputation with other academics and with prospective students. If the professional school conforms too closely to the requirements of standardized accreditation (which is the sanction of the profession) it puts itself at odds with its own university relationships and with student demands for curricular relevance. However, to ignore accrediting bodies could jeopardize the ultimate success of its graduates.

Second, there is tension over the role of the professional school as innovator within the profession. The mythology of higher education holds the university to be a critic of society and an agent of social change. However, it has not generally been so, nor have its professional schools helped change professional practice. Professional schools have usually been content to codify and pass on conventional lore to insure that their graduates are fully accepted both by the profession and by the licensing agencies.

Third, there is difference of opinion as to who should be a faculty member in a professional school. To take an example, the Stanford University School of Education is research oriented, so when it looked for a professor of junior college education, it wanted a publishing scholar. None could be found within the ranks of junior college administrators, so a publishing scholar who had had minimal contact with a private junior college was appointed. On account of this appointment, leaders among California junior college presidents attempted to boycott the Stanford program in

---

[1] This series of points is based on T. Keith Glennan (Ed.), *The Professional School and World Affairs* (Albuquerque: University of New Mexico Press, 1967), pp. 374–379.

junior college administration and even tried to jeopardize funds for the program. Very likely the trend is away from appointing practitioners to professional posts, and if it continues, new devices such as practical internships for young professors will be necessary to link the practicing professional to the professional school.

There are also unsolved and almost overpowering problems in the relationship of professional schools to the university. The magnitude of these difficulties is related by Rosenstein in connection with a study of engineering at UCLA.

The pressures upon the personnel of the professional colleges have become overpowering. The flight from teaching is well documented and the effects upon both undergraduate and graduate programs have been accumulating. It is easier to teach a mathematics or a science course than a professional course with open-ended problems. It is easier to concentrate in a specialized scientific area than to undertake the solution of substantial professional problems with a slower paper production rate. The young assistant professor has little choice. Faced with the perils of publish or perish, only the foolhardy will assume a professional stance.

Professors, like all other living organisms, tend to replicate themselves. One cannot expect a young professor who has gone directly from his Ph.D. to teaching without any professional experience to produce anything other than a Ph.D. with little understanding of the profession in which he has little desire to practice. The in-breeding consequences of the past two decades have influenced the professional curriculum. In engineering, for example, the undergraduate mathematics and science courses have received a long overdue renovation and modernization. On the other hand, the older empirically based engineering subjects have been discarded and too often have not been replaced with a modern professional stem.

The long term consequence for the professions is evident, for it is apparent that the professional schools cannot play the pure science game and survive. Nor is survival of a school for its own sake important. If the professional schools have nothing more to teach than science or mathematics or even humanities, it is doubtful that they can do a better job than the respective schools of science, mathematics, or humanities. If engineering colleges have nothing more to offer than science and mathematics or if there is nothing distinctive about any of their courses, if there is no professional design stem then the engineering school can never hope to be anything other than a second-rate school of science. Neither a change of title nor a retreat to the graduate school could hide the inferior quality or the lack of purpose and prevent the profession's ultimate departure from first-rate universities.

The raison-d'état of a professional school is not easily found in course content. On the contrary, the curriculum reflects the faculty's interpretation of the school's missions. An investigation of the role and function of the professions in the university and in society tried to determine the distinguishing features the professions had in common and to examine in detail the differences between the professions on the one hand and the sciences and the humanities on the other. The question was posed, "Is education for the professions an anachronism that should be retired?" Within the university the separate existence of the professional schools cannot be justified on the basis of the search for truth. The professions can draw support only from the American tradition of service to the community.[2]

Curricular Issues

Specific curricular issues are so closely interrelated that we cannot order issues according to importance.

High among the issues is the question of whether the professional school should concentrate on either preparing for initial job competence or providing students with a broad base of principles to facilitate long-range growth and development. This question seems especially critical in such fields as engineering, nursing, and law. As Associate of Arts degree programs in nursing have begun to produce on-line nurses, the institutions granting bachelor's degrees have moved in the direction of training supervisory nurses and nursing administrators. But if too much time is spent on organizational theory, personnel psychology, and the theory of management, the program may not develop the high technical competence the young

[2] Allen B. Rosenstein, *A Study of Progression and Professional Education* (Los Angeles: University of California Press, 1969), Vol. 2, pp. 6–8.

nurse needs in her first position. Similarly, the rationale for undergraduate programs in engineering to stress broad engineering science
together with the humanities and social sciences is to provide a base
upon which long and constantly changing engineering careers can be
built. But such a curriculum may fail to meet the expectations of
first employers that the graduates they hire will function effectively soon after starting to work. And, of course, young lawyers
have long complained that their legal education, grounded in case-
work and precedent, does not provide the skills to draw a will, plead
a case, or counsel with a client.

This issue, of course, is just a reformulation of the problem
of balance within professional curricula. McGlothlin has characterized professional education as consisting of three parts: the basic
arts and sciences, the professional sciences, and application.[3] But he
offers little help as to how a balance can be achieved, nor do the
actual practices of the various professions provide guidelines of
proportion. Architecture, for example, devotes 12 percent to arts
and sciences and 88 percent to professional sciences. Business generally seems to devote 40 percent to the arts and sciences and 60
percent to the professional sciences, while social work education,
including undergraduate work, gives two-thirds to the arts and
sciences and one-third divided evenly between professional sciences
and application.[4] But even such figures are misleading and provide
little help in resolving the issue. McGrath and others have shown
that what professional faculty members most desire for students are
really the basic biological sciences for agriculture and medicine, and
social and historical sciences for law and social work.[5]

A direction of resolution seems to be emerging from curricular reform although there are counter-currents to it. There is a
tendency to assume more and more graduate work in the professional fields, especially in business, education, and architecture. This
development allows undergraduates to concentrate on a broader
range of the arts and sciences if their faculties concur. However, at

[3] McGlothlin, *The Professional Schools,* p. 36.
[4] McGlothlin, p. 38.
[5] Earl J. McGrath, Paul L. Dressel, and Lewis B. Mayhew, *The Liberal
Arts as Viewed by Faculty Members in Professional Schools* (New York:
Teacher's College, 1959).

the same time, there are counter-tendencies in medicine and law to relax admissions requirements and accept students with less than a bachelor's degree. This has the reverse effect on the proportion of time devoted to the arts and sciences. There are also conflicting tendencies regarding the balance between professional sciences and application. The increase in clinical or field experience suggests a tendency in professional schools to train in application (previously left to the profession itself or to post-graduate training) at the expense of work in the professional sciences. But engineering schools have emphasized engineering science and reduced applied courses that really substituted for clinical experience.

Part of the confusion surrounding this matter of balance stems from the fact that in so many of the professions the responsibility for each of the three types of preparation rests with a different agency accountable only to itself. Thus the exclusively professional graduate schools (medicine, law, dentistry, and, increasingly, business) assume that the undergraduate college will provide appropriate courses and programs for the arts and sciences, but they have no direct control over actual provision of courses. Even in the undergraduate or mixed professional fields (engineering, education, and nursing) separate faculties offer the arts and science courses over which the professional school has virtually no direct control. Since the faculties of liberal arts colleges both within and separate from universities are themselves becoming more professionalized and organize their courses to conform to their own professional goals, the possibility of a seamless educational program for professional work is remote.

Curriculum theory as implied by a number of attempted reforms suggests that professional students should, for example, receive training in the social and behavioral sciences the better to comprehend their future professional practice. But if social and behavioral scientists see as their chief mission the teaching of professional science for future psychologists or sociologists, the assumptions of the professional faculties will be invalidated.

Similarly, in some professions training in application is either done in an agency different from the professional school or has to meet the requirements of a different agency for standards of performance and certification. Engineering, education, theology, law, and to some extent business, assume that training in application will, for the most part, be given elsewhere. In law, medicine, and dentistry, state licensing and certification boards set examination and experience standards without much regard for what the professional school might wish to teach or be able to teach most effectively.

In general, the professional schools know that they must teach broad principles and concepts because there is not time to offer all or even a small part of the specific information which the competent practitioner should command. But without some voice over what the undergraduate college or liberal arts departments will offer or what competencies employers or certifying agencies will accept professional curricular revision must take place almost in a vacuum.

It is this problem which gives an air of unreality to a number of attempted innovations. To say that ethical development is important and that the humanities should have something germane to contribute merely restates the problem. If the professional school does not rely on the undergraduate college, then it must rectify the deficiency itself with a consequent reduction of time for developing more practical skills and a firmer grasp of professional science.

The desire to bring professional schools closer to the university and the few attempts to restructure the university, as well as the decided interest in interdisciplinary and interdepartmental courses, seem designed to bridge the gap between education in arts and sciences and the professional sciences. If faculties of law, medicine, and engineering accept the concept of professional education as an all-university concern and are not adverse to losing some of their traditional independence through such a concept, they may be in a better position to influence or at least know about an important segment of the education of their students. If professional faculty members and humanities faculty members join in offering interde-partmental courses, a few of the fissures might be closed. At the other end of the scale—providing practical experience—the tendency seems to be to intensify practice both early and late in the professional school itself, regardless of the cost in time taken from other important matters.

A troublesome issue in the graduate professional schools is how to train both future research workers and future practitioners in the same school with the same faculty. Graduate schools of education face this problem most acutely. Schools of education in large, established universities were created to produce practitioners— teachers, administrators, and specialists. But as it became apparent that the practice of education might be improved with a broader research base and as schools of education struggled for respectability within the university, they tried to add theory and research approaches to their curricula. Consequently, a few schools have begun to add faculty members who are trained and experienced in one of the research disciplines that are relevant to the professional school: economists to schools of education, sociologists to schools of law, behavioral psychologists to schools of medicine.

However, problems of academic citizenship influence and general orientation of the school immediately arise. If a few social scientists are appointed to a law school, they may be regarded as second-class citizens in the law school; at the same time, they may be viewed as having fallen from the grace of their own discipline. Or, if the disciplinary appointees come to outnumber the application-oriented professors, as has happened in several schools of engineering and education, the interests of the practitioner are jeopardized and the influence of the applied professors attenuated. Further distortion of the balance between practitioner and research faculties has called into question relationships with the field. Practitioners expect schools to provide replacements and to service a number of their applied needs. But a school dominated by research people will consider application and practice as inferior activities which interfere with the important work of the school—research and the preparation of future research workers.

Efforts in reform have as frequently added to this problem as they have helped to solve it. The whole thrust toward more basic science and theory in engineering and medical schools seems to move them to prepare research workers rather than practitioners. The net effect of bringing the social and behavioral sciences into professional fields appears to have strengthened research rather than practice. But earlier clinical work, the descent of professional courses into the undergraduate college, and efforts to provide international experience, seem to be forces in the opposite direction.

Underlying many of the curricular issues of professional

education is the simple matter of accommodating the expanding body of relevant knowledge into the curriculum. Knowledge accumulates so rapidly that, even if human tolerance of study would permit, lengthening the curriculum would be insufficient. Both engineering and medicine have tried this approach, and medicine, at least, seems to have reached such a point of diminishing returns as to reduce admissions. Young people do not relish the thought of waiting until their mid-thirties to complete their formal education.

Many reforms, while still only palliatives, attempt to resolve this curricular issue. Interdisciplinary work might extract the essence of several fields, much as the general education program of the fifties sought to extract the essence of the liberal arts and teach them in two collegiate years. Freedom of election can add the student's own criteria of utility and relevance to the faculty criteria for selection of materials. Some of the new media, such as tape recorders and videotape programmed texts, might shorten or at least rearrange study time. Even attempts to regroup students for curricular purposes are in a way an attempt to cope with the knowledge-time equation. Since students learn so much from each other, why not exploit some free or living time for educational purposes? However, few curricular studies in the professional fields do more than complain about the knowledge issue. We suggest that until they address the problem directly, no solutions will emerge.

A group of problems emerges directly from attempts to add to or enrich clinical or field experience for professional students. The pedagogic values of trial experience for law students at the University of California conflicted with the judicial demand that only licensed lawyers practice at the bar. Financing internships in college administration is a difficult task, as is supervising cadet teachers so that supervisors are present when needed. While library students can gain applied experience and some financial support working part-time in the university library, the relatively small faculty of the library school cannot provide close supervision and the library staff itself is too busy. This limitation applies even more seriously to ministerial training. The harsh reality is that clinical experience is expensive if it is good, and few of the suggested reforms have faced this issue. It may be that simulation of experience through computer and videotape recordings can approximate some values of closely supervised clinical work, but such expedients still miss the essence of field work.

A subissue of this problem of clinical experience is the role of the clinical or supervisory professor in an academic setting. He is appointed on the basis of his experience as a practitioner, yet his experiences are different from and valued less in a modern university than the research and scholarship experiences of academic professors. In schools of education, excellent supervisors have neither time nor inclination to conform to university expectations basic to rewards. The educational clinical professor concept urged by James B. Conant, which provides for some time spent in actual practice and some time on the college campus, has not proved successful.

In schools of medicine, as the emphasis has shifted toward biochemical science, part-time clinical professors have not been able to keep up with the intellectual achievements of the rest of the faculty. But research oriented professors handling clinical work are apt to emphasize the phenomenon being observed rather than the patient, thus developing unfortunate attitudes in medical students. It is a paradox that the more professional education buries itself in science, principle, theory, and research, and the greater the prestige of the particular school, the more difficult it is to maintain the role and usefulness of the practitioner in teaching students. Yet most theories of reform reaffirm the virtues of student contact with the field and with real practitioners.

This matter is confounded by another issue, the amount and nature of research appropriate for professional schools by faculty and students. The point is emphasized by comparing the enormous research achievements of American medical schools with the general decline in the public image of the medical profession and the decline in several indices of national health. In 1950 the United States ranked sixth in infant mortality, in 1961, fifteenth, and in 1967, eighteenth.[6]

This observation holds true for other professional fields. Several of the best known professional schools—education at Columbia, engineering at Stanford, business at Harvard—gained

[6] Rosenstein, *A Study of Progression and Professional Education,* Vol. 2, p. 3.

their influence through direct and continuous concern with the practical problems of the field and through preparing the next generation of highly qualified practitioners, but as these schools turned their efforts toward more and more basic research, contacts with the field waned and the possibility emerged that their overall influence on the professions would ultimately decline.

This is a sensitive matter. Few would argue that research has no place in the professional schools, but evidence mounts that a preoccupation with research leads to rejection of practice or even of concern for practical application of research. It leads the professional faculties to concentrate more on producing new research scholars than on producing the adequately trained professionals society needs. At the same time, reform movements in some professional fields call for more and more research. One major critic of business education, for example, urges that: "The quality of business research must be greatly improved. Research should lead and advance business thought and practice, not follow it. Progress in research will give vitality to the whole of business education. There is need for more active corporate support of business. . . . Retired business executives are not regarded as promising recruits to business school faculties. Whatever their other abilities, they are ordinarily not likely to be outstanding teachers, scholars, or researchers."[7] Nursing, education, social work, and administration make the same plea, and more opportunity for students in professional fields to engage in independent research is also a major suggested reform.

Intrinsic to this problem is the question of emphasis on behaviorism and humanism in professional schools. As professional schools have plunged deep into research, more emphasis has been placed on quantification and rigorously controlled experimentation. For example, research in molecular biology now allows consideration of disease as a mathematical equation without even considering the human being who is ill. Similarly, theorists in legal and business education anticipate the day when legal or decision-making processes can be produced as mathematical models as though human beings were not actively present. This trend toward rigor and quantification

[7] Leonard S. Silk, *The Education of Businessmen* (New York: Committee for Economic Development, 1961), pp. 33–34.

has produced astonishing achievements in the acquisition of new knowledge, but at the expense of developing in students an active concern for the people they should serve. The problem is how to restore humanism to professional education so that students become reawakened to the human beings for whom the profession exists.

A last issue is the question of how long professional education should be and whether varying lengths of time for the different professions are warranted. Actual practice, of course, varies from four years for nursing and forestry to ten years or more for medicine. There seems to be a status element as other professions note the prestige and lengthy training for medicine and ponder such preparation for themselves. Further, there is a tendency for all professional programs to become longer as relevant information increases. However, status is scarcely a defensible criterion for the length of a program, and if utilization of available knowledge were used as a test, all professional curricula could be stretched to a student's lifetime.

Even within a single profession, there are programs of varying lengths. Nurses, for example, may pass the same examinations and enter into active practice after two, three, four, or five years. And both medical and law schools offer programs of varying lengths determined by what undergraduate preparation is required for admission. But there is no available evidence that length of program makes for effective practice.

These issues have reached an impasse; no definitive solutions have been found. Nevertheless, although the various innovations and attempted reforms reveal conflicting tendencies, there does seem to be an emerging pattern, the elements of which we must question.

It seems clear that professional education is drawing closer to the rest of the university to gain strength from relevant disciplines. Hospital schools of nursing are disappearing and nursing educators want virtually all nursing education to be within higher education. Almost all reports on professional education reject the separate trade school concept and indicate that only in a university setting can the requisite interdisciplinary and interdepartmental work be carried on. Professional faculties increasingly resemble professors rather than practitioners, with the role of clinical professor becoming increasingly difficult to maintain.

This means that for the most part professional curricula emphasize basic science and theory rather than applied work in the belief that training in technique is training for obsolescence. Such a posture implies that professional schools are less concerned with developing high competence for a graduate's first job than with providing a base upon which a full but challenging career may be built. Time alone will determine whether this is a tenable decision.

III

Attempted Reforms

Professional education is undergoing major transformation. Not all fields exhibit the same ferment. Librarians and agriculturists do not seem particularly active and not all schools in a professional field accept suggested reforms. But in many of the professions an identity crisis is causing serious curricular experimentation. Declining undergraduate engineering enrollments raise questions about content and method, for example. We do not know whether the experiments will work and professional instruction will improve, but we can describe the attempts under several rubrics.

Overview of Reform

In accordance with the American propensity for solving educational problems with new courses, there is much experimentation with new course and research structures. Interdisciplinary and interfield efforts are particularly popular as when psychiatrists and endocrinologists pool their efforts to teach about thyroid problems; engineers, architects and economists organize a jointly-taught sequence on urban planning; and professors from schools of business and education blend insights about the art of administration and decision-making.

Perhaps the most active cooperation is in the social and behavioral sciences. Medical educators have finally recognized that health and disease are as much social as biological matters, and now seek to use psychology, sociology and anthropology in the basic curriculum. Law schools, which had remained aloof and withdrawn from the rest of the university, have begun to bestow the accolade of law professorships on economists, political scientists, and even, as at the University of Denver, on a sociologist. Education and social work, once preoccupied with the psychological bases of professional practice, seek greater contributions from sociology and anthropology, since human change and betterment cannot be accomplished without awareness of how groups, societies, and cultures organize themselves.

In the past, graduate professional faculties disdained undergraduate teaching, on the ground that preprofessional work could safely be left to others, especially since the basic science and theory needed for professional work had to be retaught anyway. But a real detente seems in the making. At Wisconsin, Berkeley, Denver, and Northwestern, professors in law and the social sciences have created interdisciplinary courses for undergraduates on such subjects as social policy. At Stanford, distinguished historians, economists, engineers, and lawyers have created a joint sequence on international affairs.

This reawakened concern for younger students is also present in other undergraduate professional schools. Engineering educators continue the search for ways to make the undergraduate curriculum an effective blend of humanities, social sciences, and broad engineering science, leaving specialization for graduate training or work experience. Reformers in theological education see the need for a program beginning at the undergraduate level to help students think in a theological framework. They are likewise coming to see the wisdom of providing an intense period of clinical pastoral education early within the graduate program to help students decide vocational issues. Some of these divinity schools are adding Directors of Field Education or clinical professors to their instructional staffs to coordinate the preparation for active ministry. Equally practice-centered are the decisions of social work to reintroduce undergraduate social work courses and the attempts of a few law schools to offer undergraduate courses to prepare paralegal workers.

Then, too, the professional fields have finally begun to realize the contributions that the humanities long claimed they could make to the attitudes, values, ethics, and indeed the humaneness of professional people. Some educators recommend that half the undergraduate curriculum in business should be outside the professional field, and that business students should be encouraged to study art, literature, and philosophy. An applied humanities sequence at the University of California at Los Angeles seeks to show through historical study the interaction of ethics, politics and aesthetics with engineering. Some medical schools have expressed this same concern by revising admission requirements so that bright students who majored in the humanities are as acceptable to medical school as those who took organic chemistry, comparative anatomy, and the ubiquitous scientific German.

Reformers in professional education are trying many ways to reorganize and reallocate students' time. In the past, especially in engineering, medicine, and law, the prescribed curriculum was so tightly scheduled that an unfortunate lapse at registration time might jeopardize a student's chances of graduating. Now greater flexibility and freedom of election is the rule. Not all doctors need to know the details of gross anatomy, so why make it a requirement? There is the aphorism that the better the lawyer, the less he is inclined to "know the law" in the sense of possessing vast amounts of legal detail, so why require many detailed courses? Since it is true that few engineers stay with the same specialty they studied as students, why not give them a greater choice of electives?

However, more than freedom seems necessary. Much curricular thinking has been restricted by the traditional requirements of the academic calendar—four years of two semesters each. Attempts to break this pattern have been made and might even force some rethinking about curricula and teaching. Yale now views its medical program as consisting of three blocks rather than four. The architecture program at Princeton is comprised of three modules extending over six years rather than the previous monolithic five years of rigidly prescribed work. Not all medical students need a bachelor's degree nor even the junior year of undergraduate work, and some find the senior year of medicine a waste of time since it duplicates what they will do as graduate interns and residents. The Harvard Medical School is seriously considering making such freedom from required time demands possible, and respectable. Although the trimester has not proved the panacea some hoped it would be for undergraduate education, trimesters of fifteen weeks can enable students to finish an undergraduate curriculum in engineering science and a master's degree in an engineering specialty in less than the five years that the undergraduate engineering sequence had required.

There is some experimentation with a common curricular stem for related professional specialization. Not unlike the earlier suggested common undergraduate work in engineering science as a stem for graduate or employment specialization is the idea that a common first two years in basic health science might be appropriate for future dentists, doctors, and research workers in health. The Dean of the School of Dentistry of the University of Missouri at Kansas City sees this arrangement as a logical outgrowth of a center for Health Science. Some theorists in social work education are also convinced that a common undergraduate preparation for social workers, nurses, legal aid workers, and others in related professions could be useful if departmental barriers could be broken down.

Common experiences, more interdisciplinary work, and better articulation between the professional and undergraduate years suggest that appropriate administrative and organizational structure must be developed. Reformers agree that traditional school and departmental structure is divisive and tends to compartmentalize student thinking; better alignments must be found. First, professional schools should again strive to draw close to the university. During the apogee of specialization of professional education, a serious question was raised whether medical and law schools actually needed the university except as a financial base. Their professors rarely saw or spoke to those in the arts and sciences, and the professional faculties seemed able to fill students' time with their own courses. But, perhaps inspired by willingness of education faculties to consider the preparation of teachers as a university-wide affair, professional faculties have begun to ask for and offer help to other parts of the university. Through more joint appointments, cooperatively taught courses, and student enrollments from other parts of the institution, a few barriers, at least, have begun to tumble.

Even more radical changes are in the wind. A few institutions see administration as essentially the same whether it is concerned with business, education, hospitals, or philanthropy. Then why not a school for administration and policy formation? At the State University of New York at Buffalo, a single faculty responsible for administration in business, social work, and the underlying social and behavioral sciences is being contemplated. Such reasoning also suggests the breakup of the traditional school of arts and sciences, an anachronism which has lost its once presumed unity and integrity. In such a view, the health-related sciences belong with medicine, nursing, dentistry, and public health, while the social sciences belong more properly with law, administration, and social work.

If organization and curricula change, then changes in degrees and degree requirements seem likely to follow. There is widespread agreement that too many different degrees are offered by the nation's colleges and universities.

One set of reforms views the problem of degrees as follows: The number of different bachelor's degrees should be kept to a minimum, but requirements should be sufficiently flexible to allow differentiation within each degree program. Each advanced degree should be a definite recognition of a formal educational program, but should not be predictive of candidacy for still more advanced degree work; a master's degree in a professional field should prepare students either for direct employment or for further graduate work. Master's degree requirements should also be broad enough and compatible enough with work in related fields for students to change career aims without losing an inordinate amount of time in transfer to a new program. And both in the professional fields and in the arts and sciences, we should recognize reality by creating appropriate intermediate degrees between the master's and the doctorate. Regardless of degree level, we should insist that the several components—general or liberal, basic science or theory, and applied professional subjects—should not be separated into different time periods or levels.

Professional education, like all education, depends upon instruction and modes of learning, and here, while slow in coming, there is change. Professors have begun to question excessive lecturing and formal classroom experience and are willing to consider other methods of education. By far the most pervasive reform is the attempt to provide more clinical or field experience early in students' education.

In medicine, clinical experience in the first year helps motivate students for subsequent work in basic science besides contributing to their socialization as doctors. Law students should spend the summer between the first and second year in a law office, court, governmental bureau, or other legal function. Social workers need clinical work, both as undergraduates and during the second year of their graduate professional program. And future ministers need much more intensive and better supervised clinical experience than has previously been incorporated in divinity programs. The recent development of clinical pastoral education described above is a healthy sign and we suspect that, in time, the demands for this type of experience will expand significantly.

Renewed interest in individual research and independent study stresses a new faith in the student's responsibility for what and how he studies. This may take the form of a real life design problem undertaken by a freshman architecture or engineering student or independent laboratory research of a senior medical student, with research time actually allotted rather than stolen from clinical rounds and required lectures.

This thrust in individuals underlies the uses of the computer and other new instructional media. One campus locates computers so that students can use them to solve complex problems; on another campus each medical student is required to spend time in a computer-based diagnostic center, testing his own patient assessment with that made by a computer which knows every case in the history of the teaching hospital. Video-tape and sound tapes allow storage of lectures, operations, clinical interviews, and technical procedures to which students can refer when they feel the need. In one school of dentistry, for example, movie films of fifty complex dental procedures are stored in the clinic with nine projectors. A dental intern who is unsure of how to proceed, can stop, view the filmed procedure and return to his patient, presumably with greater understanding. Nurses with a five-minute film clip, several oranges, and a hypodermic needle, apparently developed greater skill in giving injections on their own than in the presence of a teacher, and television allows large numbers of students to view intricate surgical procedures at a very close range.

Before World War II most American professional schools assumed that their graduates would practice in the United States and that there was no need for the curriculum to transcend American culture. But faster transportation and communication, the nation's involvement in world affairs, and the internationalization of knowledge, have rendered such assumptions obsolete. While sometimes grudgingly, all professional schools have reexamined their curricula with a view toward internationalization. Medicine tries to give professors international experience, law professors contribute to undergraduate general education in courses in international law and foreign trade agreements, and some schools have presented foreign concepts with courses in anthropology and the study of comparative cultures.

Two other moves toward reform are expressed more as statements of concept rather than of specific accomplishment. The first is the quest for better ways of developing a personal professional identity in students. Through relatively close contact with professional faculty members, the student is expected to acquire, almost unconsciously, ethical principles to guide him in his practice, but for many reasons—increased numbers of students, more complicated ethical dilemmas (heart transplant, dealing with organized crime), and delocalized collegiate institutions—the more informal ways no longer work and new ones must yet be found.

Secondly, since it is generally agreed that the half-life of knowledge in a profession has shrunk to perhaps five years, those in active practice should constantly seek reeducation. But while everyone knows this, institutions have not yet seriously thought through content, organization, or methods of financing for continuing education for professionals. Except in education, agriculture, and to some extent in administration, continuing education programs for professionals are rare in universities.

These needed reforms are not isolated phenomena peculiar

to professional education. Similar changes in all of higher education exhibit many of the same weaknesses and lack of systematization.

Reform in Undergraduate Education

Colleges and universities have begun to make curricular changes, sometimes in response to student needs and demands, but as frequently on account of other forces and factors. The success of these reforms appears to depend in part on the primary reasons for initiating change. Several, brought about for economic reasons or to satisfy faculty desires, appear largely irrelevant to the educational needs of college students or even antithetical to them, and some have failed to achieve the purposes for which they were attempted.

Consider first the decline of general education as a distinct function. General education really began at Columbia in 1918, took on characteristic form at the University of Chicago in the 1930s, spread through several of the great midwestern universities in the 1940s, and gained respectability through the publication of the Harvard Report in 1947.

It consisted of interdisciplinary courses seeking behavioral objectives linked to man's non-vocational life. While the number of required courses has not shifted appreciably since 1947, the character of those courses has changed and will do so more rapidly in the future. General education is being replaced by the distribution requirements popular in the 1920s and 1930s which asks students to take courses from each major division of knowledge.

Ostensibly, this shift provides greater flexibility for students; in fact, the reform of general education does not seem likely to improve the curriculum for students because the distribution system fails to force faculties to create courses for the non-major. Even if the system proceeds as it has in a few places to the free elective system, first popular in the nineteenth century, it still will not bring improvement.

The shift to distribution requirements arose from unwillingness of professional faculty to teach non-departmental and staff courses. The academic climate was such during the 1960s that young Ph.D.'s would not accept a position in which they would teach a staff course; they saw their own future related more to the department and to departmental offerings.

A second category of reform most starkly stated consists of changes in academic calendars. Pittsburgh really began the movement when it created the trimester to enable fuller utilization of scarce classrooms, laboratories, and equipment. That effort was followed quickly by other attempts to gain year-round operation. Schools on the semester system changed to a four-quarter plan and schools on the quarter system either tried the trimester or emphasized that the four quarters already insured year-round operation. Then came a flurry of other modifications. Some tried the 3–3 (three courses in each of three terms), 4–1–4 (the "1" being a month of interim studies), 4–4–1, a three semester academic year (starting the year in early September so the semester ended before Christmas), and even a revised single course plan (one course taught in seven weeks). These were spawned for several reasons. Calendar change is easier than real curricular revision, makes a school feel it is accomplishing something, and can boost faculty morale or attract attention to the institution. Perhaps the most cynical attempt was that of a major university on the quarter system which divided each quarter in half so that professors would teach the first five weeks and students would do independent study the second part, thus allowing senior faculty more time for their own work. Only with such a bribe could senior professors to persuaded to teach lower division courses.

Third are reforms in techniques using the media. These include open and closed circuit television, computer based or computer assisted instruction, language laboratories, tapes, recordings, multimedia classrooms, and programmed learning. Once again, economics has motivated experimentation. Was it possible through the use of technology to bring about savings in the instructional budget by presenting a professor to a larger number of students, shortening the time required for students to master something, or making students responsible for more of their own education, thus increasing the student-faculty ratio? By and large this goal has not been attained, although use of the media has become central in higher educational practice. There are, to be sure, thousands of experiments, but the bulk of the college curriculum has continued as though the electronic revolution had never happened.

A fourth major category of reforms consists of newer ways of grouping students and teachers. These arrangements seem to have been stimulated more by educational needs than were some other reforms. New groupings include team-teaching at Chicago State College, the house plan at Stephens, the experimental college at Hofstra, block scheduling at Florida State, cluster colleges at Michigan State and the University of the Pacific, and the creation of the Santa Cruz branch of the University of California with its separately housed colleges of six hundred to one thousand students. These seem designed to capture something of the spirit of the older, small residential colleges in a larger, more economical institution.

Descriptive reports indicate some success; students do like the smaller groupings, and when students get to know one another well by being in a series of the same classes, they seem to develop more rapidly. If the serious problems of cost and faculty satisfactions can be solved, some form of regrouping may prove a fertile approach to reform. However, in the enormous state colleges and universities with older ways of organizing built into the physical plant, the possibility of affecting large proportions of students seems remote.

Efforts to change the curriculum in response to student needs are noted in the many attempts to create ad hoc issues-inspired courses and courses of differing lengths. This effort seems to have originated from student creation of free university sorts of courses. Each set of recommendations that has followed a campus upset includes ways of offering new style courses and of getting them approved through the administrative curricular apparatus. Such examples as the experimental courses at California State University, San Francisco, freshman seminars at Stanford, and the new freshman year program at Antioch appear well received. But difficulties abound. Quality control is an issue—that is, how to insure professional competence to teach a wide-ranging problems-centered course, or, if teams of faculty are used, how to finance it.

Logistics are also involved—how to accumulate library holdings and make them available for constantly changing course titles. At Stephens College, for example, a seminar required of all junior year students changes its focus each year; the library certainly has not been able to keep up, but above all, there persists the same problem that plagued the older general education interdisciplinary courses: how can we prevent ad hoc courses from being superficial, offering a false sophistication to students who experience them? Older courses in personal adjustment or functional mathematics failed; new style courses may fail as well.

Still another promising reform consists of providing off-campus experiences that enable students in theory at least to test academic ideas in real life. Well organized and financed efforts frequently have produced dramatic results. Cooperative work/study at Antioch or Northeastern seems essential to the impact those schools have had on students; and at Northeastern, a university of 26,000, the cooperative work/study program allows it to compete with lower tuition public institutions. The overseas campuses of Stanford University, Gonzaga University, and Loyola University of Chicago appear to be among the more impressive elements in the undergraduate education at these institutions.

Several questions arise, however. If every institution attempts overseas experience, are there enough places abroad to put students? Even now parts of Europe that once welcomed students are much less open and receptive. The European ghettos cannot absorb too many more transients. Even an expanding economy would find difficulty accepting over two million cooperative study students from freshmen classes, and of course, cost is a factor. Smaller institutions already facing serious financial crises find the administration of a full off-campus program too expensive, and if junior colleges become the main route for lower division education, can fruitful off-campus experience be fitted into a two-year program?

Having viewed higher educational reform in general, we can now examine in more detail curricular reform in professional schools.

New Courses and Research

Interdisciplinary and Interdepartmental Courses. There is widespread belief that courses have tended to be too narrow and too closely tied to traditional departments, and this has led to experimentation with interdisciplinary or interdepartmental courses. In medicine, for example, there have been attempts to provide a new integrated interdisciplinary approach to an orthodox course such as pathology. At Johns Hopkins the course in the science of disease is divided into several aspects of disease. Students move from clinic to laboratory autopsies and then move into the various basic science laboratories of biological, chemical, and microcellular pathology, and bacteriology.[1] Such attempts are based on the widely shared belief that traditional curricula based on departmental autonomy are obsolete and restrict collaborative teaching and effective learning.

A few institutions of theological education are seeking to cross or even eliminate departmental lines and divisions. The United Theological Seminary of the Twin Cities begins the student's training with courses in the Christian faith and the social order, the Christian faith and human personality, and the Christian faith and the economic and political orders. Only later are students allowed into more restrictive courses such as biblical theology and interpretation of historical theology. Study at the Graduate Theological Union in Berkeley is divided into eight areas, several of which are highly interdisciplinary, and most of the doctoral instruction is carried out in full cooperation with the appropriate departments of the University of California at Berkeley. At Princeton a new theory for architectural planning has become the focus of the curriculum which invites major contribution from professors and students in engineering and the Woodrow Wilson School of Social Policy. These combined efforts are integrated through an actual design study of some real urban area on the East Coast. The School of Engineering at Stanford uses a similar approach and has brought together people from architecture, economics and business to offer joint courses on planning, on the assumption that no one point of view is adequate for instruction in planning and design.

We can see the problems created by necessary interdisciplinary courses in recommendations from several professional school associations. In a survey of recent trends in engineering education the problem or task course as a modern offspring of earlier general education courses appeared promising. The alternative to the survey course need not be a disciplinary course, but rather an offering of courses that focus on a particular set of problems and bring various disciplines to bear on them.[2]

[1] John H. Knowles, *Views of Medical Education and Care* (Cambridge, Mass.: Harvard University Press, 1968), p. 153.
[2] *The Journal of Engineering Education* 49 (December 1968): 313.

The nursing curriculum generally appears less fragmented than it had previously, with such highly specialized courses as Disaster or Operating Room Nursing replaced by broader emphasis on health, the community, and collaboration with the health team. Social work education is moving away from an earlier isolation and is searching for ways to emphasize interdisciplinary in-service teaching and research programs to make greater use of the teaching staffs from other professions and disciplines.[3] Some schools of education have also begun the slow but essential task of cutting back on specialized courses in favor of broader offerings. At Harvard, for example, six or seven previously offered foundation courses have been eliminated and replaced by a staff-prepared course, Introduction to Education, that utilizes a case approach, tutorials, field experiences, and a series of written exercises, called briefs, with information and insights from a number of relevant disciplines needed to support a position.[4]

It should be clearly understood that these efforts are just beginning and as yet there is no real evidence that interdisciplinary work can be carried out successfully. Both the intent and the state of this development are revealed in a remark made by Paul Sanagaro in connection with a study of theological education: "Speaking of the development of the student as a professional person, the simple fact of the departmental autonomy in medical schools is a major barrier to his developing a unified view of the profession . . . the attempts to overcome this by conjoint teaching and integrated teaching having all come about in the last few years and are notable for their lack of success."[5]

Social and Behavioral Science. One variant of interdisciplinary work—the attempt to use materials from the social and behavioral sciences in the preparation of professionals—must be treated as a major category of reform. Whether in medicine, law, theology, library science, or dentistry, there is widespread belief that

[3] Kurt Reichert, "Report of the Fifth International Survey of Training for Social Welfare" (n.p., n.d.).

[4] Theodore R. Sizer, *The Graduate Study of Education* (Cambridge, Mass.: Harvard University Press, 1966).

[5] Cited in Kenneth Underwood, *The Church, the University, and Social Policy* (Middletown, Connecticut: Wesleyan University Press, 1969), vol. 2, p. 302.

these sciences can be useful and that they are sufficiently advanced and productive to make definite contributions to professional training. Further new appointments and curricula reflect the belief that "the growth within medicine has brought it to a period of transition and movement not unlike the situation it faced a hundred years ago. In response, it is again reaching outside itself for help. Secure in its century-old partnership with the natural sciences, it now seeks the added collaboration of the social and behavioral sciences."[6]

In autumn 1966, there were five thousand behavioral and social scientists employed in 447 professional schools lodged in doctoral institutions. Medical schools were by far the largest users of behavioral scientists, with psychiatrists and psychologists the best represented and with a fair sampling of sociologists. Business schools, next in rank, chiefly employed economists, psychologists and political scientists. Schools of education and public administration also employed large numbers of behavioral scientists.

While the need for social and behavioral science materials in professional education is generally recognized, attempts to include them are still a matter of trial and error. The Law School at the University of Denver has a broad interdisciplinary program in judicial administration, an important ingredient of which is a seminar, Methods in Social Research, in which law students are taught to use social science research on legal problems and questions of justice. At Wisconsin graduate students in several of the social sciences have been accepted into law courses and some law students have been accepted for tutorial work in social science departments. Wisconsin is also developing law minors for Ph.D. candidates. A recent study in legal education conducted for the Carnegie Commission on Higher Education suggests that such trends may well increase, especially as the American Bar comes to grips with the thorny problem of sub- and paraprofessionals in the legal profession.[7] While the social and behavioral components of the normal medical curriculum are still minimal and in most schools token, the growing body of research on medical problems from the social science

[6] Lester J. Evans, *The Crisis in Medical Education* (Ann Arbor: University of Michigan Press, 1964), p. 1.

[7] Herbert L. Packer and Thomas Ehrlich, *New Directions in Legal Education* (New York: McGraw-Hill, 1972).

framework is generating increasing willingness to accept such a dictum as: "The sources of human wellness and disability are social, behavior and biophysical in nature. It follows then that medicine, in the aggregate, must develop the ability to identify and to deal with all of them."[8]

Undergraduate Courses. Although some see most professional education as moving inexorably away from undergraduate and into the graduate years, a number of professional fields are entering or reentering undergraduate education for a number of reasons: (1) to allow professional fields to contribute to students' general education; (2) to help guide undergraduates to decide on professional careers; (3) to prepare sub- or paraprofessional workers for whom a bachelor's degree is sufficient; (4) to gratify professional faculty who want more contact with younger students; (5) to experience interdisciplinary insights that can come from working with undergraduate problems in issue-focused courses; and (6) perhaps most important, to bring the professional schools back into the mainstream of the university. Since this movement is still so new and experience so limited, no comprehensive resume is possible, but some appraisal of the developments may be obtained by looking at a few examples.

At Stanford a revised undergraduate curriculum anticipates that ultimately all freshmen will take seminars, many offered on an overload basis by senior professors from the graduate professional schools. Illustrative of these freshman courses are the following:

> *The Evils of Sociological Planning*, Roy Cohn, Professor of Surgery. Using medicine as a focus, examples of the failures of sociological planning will be presented. The constant conflict between the good for the individual and the good for society will be emphasized.
>
> *Distribution and Delivery of Mental Health Services*, Thomas A. Gonda, Professor of Psychiatry. This seminar will examine the diverse factors (biological, psychological, social, economic, and political) that are contributing to the dramatic change in the patterns of distribution and delivery of mental health care services.
>
> *Technology and Society*, Steven J. Kline, Professor of Mechanical Engineering. This seminar will examine the rela-

[8] Knowles, *Views of Medical Education and Care*, p. 48.

tions of technology and society with emphasis on concepts and
tools that allow better understanding of decision making . . .
where both technics and social values are important. It will
include materials on the viewpoint of the scientist and tech-
nologist and on how technology operates, using both literature
and indepth current examples . . . [and] discussions of personal value systems and how they influence social decision
making processes.

A conference held by the Catholic University of America to
consider The Law in the Liberal Arts: The Social Dimension, revealed something of the needs as well as the issues of this intrusion
of professional work into the undergraduate years. According to
conference participants, law should be returned to the undergraduate
school because concerned students are asking legal questions that
can be adequately answered only by people schooled in law. While
some law faculties seem uninterested in teaching undergraduates
and there is a lack of materials appropriate for undergraduates, this
condition can change. In fact, the West Publishing Company, a
pioneer in legal textbooks and materials, has recently produced
some texts that are specifically aimed at an undergraduate audience.
If lawyers will not come to the undergraduate schools, people trained
in labor or political science may have to obtain some background in
law to offer the desired courses.

While the undergraduate school should not be turned into
a preparatory school for the graduate study of law, an appropriate
undergraduate course could provide a guidance function. Probably
the ideal undergraduate course should not teach substantive law, but
rather approaches to, or methodologies of, the law and the relationship of law to other knowledge. This would have a liberalizing effect
and would remove some of the veil of mystery that surrounds professional practice. In effect, such a course should: "give the student
an appreciation of the method of law's evolution to give him some
notion about the efficacy or the adequacy of its functions, the notion
of its methods, and the ways in which change is achieved in the law,
because if a student sees law as something that is static and
irrevocable, then he becomes addicted, perhaps, to the notion that
this is something which can be learned for now and all time, and to

form a highly warped notion of at least American legal institutions."[9]

At this same conference, possible approaches to law courses for undergraduates were described. These analyses stressed the differences in purpose between undergraduate and professional education and how the differences dictated the methods. For example, this notion was revealed in one course:

> There are at least three different functions that a course on the legal system for undergraduates in a liberal arts college might fulfill. The first would be that of acquainting students who are not prospective lawyers with the legal system and its role, past, present, and future.
>
> The second function of such a course would be as a vehicle by which to interest and to thereby recruit able undergraduates for the legal profession.
>
> The third different function such a course might have is to serve as a vehicle by which prospective law students could evaluate their aptitude for the study of the law. . . .
>
> The materials that I would propose would frankly seek to be a survey. They would seek to give a macrocosmic rather than a microcosmic view of the legal system. Now such a course might cover all or some of the following topics: the development of legal systems; the development of the common law system; using discursive material; the Anglo-American legal system; and the nature of legal analysis. There should also be some kind of brief discursive treatment of the nature of the system itself, even including undergraduates. A brief discussion of the role and structure of the court system, the legislature, and the executive might be necessary.
>
> Then, there are essential or significant aspects of the legal system: the men who made this system and who make it; the titans of legal systems, the great judges and the great lawyers; and why. I think we ought to let the students see the anatomy of a legal case and what documents look like, and we would talk about what we had seen. Finally, there is great rhetoric in the law; for example, Justice Frankfurter's concurring opinion in the case of *Wieman v. Updegraf* involving the loyalty oath or some opinions by Justice Jackson. Then one

---

[9] Albert Broderick, *Law and Liberal Arts* (Washington: Catholic University of America Press, 1967), p. 66.

could raise some of the questions about what are the alternatives to the Anglo-American legal system, the influences of society on the law, and the presuppositions of the legal system. Still other potential topics might be: the different conceptions of the way in which disputes might be resolved; the adversary system versus alternatives to it; the economic assumptions of a legal system; the conceptions of justice and the conceptions of freedom; and finally, alternatives to legal systems themselves.[10]

The movement of social work, long restricted to the graduate years, into undergraduate education is in response to some similar, but other quite dissimilar, motivations compared with law. We now recognize that history, philosophy, literature and other arts can illuminate human problems and aspirations and thus edify social workers. Thomas Walz has summarized the justification and aims for an undergraduate social work program. This analysis could apply to most professional fields:

> [An] important demand for undergraduate social work programs is coming from the college students themselves. Many of them are socially concerned. They seek social welfare as a career which can offer them the meaningful investment of self that they are searching for. . . .
> If we recall the original conception of a liberal education as a moral education and as an education for knowledge for social betterment, we can see how an undergraduate social welfare curriculum makes a distinct contribution to the liberal arts programs. It offers a look at societal values and their implications, and it does not skirt discussing values in the objectivity of science. . . .
> A further argument for an undergraduate social welfare program relates to the self-interest (survival needs) of the university itself . . . the university has needed to demonstrate to its own students and to the community its concerns with the basic domestic issues of the time.[11]

[11] Thomas Walz, "The Philosophy and Objectives of Social Welfare Institute.

[11] Thomas Waltz, "The Philosophy and Objectives of Social Welfare Education," in *Issues in Planning for Undergraduate Social Welfare Education* (Atlanta: Southern Regional Education Board, 1970), pp. 9–20.

Humanities. Another belief now pervasive in most professional schools is that the humanities should be an important part of the curriculum. While the idiom may differ slightly from field to field, the central thrust of the argument is common. For medicine the hope is that work in the humanities will produce doctors with enlivened consciences, increased responsiveness, broadened interest, clarified purpose, and, in the end, a quickened ethical sense. From engineering comes the cry that the estrangement between the humanities and the professional schools must end, for without deep appreciation of an active participation in all phases of the humanities, the professions become sterile and lose relevance to society. To prepare business students for life and not just for their first jobs, at least half of the undergraduate curriculum should consist of courses in the liberal arts. These can start an individual on the process of developing analytical ability, balanced judgment, vigor of mind and imagination, and an understanding of men and social forces conditioning the times.

These hopes are somewhat dashed by the preferences of professional faculty members for required courses in the humanities. Although the picture may have changed somewhat, the actual curricular preferences as shown in recent writings seem to conform generally to those revealed in Table 1. The liberalizing courses professional faculties most prefer are those with the closest affinities to actual professional work.

Nevertheless, most professional schools are in one way or another trying to fit more of the humanities into their curricula. Undergraduate professional schools are loosening professional requirements and recommending work in the humanities or requiring some variant of distribution requirements. The graduate professional schools encourage preprofessional students to take work in the humanities and modify entrance requirements to insure that applicants are not penalized for doing so.

Doctoral students in the School of Education at Stanford are required to take approximately twelve hours in normative studies—history, philosophy, literature—to develop a broad perspective for the practice of education. An engineering curriculum study at the University of California at Los Angeles has urged the engineering school to develop a sequence of courses in applied humanities begin-

Table 1.

PERCENTAGES OF COMBINED PROFESSIONAL FACULTIES FAVORING
CERTAIN POLICIES TOWARD LIBERAL ARTS SUBJECTS

Subject	Required of All	Optional But Encouraged	Optional	Discouraged or Prohibited
English				
Composition	96.4	2.2	0.6	0.2
Mathematics	64.1	17.6	15.6	1.5
History	56.5	29.6	12.4	0.8
Chemistry	51.6	19.0	24.7	3.7
Speech	50.7	28.3	17.8	2.3
Physics	47.5	24.2	24.9	2.4
Economics	45.1	28.7	22.8	2.5
Literature	44.3	32.9	20.6	1.1
Psychology	42.1	31.0	24.1	1.8
Biology	42.0	22.7	29.4	4.7
Sociology	32.1	32.5	30.7	3.5
Foreign				
Language	30.5	34.9	30.8	2.9
Philosophy	27.0	41.1	29.3	1.6
Physiology	27.0	18.8	44.8	8.3
Political				
Science	26.8	36.0	32.1	4.1
Music	13.0	19.1	58.0	8.4
Art	12.1	24.7	55.0	7.1
Religion	7.7	20.9	61.7	8.7

Source: McGrath, Dressel, and Mayhew, *The Liberal Arts as
Viewed by Faculty Members in Professional Schools,* p. 35.

ning in the freshman year and using a sequence of critical periods of
man's social evolution to develop a foundation for later work in the
humanities and to display their role in the profession. The sequence
offers examination of the forces, interests, and activities which make
up the community of man.

Temporal Arrangements

The second major category of reform consists of new temporal
arrangements. As a result of the enormous increase in knowledge in
professional fields and the American curricular tendency to accommo-

date new knowledge in new courses, the time required for basic professional training has increased. Further, the quantity of prescribed course work deemed essential in most of the fields has also increased so much that students have had little time for reflection and virtually no time for individual interests. These trends have risen in part from the widespread belief in a core of knowledge that every practicing professional should possess, but it has derived even more from the concept of preparing the generalist.

Flexibility and Electives. The reforming response to these changes and problems has been various. First and probably most important is experimentation with curricular flexibility and freedom of election. Education in architecture, for example, was once a monolith of five tightly prescribed years. A suggested change calls for a curriculum of three modules. The first follows a somewhat common course pattern for two years. The second culminates in an A.B. degree which allows a relatively freely elected concentration in related fields. The third, culminating after the sixth year in a first professional degree, provides time for intensive specialization.

In medicine there is a concerted movement to curtail the time students spend in formal classes and laboratories so as to allow them more time for study, reflection, and independent research. One suggested curricular revision in medicine assumed that an educational program was a continuum from elementary school to professional practice, which, if approached creatively, could be shortened and made more effective. It conceived of medical education as eight to ten years, divided between three years of undergraduate work, three of medical school, and two to four years of graduate education.[12]

Theological education seems to be moving away from the prescribed core of courses once thought essential to insure quality. In 1972, Andrew J. Dufner of the Jesuit School of Theology at Berkeley developed a two-track program leading to the Master of Divinity degree at that institution. The first track, called the Curricular Program, allows a classroom-oriented student the opportunity to complete his education by selecting from a variety of courses offered within each major theological area. The second track, or

---

[12] Knowles, *Views of Medical Education and Care,* p. 160.

Modular Program, designed for more independent students, allows the student to design his own theological program from a wide variety of classroom, tutorial, reading, and independent study experiences. Quality control of the modular program is maintained through a series of diagnostic and prognostic examinations that each student takes when he feels he has achieved sufficient mastery of a body of theological material.

The two major critical reports on business education also see free electives inside or outside the business school as a desirable third of the total program.[13]

In engineering the general tendency is to make curricula more flexible and give students greater freedom of choice, although many still question the value of this movement. Greater freedom can militate against any overall view of the interrelations among the elements of professional education.[14]

Representatives of engineering education have in fact been more consistently introspective about curricular matters than any other professional group. Their comments in *Goals of Engineering Education*[15] could stand almost as the credo for flexibility as a matter of reform for most of the professional fields:

> (1) *Existing programs should be made flexible* . . . tightly specified curricula tend to delay modernization and discourage valuable experimentation. Provision of free electives with an effective advisory system would permit student to follow programs which offer the greatest challenge to their abilities and the best preparation for their next steps after graduation.
>
> Flexibility of individual programs is needed to allow for the diversity of interests and talents of particular students and provide engineers with a wide range of competencies to meet the needs of industry and government.
>
> The principle of flexibility will permit engineering

---

[13] R. A. Gordon and I. E. Howell, *Higher Education for Business* (New York: Columbia University Press, 1959), and T. C. Pierson, *The Education of American Businessmen* (New York: McGraw-Hill, 1959).

[14] Pusey and Taylor, *Ministry for Tomorrow*, p. 93.

[15] *Final Report: Goals of Engineering Education* (Washington, D.C.: American Society for Engineering Education, 1968).

schools to offer their strongest programs, building upon established strength free from constraint to offer programs they are not prepared to administer.

(2) *Expanded opportunities for interdisciplinary study are needed.* Many of the recommendations for curricular changes suggested by engineering graduates point to the existence of a clear demand for and interest in interdisciplinary programs. Some students may have the ability and desire to begin interdisciplinary work during their baccalaureate programs, but some programs are so specialized that the student has no opportunity to study any engineering subject in depth outside of his own field.

(3) *Credit hour requirements should be reduced.* One of the aims of educators has been to find the balance of courses needed to make engineering education a general scientific, technological education. The movement toward general education has often meant addition of new courses to the curriculum to the point that it has become difficult to obtain a bachelor's degree in eight semesters. Compared with requirements for a bachelor's degree in mathematics, physics, and chemistry, engineering demands almost an additional semester's work.

The restrictive effect of an excessive academic load often prevents the student from engaging in other worthwhile activities of college and community life, and in courses outside of his major field where he might gain the breadth of perspective and develop the creative imagination needed by the engineer of the future. There appears to be a lack of evidence that credit hour requirements for graduation are correlated with the quality of the products.

(4) *Many prerequisite courses should not be required.* The requirement of many prerequisite courses often unnecessarily discourages qualified students in one area from taking courses in other fields. Wherever possible, prerequisite material . . . should be required through self-directed study.

(5) *Provisions for transfer into engineering are needed.* Too many engineering colleges make it almost impossible for students to transfer to engineering above the freshman level. There is real opportunity to increase the enrollment of first-rate students other than through the freshman class.

(6) *The role of cooperative education should be recognized.* It is generally recognized that actual practice of engi-

neering periodically interwoven with classroom and laboratory instruction can provide . . . balance of their intellectual development. Currently fifty colleges of engineering in the United States provide curricula on the cooperative plan largely at the baccalaureate level. These curricula have much to offer to engineering education of the future, both undergraduate and graduate, basic and advanced . . . With increased emphasis on continuing education throughout a professional career, early development of a capacity to deal with alternative methods of study and practice has many advantages, and the cooperative plan extends educational opportunities to talents of students of limited financial resources.

Changes in the Calendar. Professional fields have found traditional ways of dividing the academic year, and academic programs are awkward and inhibit change. Over the generations, practices and procedures of a two-semester or three-semester academic year, four-year bachelor's degree, and one- or two-year graduate program, tend to crystalize, harden, and become almost sacred. One way to break the calendar-imposed lockstep is to revise the calendar. Calendar revision, important in undergraduate college reform, is now considered seriously in the professional schools. Although examples are still limited, they may be predictive of the shape of things to come.

The Yale Medical School has rejected the four-year concept in favor of a plan which divides the medical curriculum into three approximately equal time units. This is consistent with the recommendation of the Association of American Colleges Curriculum Workshop that medical schools should individualize the education of physicians to the extent that some students could accelerate their programs and graduate in less than the standard four years.

Both social work and nursing have accepted two-year junior college training for some kinds of practice. At least one school of veterinary medicine has constituted a trimester system of forty-five weeks which allows a student to complete degree requirements in slightly less than three years rather than the orthodox four.

The Master of Arts in Teaching builds a full calendar year of clinical experience and instruction on the base of a bachelor's degree, and a supervised year of paid internship in place of a pre-viously accepted academic year-long master's degree in education.

Underlying some attempts to modify the calendar and, if possible, reverse the century-long steady increase in the time required for professional education, is the notion that separation of basic education in a profession from specialization can somehow prove more efficient. An early manifestation of this idea appeared in the engineering science movement. The argument ran that several specialties in engineering—mechanical, civil, electrical, and so forth—should be developed on the job or in graduate school, and that the undergraduate school should stress basic engineering science. The idea has not been universally accepted. Some schools, especially those in state colleges, feeling pressures from employers, have insisted on special training in the undergraduate school.

However, the majority opinion of professional educators favors some variant of this concept. A few institutions have insisted that there should be no undergraduate school of engineering at all. At the University of California at Santa Cruz, for example, it is assumed that the master's degree in engineering should be the first professional degree. There is some emerging belief that the various health-related professions might be based on a common core of basic health science. The future physician, dentist, or Ph.D. in a health science would take two years of a common curriculum. Then, at the point of intensive clinical experience or research effort, the specialties would separate. The reports on business education pre-viously mentioned also move in this direction. Both believe that the undergraduate curriculum in business should stress the humanities, mathematics, statistics, economics and the social sciences, a strip-down program in functional business subjects, and a few broad courses in business policy, principles, and organizational theory.[16]

Only slightly presumptuous is the claim made in the name of social work education that the best undergraduate preparation for the helping professions, whether the graduate goes to work or pro-ceeds to graduate studies, is a sound general education in the liberal tradition. The biological and behavioral sciences comprise its

[16] Silk, *The Education of Businessmen,* p. 30.

scientific foundation; its roots in the democratic social values are nourished in the humanities; and aspiration and human potential are illuminated in philosophy and in the arts. "The cluster of occupations with which we are concerned have much in common. They share a base in the biological and behavioral sciences. They also hold in common human values. These scientific and value elements made explicit link liberal education and preparation for the human service professions."[17] The presumption is that there could be a core base for a number of helping professions.

New Organizational Patterns

Pervading the several attempts to restructure programs in the professional fields are designs to link the professional schools closely to the university. Reformers agree that traditional school and departmental structure is divisive and tends to compartmentalize student thinking. Better alignments have to be found. During the apogee of specialization of professional education, a serious question was raised as to whether medical and law schools actually needed the university except as a financial base. The faculties of the arts and sciences contributed to this split by coming to resemble another professional school themselves. However, pressures have begun to operate in the opposite direction. Through more joint appointments, cooperatively taught courses, and student enrollments from other parts of the institution, the university may become reunified. This will never be an easy task; the divisive forces are enormous and the existence of a multiversity is a reality, with all the lack of cohesiveness that term implies.

New Academic Units. One device for bringing together the disciplines and professional fields that need each other is the experimentation with new groups of academic units. Centers of health services which bring together medicine, dentistry, nursing, and paraprofessional fields now exist. There are also attempts to place in one school or college responsibility for preparing people for administration. On the premise that all administration is the same—

[17] Virl S. Lewis, "The Relevance of Social Welfare to the Liberal Arts," in *Issues in Planning for Undergraduate Social Welfare Education* (Atlanta: Southern Regional Education Board, 1970), p. 5.

public or private, educational, philanthropic, or business—a few attempts have been made to create a school of administration and policy science. Several rather extreme departures from orthodoxy may illustrate the directions and purposes these new administration alignments are taking.

The University of Wisconsin at Green Bay has focused its entire curriculum and administration structure on ecology, and because ecology is pandisciplinary, it has organized its colleges in the framework of environmental themes rather than according to traditional fields or disciplines. Thus, there are the colleges of environmental sciences, community sciences, human biology, creative communication, and professional studies (business, public administration, teacher education, leisure sciences, mass communication, and social services).

The State University of New York at Buffalo has adopted in principle a new organization consisting of a university college into which all students are matriculated as freshmen. The college is made up of the following faculties: arts and letters, educational studies, engineering and applied sciences, health sciences, social science and philosophy, law and jurisprudence, and applied social science and administration. There is intent in this structure to end professional education for undergraduates, although this is not yet accomplished. More explicitly, it was created so that various departments could participate with greater ease in the programs of more than one faculty. In theory, no faculty would be purely professional. For example, the faculty of law and jurisprudence was expected to offer work for undergraduate students. Originally applied social science and administration were intended to provide undergraduate work as well as professional work in business, social welfare, and probably library science. However, these last-named departments have not been put into effect.[18]

Changed Admissions Policies. Another innovation in administration is a revised admissions philosophy. Faced with anticipated increases in demand for professional services and with trends to

[18] James S. Schindler, "Emerging Patterns of Management Education on the State University of New York at Buffalo Campus," in *The Next Half-century in Higher Education for Business* (St. Louis: American Association of Collegiate Schools of Business, 1968), pp. 17–19.

bring more minority groups into the professions, several professions have revised their position. The Workshop on Medical School Curriculum argued that only by increasing the size of entering medical school classes and by reducing attrition can the nation's need for more doctors be met. Medical schools should search out prospective students from deprived backgrounds, and when students deficient in educational background are admitted, tutorial help and additional time to complete degree work should be provided. Professional schools have begun to recruit actively from minority groups and to experiment with new courses to cope with minority experience in the curriculum. The law school of the University of Washington became involved in a court case for accepting less qualified minority students over more qualified white students. The University of Michigan has set an overall university quota which requires all professional schools to increase the proportion of minority group members. However, there is little evidence as to how effective new predictive devices are.

Academic Degrees. Last among these administrative approaches to curricular reform is reconsideration of academic degrees. While there is no absolute agreement, there is a trend for the master's degree to become the first professional degree. In those fields in which this is most decided, several patterns occur: (1) Undergraduate work in a profession such as business followed by a master's program in the same field. (2) Undergraduate major in the liberal arts followed by a master's program in a profession, for example, social work after a sociology major. (3) Undergraduate program in a profession—say, education—followed by a substantive master's degree in one of the liberal arts. (4) A five- or six-year professional program yielding either a bachelor's or master's degree, as in architecture or engineering.[19]

Since degree requirements do define the parameters of a curriculum, educators are reconsidering the principles of degree structure. Spurr has developed five such principles which could be the basis for widespread reform. (1) The number of degree titles should be kept as low as possible, allowing for substantive variation within each for subject matter, emphasis, quantity, and even quality of effort required. (2) Degree requirements should be flexible with

[19] Steven H. Spurr, *Academic Degree Structures: Innovative Approaches* (New York: McGraw-Hill, 1970), pp. 75–76.

respect to time necessary for completion. (3) Each degree should mark a successful stage of academic progress without implication or prejudgment as to a student's capacity for the next stage. (4) Degrees should be so interrelated as to facilitate opportunity for student motivation, interests, and intellectual achievement. (5) The various components of education (general, basic, theoretical, and professional) should not be separated into discrete time periods.[20]

Application of these principles to a professional field—for example, social work—would produce a B.S. with perhaps a major in one of the social or behavioral sciences, and a Master of Social Work which could variously be completed in one, two, or more years and which would lead equally into practice or consideration for doctoral candidacy. The requirements for the master's degree would have enough in common with some other professional fields to allow students to change emphasis without retracing a full master's program.

Techniques of Teaching

Important to these attempts at curricular reform are innovations in teaching techniques. Perhaps the most pervasive tendency is to increase clinical or field experience and to introduce this much earlier in the student's educational career. This means that in medicine, students would be introduced to clinical work within weeks of entry into a program. At Case Western Reserve, for example, each freshman assumes responsibility for working with a pregnant woman. He gets to know the family, follows the case through delivery and the early years of the infant's development. By the time he graduates, he is actually rendering medical service to that family. At Yale, first period students serve in neighborhood clinics on the theory that work in basic science will be much more humane when students can relate it to the needs of their personal experience. In addition, the process is designed to bring the patient back into primary focus in medical practice.

Some teacher preparation programs now provide teaching experience for college freshmen as vocational guidance, and others are seeking to attain clinical experience with a semester of observa-

[20] Spurr, pp. 26–27.

tion and a year of supervised teaching. At Carnegie–Mellon, for example, students spend a term observing and helping in a laboratory school, a term observing in a public school, and a term of supervised teaching.

In law there is a growing feeling that such experiences as a moot court (trial) are too artificial and that students, preferably between a freshman and sophomore year, should spend an intensive summer in a law office, governmental agency, or court. Greater opportunity for law review for more students is also sought. Social work now accepts an undergraduate major, which would intensify clinical work in the second year of graduate professional study. A proposed reformed curriculum for theology puts field experience, often in the form of clinical/pastoral education, at the heart of the first year of professional education, and seeks to relate academic subjects to that work. Architecture and engineering students are given a real life design problem and are expected to assume professional consequences for the solution.

In effect, most of the professional schools actively seek for their students the clinical exposure that medicine, nursing, and dentistry are presumed to have been providing. The health fields are also trying to connect clinical experience more closely to work in the basic sciences and theory.

The approach used by the University of Connecticut in law illustrates the problem and how it might be solved.

> The law schools employed three lecturers-in-law (legal interns) to assist the clinic director in the development of a closely supervised clinical experience for more than thirty second and third year law students. The program was restricted to clinical training in criminal law because of the lack of faculty personnel to supervise a civil division.
>
> The interns completed a six-weeks training session in Connecticut criminal procedure prior to their admission to the state bar in mid-September. Since then they have accepted fifty-four cases involving the defense of indigents accused of criminal offenses in both state and federal courts. In each case two students have been assigned to assist them with the investigation, research, and courtroom presentation. Although Connecticut students are not yet permitted personally to represent

clients, the present program allows them otherwise actively to participate in the decision-making process. In a pyramidal supervision system analogous to the clinical procedure of medical schools, the clinic director is involved in each case as an aggressive advisor and accompanies the intern student team during every important courtroom appearance.

The clinic staff complements the criminal defense cases with a two-hour seminar session every other week. The classroom phase of the program attempts to bind together the clinical experiences of all students and relate them to traditional legal materials. As a result of a recent devaluation, the format has been altered so that many sessions will focus on in-depth analysis of one case, including all the motions, memoranda, and transcripts of court proceedings in the light of tactical, ethical, and legal considerations.[21]

This pilot program proved successful, but one-sided because students gained experience only with criminal defense. A next step would be to devise a similar context for work with prosecutions and corrections.

[This clinic program described above has] the virtue and the vice of being within the general pattern of other clinical experiments being conducted in a number of law schools. Although Connecticut appears to be unique in using interns as teaching supervisors, it follows the approach of other schools in segregating the clinic from the mainstream of legal education. Thus, the clinic has become a separate and distinct course at most law schools (including Connecticut) instead of *the clinic method* becoming an essential teaching tool in many traditional law courses. As a result, the clinic staff has been set aside to supervise its own narrow specialty rather than being employed as an immediate available resource by the rest of the teaching staff.

Those involved in clinical education constantly speak of the "feedback" and "enrichment" that the clinic will furnish to the rest of the curriculum. Assuming the validity of these statements in the absence of available and measurable evidence, it is

[21] *Council on Legal Education for Professional Responsibility,* Feb. 1970, *3* (7).

suggested that the "feedback" and "enrichment" would be more meaningful and apparent if the clinic experience were tailored to meet the narrow educational needs of appropriate law school courses. To achieve this result, it is not proposed that each law professor need become a clinician. Rather, it is urged that the clinic staff lend its expertise to a number of teachers who desire to heighten student interest through the clinic method. In effect, clinic personnel will be brought in to teach the traditional course with the regular professor.[22]

The experience of this law school is repeated in most attempts to develop clinical experience. The two major tasks are how to prevent the work from degenerating into routine tasks and how to insure adequate supervision. Only the health fields have solved the problem, but at enormous expense.

Independent Study and Research. The movement to have students gain a different sort of experience through independent study and independent research modeled after Ph.D. programs is another innovation. Those interested in reform are convinced that there has been too much formal classroom work, too much lecturing, and too frenzied a pace for students in highly organized sequences. As a remedy, medical students are given time especially in the last two years to work on independent research; social workers are encouraged to do research in connection with their clinical work; and lawyers, particularly in those schools trying to relate the social and behavioral sciences to law, undertake original research.

Actual practices range from individualized, paced learning in schools of business to placing nurses in a community with instructions to identify a problem and produce an independently prepared solution. The most common practice however is for each professor to be assigned an independent study course number which he uses to allow each student to pursue his own interests in the last two years of a program.

New Technology and the Media. Few educators discuss in any systematic way a group of technologically based techniques which affect curricular substance as well as process. Widespread use of computers in educational programs is judged a real potential.

[22] *Council on Legal Education. . . .*

There is growing demand for computer services in academic research, and graduates in an increasing number of fields use the computer as a professional tool on the job. There is a great demand for computer scientists and technicians in all major occupational sectors, and there is widespread interest in research and development in the computer sciences and related disciplines.

The University of Missouri Medical School regards the computer as such a potentially powerful diagnostic tool that a separate computer center has been created with computer-based diagnostic rooms so that every medical student can spend time making diagnoses with the assistance of a data bank of medical histories from both in and out patient records for the entire history of the school. In many of the programs at the University of California at Irvine, the computer is an instructional device. For example, genetics is currently being taught through computer-based simulation which makes it possible for students quickly to solve complex problems of genetic drift. A few institutions have provided computer outlets at various places on the campus for student use in problem solving. The University of Massachusetts at Amherst anticipates forty such outlets, expecting that each professional school and academic department will be responsible for training its own students in computer uses. Faculty members from several large computer science programs offer short, practical courses for faculty and students.

However, the bulk of the literature on curricular reform in the professional schools proceeds as though the computer did not exist. This is somewhat strange in view of widespread published predictions of what computers and other of the new media will accomplish educationally. But, at the very time when professional schools are introducing greater variety into their curricula to appeal to differing student interests, to emphasize computer instruction from stored information might produce a uniformity that is intolerant of the random and sometimes aberrant thoughts essential for creativity. Thus, for the moment, we must judge the computer as only a potentially powerful factor in curricular reform.

Similar statements can be made about other educational media or technology—television, tape recordings, multimedia classrooms. Many professional schools have adapted some media, but few have made media-based instruction central to the professional curriculum. All academic departments of the school of medicine and the school of nursing at Duke University use television in teaching, but few departments substitute television programs for live teaching. Duke videotapes psychiatric interviews exhibiting nonrepetitive examples of patient care so that student therapists can review these episodes. And television equipment is available in patient examination rooms in the outpatient clinic so that the student physician can play back immediately his procedures, thereby improving them.

The self-learning center at Oregon State University School of Forestry, equipped with study carrels, work tables, cabinets, recorders, and slide projectors, proved useful once instructional materials in forestry were assembled. Students unable to attend lectures can listen to recordings of them. Instructors absent from class sessions can learn from tapes what progress has been made. Instructors tape exercise instructions and leave them at the center for subsequent student use, and slides and other visual materials, first used in class, are deposited at the center for student viewing at leisure. Notes and photographs from required summer field experiences are also lodged in the center.

Lecture rooms in the School of Medicine at the University of California at San Diego are equipped with electronic response systems for use during lectures which allow students to transmit anonymous answers to multiple choice questions and to queries raised by the instructor during his discussion. The University of Michigan School of Nursing uses videotapes to teach the preparation and administration of medications, and uses the School of Social Work videotape equipment and correlated programmed instruction to develop student skills in interviewing. Carnegie Tech teaches basic circuits and field courses by programmed texts. The Center for the Study of Medical Education at the University of Illinois designed a series of clinical and laboratory simulations which require sequential decision-making as data accumulated. The materials are printed with opaque overlays to move students along the various steps.

The relative unimportance of media in the professional schools is illustrated by the fact that in a comprehensive résumé[23]

[23] Association for Educational Communications and Technology, *New*

only a few of the several hundred examples of media use described come from the professional schools. Nevertheless, if curricular reform proceeds, these techniques are likely to become more useful and important.

International Education

A unique element of curricular reform, the magnitude of which is only gradually emerging, is the attempt in professional fields to add internationalism to the curriculum. The reasons for this development are quite obvious: "Professional people from every field, from medicine and law to social work and education, are prominent in the ranks of the overseas Americans; the professions have developed an international emphasis for the simple reason that the functions they serve must be performed in all societies."[24] A brief résumé of practice and recommendation for international education in several fields illustrates how professional education is responding to this change.

For schools of business administration and public administration, it is suggested that every school should study the nature, extent and timing of its involvement in internationalism. Every school should have some world affairs content in its curriculum. The schools should sponsor lectures on international matters; students should be encouraged to enroll in international courses elsewhere in the university; faculty members should be encouraged to seek international experience; schools should accept qualified foreign students and faculty; and students and faculty should both be encouraged to learn foreign languages. Some schools could go further by introducing comparative and cross-cultural materials into their existing courses. They could initiate courses of specialized international character and could support faculty research of an international nature. Michigan State University follows most of these recommendations. Faculty members have accepted a number of contracts for overseas service. They take graduate students to the host institution, provide service, conduct research, and in the process gain an international perspective.

Media and College Teaching (Washington, D.C.: National Education Association, 1968).

[24] Glennan, *The Professional School and World Affairs,* pp. 1–2.

Generally, schools of agriculture have participated in international projects but have moved slowly to undertake curriculum revision with an international component so as to prepare students for international service. At present there seems to be a struggle in agricultural colleges over how to incorporate overseas experience into campus programs. While performance has been less than adequate, several imperatives emerge. Each school has the responsibility to give its graduates a reasonable comprehension of world affairs. Colleges of agriculture should provide students with training in a selected technical field, augmented by studies leading to an understanding of the interrelationships among people and countries of the world, which might be developed in seminars on international agricultural development. All colleges should insist on an adequate foreign language requirement.

While engineering schools have attracted large numbers of foreign students, only Michigan State University has made a serious effort to develop comprehensive programs to bring internationalism into American engineering curricula. Since American engineering schools should help build engineering schools abroad, they must produce specialists who have both technical competence and understanding of the international scene. Clearly, such specialists should be able to speak the language and should be exposed to the history, manners, customs, and social mores of the region in which they will likely work. Engineering schools should also pay more attention to the needs of foreign students studying on the United States campuses, not only for the sake of these students, but for the further edification of our American students.

Law schools present still a different set of problems. Currently, in contrast with earlier years, more law school professors are teaching courses in the international field. More students are taking these courses, and more students and lawyers are coming to the United States from other countries for legal training. American law schools have made their greatest progress in developing courses and teaching materials dealing with comparative law, public international law, international business transactions, and international organizations. However, few law graduates will be primarily engaged in international practice. Thus the predominant need for legal education in the United States will be in the general education of the larger body of students who will not specialize in international law, but who should get a basic understanding of the problems and limitations of law and of legal institutions in an international context.

As for the professional component of law schools, there are several urgent recommendations. There is a need for greater emphasis on empirical and process oriented research on the relationship of law to economic and social development, and on courses and experiences showing the role of law in land reform, economic development, regulation of business, and other fields acutely relevant to developing countries. Law schools should be increasingly involved in legal assistance activities. They should seek techniques for greater cooperation among law schools in such activities as selecting foreign students and meeting the requirements of legal assistance work abroad.

"Increasingly medical schools have become concerned with international medicine. The interest may stem from global epidemiology, medical missionary education, the desire to expose physicians to medicine in another cultural setting, observations of rare diseases, preparation of teachers or members of the Peace Corps, international health organizations, and the broad influence of travel."[25] Medical schools have tried to meet these needs by increasing emphasis on the social environment. This is reflected in the way several new schools are pioneering with departments and curricula that stress community medicine and preventive medicine programs, departments of behavioral sciences, and interdisciplinary activities. Overall, there seems to be the feeling that students are most in need of experience in overseas programs and work with physicians and students from abroad. Thus, the major reform in medical education will likely be increased participation in world and international health programs.

The thirteen accredited schools of public health in the United States have long been involved in international service, but have only recently begun to formalize their training programs to meet increasing demands for personnel to work in international organizations and on problems involving more than a single country. Several reforms suggest themselves. Students should be taught the elementary

[25] Glennan, p. 234.

steps in preventing or reporting any disease recently arrived from abroad, the immunization protection needed by American citizens traveling abroad, and awareness of how international health services are organized. Students also should be taught to use innovative procedures developed by other countries when they are appropriate to use in the United States. They should be given an understanding of the relationship among other countries between public health and organized medicine, and should be trained to deal with health professionals from other countries.

Until recently, schools of education have given little or no attention to international opportunity and careers except in several surveys, notably *Undergraduate Education in Foreign Affairs* (by Percy Bidwell) and *Non-West Studies in the Liberal Arts College.* While a few outstanding programs have been created, the overall picture is found to be rather impoverished. To rectify this condition, several recommendations have been made. First, each institution should create formal guidelines to help determine the desired contributions of courses in history and the humanities to the student's world view. The undergraduate course requirements of a prospective teacher should probably include some study of a foreign, preferably non-Western, culture. The social and behavioral sciences contributing to the study of education should be used to introduce more comparative data. Such comparative social sciences, as anthropology, should be used more frequently in the preparation of teachers. Curriculum reformers thus suggest that the education of American teachers in the past has overemphasized the behavioral sciences and understressed the social sciences which have the greatest potential for generating international insights.

Ethics and Professional Identity

Only two other major rubrics of curricular reform need to be considered. The first of these is a sustained quest on the part of professional schools to develop in the student some feeling of being a professional and, concomitantly, to identify better ways of developing in students workable and acceptable professional ethics.

The barriers that professional schools currently encounter in developing a professional self-image and a system of ethics for students are illustrated in the perplexities of medical education. In contemporary medical schools, it is difficult for medical students to acquire a unified view of medicine, or a clear concept of their role and their obligations in medicine. Medical education itself, in the formal sense, does not have a rational basis, deriving rather from historical, cultural, traditional, and accidental factors. Thus, there is really no solid base upon which to develop substantive curricula, much less a base which leads to an awareness of moral problems.

The lack of relationship between medical education and the medical profession causes further difficulties. Most medical schools provide either no formal instruction in ethics or only principles more related to economic conditions of the profession than to the larger social issues. Some medical educators have felt that professional schools should rely on undergraduate colleges to develop a sense of moral responsibility. However, not all educators in the undergraduate college will accept this as their responsibility.

Still a further barrier to the development of professional morality in students is the division of medical schools into departments whose very independence and autonomy inhibit meaningful synthesis of disjointed educational experiences. Fundamental biological research, and not human problems, has become the guiding force in medical education, partly in reaction to the charge of being a trade school and partly because of the availability of important federal fundings. Perhaps the grossest example of the clash between professional ethics and the demands for research is the now famous Tuskegee study of syphilitics which first became public knowledge during the summer of 1972. That study, begun in 1932 under the auspices of the United States Public Health Service, included six hundred participants—all Alabama blacks—of whom four hundred had syphilis. Half of the syphilitic participants were denied proper medical treatment, even after the discovery of penicillin, so that doctors could determine through autopsies what damage untreated syphilis does to the human body. Public Health Service officials are now of the opinion that proper care, even fifteen years after the beginning of the study, would have saved most of these unfortunate victims.

In response to the moral and ethical nightmares similar to the one reported above, most major hospitals have now instituted the equivalent of a human subjects committee that must approve any experiment to be performed on a live subject, and while these committees have been quite successful in preventing much questionably ethical experimentation, the fact that one such committee at a prestigious American medical center turned down 60 percent of the applications for experimentation on human subjects shows quite clearly that the profession has not yet reconciled the contrary demands of medical ethics and research. We are of the opinion that the best place to begin the inculcation of medical ethics is in the medical school.

But even when medical faculties approach important ethical questions, the current emphasis on research weights opinion against the ethical nature of practices. A number of distinguished medical professors have been reluctant to see federal restrictive policies to prevent abuse of drug experimentation. If regulations were drawn so tightly as to place the safeguarding of the health of the patient above research aims, fundamental research could conceivably be seriously retarded. Several other minor elements intrude. Drugs are used so frequently in medical schools that students come to accept as normal the use of powerful drugs without realizing the psychological or physiological changes that so many new medicines can induce. Using students as volunteers in experiments, a practice that has grown up in part because of the financial needs of students, gives students the feeling that experimentation with human beings is appropriate and normal.

The increased use of electives allows students great choice, but it does tend to break down the cohesiveness of a medical class. Thus, one further device for acculturation has been weakened. Over half the medical students are married by the time they graduate and have lived part of their lives away from the medical school, a separation almost guaranteed to prevent intense identification with the profession and with the ethical concerns that perplex it.[26]

Continuing Education

The last element of curricular reform, continuing education, has developed from an impressive set of premises, but has turned

[26] Kenneth Underwood, *Church, the University and Social Policy,* vol. 2, pp. 299–307.

out to be a puny effort on the part of the professional field. A few schools of business and engineering have created master's programs to retrain people from one profession for another—notably bachelor's degree holders in engineering receiving a master's degree in business. Schools of education conduct summer programs to upgrade the education of teachers. Colleges such as Sarah Lawrence have begun programs for matriculating mature women and preparing them in mid-life to go into new careers of teaching. A few land grant institutions have created elaborate extension divisions with the avowed purpose of upgrading continuing education. But even at land grant institutions, which probably have the best record in continuing education, the picture is far from bright. Ralph Tyler states that while almost all the institutions participating in general extension reported programs of continuing education at technical, professional, and postgraduate levels, the catch is that most of them are for public school teachers and administrators who in most states get more pay if they have advanced degrees or have completed certain amounts of work toward them. A large part of the work for other groups is of the short course variety which is likely to emphasize immediate answers to pressing problems, rather than the developments of broader and deeper understanding and the use of new concepts and techniques.[27]

But if achievements have not been great, concerns on the part of professional schools are emerging clearly and from those concerns we can infer something about the curricula of the continuing education effort. From engineering comes this prediction:

> It is clear that now and in the future basic engineering cannot presume to teach students all they need to know. Accordingly, the profession and academic institutions which serve it must look forward to a growing activity in continuing engineering studies as a distinct educational function outside of advanced degree programs. This is not merely a matter of dealing with current obsolescence, retreading, retraining, or any of the other popularized versions which have been developed, sometimes almost frantically, to satisfy urgent localized needs.

[27] Herman R. Allen, *Open Door to Learning* (Urbana: University of Illinois Press, 1963), p. 16, quoting Ralph Tyler.

It is rather a matter of establishing an entirely new dimension of personal development throughout the engineer's career. It is a matter of taking a long-range look at the ever-increasing rate of technological change and then deciding what now needs to be done to ensure the continuing effectiveness of the profession in the 1970s and beyond. In this sense, the limited activity in educational institutions, even in recent years under the broad title of continuing education, cannot be considered as adequate for the need and service that is being considered today.[28]

Stressing similar points for continuing theological education, Pusey states:

We express one particular concern that the education of ministers after ordination be of different type now characteristic of the B.D. course. It should not be purely intellectual nor pedantic, but take into large account the work of the minister in his particular station and the experience he has had of human hungers and theology's relation to life and what he has learned in prayer and worship about the deep places of his own and others' innermost hearts. We do not separate intellectual stimulation and spiritual growth. Both are needed. We are concerned for the former, but the non-cerebral factors in education must not be omitted. The Church has an obligation to feed the intellectual fires it has kindled. It must also help a man to grow in the knowledge of what sort of person he ought to be and in the ability to practice that which he ought to do.[29]

Finally, from legal education comes this criticism and advice:

There has been a great effort to promote the continuing legal education of lawyers during the past twenty years. Efforts in this direction have gone on much longer than that in certain localities, particularly in some of the larger states and cities; but by and large nationwide, very little attention has been given to bringing lawyers in practice up-to-date, particularly the sole practitioner who needs it most. . . .
State administrators of continuing legal education have

[28] *Final Report: Goals of Engineering Education,* p. 58.
[29] Pusey and Taylor, *Ministry for Tomorrow,* p. 110.

been appointed in all but nineteen states. Only a few had existed earlier. Much more needs to be done to develop their activities more fully and to raise and maintain the quality of the continuing legal education offered and to persuade lawyers far more generally to make use of it. Much needs to be done to coordinate continuing legal activities throughout the nation to make them more efficient and to improve the quality. The instruction should not be limited to how-to-do-it courses for practicing lawyers. There ought to be more emphasis on high level courses and on professional responsibility.[30]

Illustrative Cases

Illustrative of professional schools that have given a great deal of thought to curricular reform are the School of Medicine at Yale, the School of Law at Denver, and the School of Architecture at Princeton.

School of Medicine at Yale. This school is undertaking its first major curricular reform since 1928 when the school shifted from reliance on part-time teachers to a large core of full-time professors. During the decades after that reform, some minor changes were made in the curriculum, and an occasional addition, as when psychiatry was included among the specialties. In 1968, the college conducted a major curricular restudy. It was assumed that whatever evolved would be based on important elements of the Yale system which has traditionally emphasized freedom for students both to attend lectures and seminars as they wish, and to choose from a number of electives.

Generally, the four years of medical education have now been divided into three approximately equal blocks of time. Students in the first block will receive intensive instruction in basic science, an introduction to clinical medicine, which will develop facility in history-taking, methods of physical examination, basic vocabulary, and basic diagnostic patterns, so that toward the end of that first block the student can enter some clinical work. During the second block of time, approximately a year and a half, students will be given training in specialties, and this will allow them to concentrate

---

[30] David Haber and Julius Cohen, *The Law School of Tomorrow* (New Brunswick, N.J.: Rutgers University Press, 1968), p. 219.

on the specialty of their choice. The final block will return to basic sciences and a great deal of clinical work, with the opportunity for some further electives. In the third block there will be a serious attempt to correlate closely the basic sciences needed for the clinical specialties in which the student is working.

It is hoped that this new arrangement will accomplish several purposes. First, if a student has had some clinical experience before he undertakes work in specialty and basic science courses, it is presumed he will be more highly motivated to get at the scientific roots of problems he has encountered at the bedside. Second, it is hoped that earlier contact with patients will infuse humanism into the curriculum. Since Yale has always emphasized specialization, students have tended to become preoccupied with either a basic science or a disease syndrome. The new curriculum is designed to bring the patient back into the picture. The success or failure of this particular element of curricular reform is going to rest largely on whether or not the faculty will be willing to rearrange time to provide students with the individual supervision they need in the two clinical periods, and whether the faculty will be willing to engage in more conference style teaching and seminar work in place of the easier lecture. The college anticipates offering five major tracks: clinical medicine, basic science (primarily for those who anticipate specializing in research), health delivery services, psychiatry, and the behavioral sciences, and a track for the primary physician, who Yale professors feel will begin to act like a specialist.

Greater emphasis will be placed on the social and behavioral sciences, particularly in restoring humanism to the curriculum. Students will be able to shift in mid-career from an M.D. program to a Ph.D. program without serious loss of time. The approach to the basic sciences will differ substantially from past efforts because of the enormously expanding body of basic science knowledge; only those portions clearly relevant to the physician can be dealt with in courses. This restructuring of course work will be attempted partly in the School of Medicine, but partly through cooperation with the basic science departments in the rest of the university. In the past in some basic science departments, M.D. candidates were considered second-class citizens. However, because the university has begun to reemphasize the values of professional education, the time seems ripe for a rapprochement between the medical school and the basic departments. If plans go as hoped, the result might well be single departments in the basic sciences serving both the graduate and medical school. Already three departments have been combined in the medical school which forces faculty to discuss common curricular problems, and distribute a common budget.

Another important element in the Yale pattern is a fundamental belief that the institution itself should be concerned with the delivery of health services, and should sensitize its students to this responsibility. The University plans to establish and conduct community health centers which, after starting off with some mental health services, will move to pediatric, then gynecological, and eventually surgical and internal medicine services. Medical students, particularly first year students, will be active in these centers which should also in time provide important research information about incidence of disease, epidemiology, and the like, for certain areas in New Haven. These centers are also planned to serve as models for other urban centers and nations.

Especially promising will be the experimentation with group practice that the neighborhood centers will provide. The Yale faculty is convinced that group practice and group delivery of medical service, especially in relationship to government programs, will play an important part in future developments. Student and faculty experience in creating and developing the centers should also give medical workers experience in working with laymen in the community.

The medical school has considered other reforms including the training of nurses to become almost the equivalent of the old-time general practitioner. They believe that a well-trained nurse with the services of the computer and biochemical laboratory can render more effective primary medical service than can the M.D. who has gone through intensive specialization training. The university accepts as axiomatic that the computer is an essential part of medical practice. Students will be given training to use the computer and computer-based information.

School of Law at Denver. The Dean of the Denver Law School is convinced that lawyers and legal education too often focus on the past, partly because of the preoccupation of law schools with precedent as a means of teaching and analysis. Obviously there must be a mix of past, present, and future in legal education, but an overemphasis on precedent is unrealistic. As a first step, the dean wants the law faculty to start thinking about the present and the future and to engage themselves in research appropriate to those time periods. One focus for this new emphasis very likely will be concentration on policy sciences. Lawyers thoroughly immersed in social and behavioral sciences could become the policy scientists of the future. Such a notion might provide a viable alternative to the preoccupation with precedent. Through use of computer and game theory, for example, lawyers might even instruct judges and practicing lawyers in alternatives to precedent. Thus, in the future social and behavioral sciences will play a major part at the University of Denver Law School. Six non-lawyers, including one theologian, who already are full-time members of the law school faculty, are charged primarily with bringing the insights of their disciplines into the study of law. The pattern of research will also be affected. Schools of law do not conduct much research other than orthodox precedent research. However, increasingly the law faculty must be led to involve students in research of the policy sort entailing both law and social and behavioral science disciplines in interdisciplinary effort.

In the past, legal education has attempted to train all candidates in all branches of the law, for the most part through fear of the bar examination. The University of Denver adopts the stance that law, as all other professions, is increasingly specialized and that there should be curricular recognition of this fact. Thus, it is anticipated that first-year students will study the basic sciences of law—contracts, torts, constitutional law, and so forth—and then spend the next two years electing rather widely from law courses and behavioral science courses that seem appropriate for each individual's specialized needs and aspirations. It is assumed that social and behavioral science materials and specialization can be injected into the law curriculum without a major extension of time by cutting out irrelevant curricular materials and stressing free election of specialized courses. Law students will have their introduction to applied experience by helping staff community service centers which should be a responsibility of law schools. Generally, however, the University of Denver sees practical experience as summer activity not to be injected into the normal academic year because there is time for practice after leaving school, and the primary mission of the law school is to help students to see the full legal system in relation to society.

Just as Yale has begun to think about nurses, Denver has begun to think about the roles of paraprofessionals in legal work and is seriously considering creating programs leading to the preparation of insurance adjustors, probation officers, and estate planners. The bar generally has been reluctant to see law schools train people other than practicing lawyers, but the need for these paraprofessionals is so great that the law school must meet it. Packer and Ehrlich have pointed out that the day of the legal paraprofessional is already at hand, and that once the bar associations have taken official notice of this fact, law schools will have an even greater responsibility to design programs to meet the ever-growing need in the legal field.[31]

Two other developments should be mentioned. The university is convinced that continuing legal education has been handled deplorably in the past, concentrating largely on bringing practitioners up-to-date on specific legal matters. A more broadly conceived continuing education can bring practitioners to view the law in a wider context. Some of this broader retraining of practitioners can be accomplished in the newly created centers for blending law and the social and behavioral sciences. At present there are four of these centers, at Berkeley, Denver, Northwestern, and Wisconsin, and at each of them law professors and social and behavioral science professors come together to offer interdisciplinary interpretations of legal matters. The centers which function most effectively are those which are lodged administratively in the law school.

School of Architecture at Princeton. Here, the architecture program has, in the past, been a monolithic, five-year, for the most part prescribed, program leading to a professional degree in architecture. Princeton visualizes architecture consisting of modules normally of two-year duration in future years. At the end of the second module a student will receive a bachelor's degree and at the end of the third module, his professional degree in architecture. During that second module students can elect appropriate special-

[31] Packer and Ehrlich, *New Directions in Legal Education,* pp. 15-20.

izations. Thus, one student might concentrate on engineering, another on planning, and still another on architecture *per se*. Using these modules and the new flexibility, it is hoped that architecture can make much greater use of social and behavioral sciences than it has in the past. Historically there has been a good connection between architecture and the technologies and art, but social and behavioral sciences have been underutilized. With the present interest in leading architecture toward planning, the time seems right to bring in these people-concerned subjects.

As the school tried to establish a rationale for its new curriculum, its faculty used the ideas of Benjamin S. Bloom in *A Taxonomy of Educational Objectives: The Cognitive Domain* and the approach to curriculum construction first elaborated by Ralph Tyler. These consist of trying to specify the behavioral objectives that people who go into architectural planning or engineering actually need, and then contriving a curriculum appropriate to the development of those behaviors.

Urbanism is another element of architecture design that will likely be an important concern of the school of architecture at Princeton. Already an inter-university committee has been set up, consisting of the dean of the Graduate School and the deans of Architecture, Engineering, and the Woodrow Wilson School of Public Policy, to create a Center for Urban Studies which will draw on many of the disciplines and the professional fields to reinforce and enrich the preparation of professional students.

Princeton has arranged work-study programs in the summer for most architecture students as an additional way to branch from a common core of educational experiences into a specialty. While the greatest effort at curricular reform has dealt with the undergraduate program and the program leading to the first professional degree, there is similar concern with graduate work in architecture. In the past, doctoral students in architecture have concentrated on historical or critical studies. It seems likely in the future that they, too, will be combining architecture, the social and behavioral sciences, and real life problems as they prepare themselves for important work in urban design.

IV

Models and Criteria

There is no common theory of curriculum construction nor any generally accepted model for professional education with the exception of the efforts of professional schools to pattern education after the medical school. Nor should there be, because there are essential differences in the professions, and even individual schools serving the same profession have different missions. But there are common problems and common attempts at reform that suggest principles or ways of conceptualizing the curriculum which could be effective in most of professional education. There have been few efforts to create generally acceptable models or sets of principles.

Models for Reform

In a sense, the composite of current reforms implies one model, although without including all of the elements required by professional curricula. For example, there is the proposition that professional schools belong in a university context and that full professional preparation should include graduate and undergraduate education and some educational experiences in the arts and sciences, the professional sciences, and in application.

If faculties understand the requirement of actual practice, they should be able to list the specific skills and competencies that every graduate needs. The list need not be infinite and ways of developing these capacities are not beyond the abilities of a school seriously interested in a serviceable curriculum. Somewhat more difficult but possible is arranging a variety of experiences to contribute to the development of a professional person. For example, every professional student should have clinical or field experience, work with a group of peers on a professional problem, close identification with at least one member of the faculty, observation of practitioners in action, work with people from related professions, and exposure to some foreign culture. A program could be devised which would insure that all students would enjoy these experiences.

Organization for balance between general and specialized studies suggest a second model. We have argued elsewhere that the undergraduate curriculum should consist of at least four components, each demanding about a fourth of a student's time. Certain common learning should be the shared heritage of all and should create a common universe of discourse. Then there should be specialization requiring no more than a fourth of the student's time lest he become too one-sided in perspective. To enrich specialization another fourth of the curriculum should directly relate to the field of specialization and should provide a context for it. The last fourth should be intended to insure time for students to broaden themselves, to explore matters which particularly interest them, and to achieve greater insight into a more general culture.[1]

This conception will have various applications for different professions. For bachelor's degree in engineering it is easy to visualize one fourth of applied engineering courses, one-fourth of mathematics, physics and chemistry, one-fourth of common studies in humanities and social sciences, and one-fourth spread over subjects in business, the arts, or law.

[1] Lewis B. Mayhew and Patrick J. Ford, *Changing the Curriculum* (San Francisco: Jossey-Bass 1971), pp. 150–151.

For graduate social work, we would put field work in the area of concentration and assign one-fourth value to it. Contextual studies would be courses in social work theory. Courses in sociology, psychology or anthropology would provide a common background of discourse about the nature of society and of social problems. The fourth allowed for electives might see students taking work in nursing, education, law, the arts, or even in urban design.

Law schools might use slightly different proportions. Thus one-third could be comprised of basic legal science courses, one-third of specialized work, and one-third contrived to force law students to broaden themselves through instruction outside the law school. We stress again that such a scheme which may sound mechanistic is no absolute model but just another way of considering the curriculum.

A third form of model can be based on the assembling of groups of general principles to be considered in curriculum construction. McGlothlin sees three major problems: curricular content; curricular length; and curricular organization.[2] Within each area he seeks to identify the critical issue and then to elaborate principles helpful in resolving it.

Principles for curricular content:

(1) Obviously content should reflect the aims of professional education and since those are broader than that of mere technical competence, curricula cannot be governed by job descriptions alone.

(2) The professional curriculum should make explicit provisions for developing social understanding, ethical behavior, and a lively scholarly interest.

(3) The professional curriculum should be considered as the totality of work in the arts and sciences, professional sciences, and the arts of application. Thus, the content of undergraduate education is properly a concern of professional education. Cooperation between each school or agency having responsibility for an aspect of the education of professionals is necessary.

(4) Professional schools should continuously inventory new knowledge for new insights and theory for professional practice.

[2] McGlothlin, *The Professional Schools,* pp. 32–54.

(5) Professional education should develop in students an understanding upon which specific techniques and methods can be based consistent with the individual's own personal style.

(6) The content of the curriculum should be limited so as not to overwhelm students.

Principles for curricular length:

(1) Since the needs for each profession differ, there should be no attempt to maintain uniform curricular length in each field.

(2) The sole criterion for length should be the time an average student requires to master the knowledge and skills necessary for entry into practice and the base for future development. Since new knowledge constantly emerges, the length of the curriculum should never be considered as fixed.

Principles of curricular organization:

(1) The curriculum should be organized to move from the elementary to the advanced, to move students quickly into practice and integrate difference experiences.

(2) While early practice is desirable, so is early mastering of fundamental concepts.

(3) Closely related courses should parallel each other to enable students to understand the relationships.

(4) Problem solving should be a central focus of the professional curriculum.

(5) Integration of knowledge is best achieved through application, hence every professional school should make some provision for clinical or field experience.

(6) Curricular experimentation should be the rule.[3]

A more generic way of studying the professional curriculum is illustrated by Tyler's principles of curriculum construction as elaborated by Bloom's studies of educational objectives. The process of Tyler's conception is a laborious one, but seems almost the only possible approach if curriculum construction is to be a rational act.

[3] Ralph W. Tyler, *Basic Principles of Curriculum Construction* (Chicago: University of Chicago Press, 1929).

The first step of this approach is to establish educational objectives which are really value statements of broadly held cultural aspirations, for example, to produce lawyers sensitive to rapidly changing social and economic conditions. Ideally, these objectives should be stated as precisely as possible. Then they must be converted into descriptions of the actual behavior of a person exemplifying the objectives, for example, to produce a lawyer who understands basic economic principles and the relationship among social institutions and who has the ability to acquire and apply new knowledge. These specifications should point to appropriate educational experiences to produce the desired changes in behavior, for example, exposure to a course which develops understanding of statistics, skill in using data from a computer, and familiarity with sources of information on changes in society. At the same time effective specifications of behavior should suggest techniques of evaluation so that the professional school can discover how effective its educational program is.

Tyler's model has been available for almost forty years, but apart from attempts by nursing educators to apply it to professional curricula, the professional field has only recently become aware of its potential. Whether that potential will be realized depends on whether professional schools and organizations are willing to devote the enormous amount of time systematic curricular construction requires.

Criteria

Systematic Planning. Several criteria should be considered if professional curricula are to be more effective. The first of these is so obvious that one wonders at the rarity of the practice in the past. This is continuous, systematic curricular planning in the professional school. Too frequently courses have reflected chiefly interests of faculty, practices copied from prestigious institutions, unverified requirements of the professions or their accrediting bodies, or historic institutional emphases and interests. In a rapidly changing and expanding profession, these will not suffice.

Systematic curricular planning requires first of all careful attention to the needs of society for professional services and manpower not only for the moment, but for at least several decades in the future. Until quite recently necessary information on these needs was not available. Presently, however, as the study of manpower becomes professionalized, there is reasonably reliable data. For example:

> The demand for persons with legal training for the next two decades is likely to be sufficient to absorb all the graduates that law schools can produce.
>
> [The] principal hope for improving medical sciences in the next decade is the possibility of further increasing physician productivity.
>
> While enough young people are interested in engineering as a career, the attrition rate from schools of engineering is so high as to create a shortage of highly capable engineers.
>
> Engineering schools would do well to follow the example of medical schools which have recently made intensive studies of factors affecting retention of students in their programs.
>
> [During the next decade] the supply [of elementary and secondary school teachers] will not only be equal to the demand for teachers, but also to the projected need as defined by the National Goals Commission.[4]

Planning also must consider such factors as obsolescence of knowledge and such concepts as the half-life of a curriculum—that time during which half of the content has been replaced by newer knowledge and concepts. Because of the exponential increase in relevant information, the half-life of a number of professional curricula is now about five years. One can argue that as the half-life of a curriculum is approached, major curricular overhaul is needed.

The processes of curricular planning need careful study. By 1970 enough institutions had finally begun to examine their curricula so that patterns and principles began to emerge. Dwight Ladd concludes that curricular reform will take place only when a large proportion of the faculty accepts the desirability of change and when there is strong and skilled administrative leadership. He suggests

---

[4] John K. Folger, Helen Astin, and Alan E. Bayer, *Human Resources and Higher Education* (New York: Russell Sage Foundation, 1970), pp. 75–146. This book is illustrative of new information now available for planners.

that curricular planning can no longer be conducted by faculties alone as in the past. Some new mode of decision-making may be essential to keep curricula useful and professional schools responsive to the supporting society. It seems logical that greater interdepartmental and interfield work will characterize professional curricula. This in turn will demand planning and decision-making that will transcend the parochial interests of any individual department, school, or faculty. One way may be to develop a system akin to ministerial government in the parliamentary democracies. After appropriate consultation someone must have the power to make decisions.[5]

Contributions of Social and Behavioral Sciences. Virtually every reform effort in the professional field has assumed that in the future social and behavioral sciences will make serious contributions to professional curricula, that these disciplines have matured sufficiently to become full partners in professional education. But there has been little or no evaluation as to whether this hope is warranted. There is some reason to believe that the reverse is more nearly true. Psychological research, for example, has contributed little of direct application to the practice of teaching. Strong sociology departments, active in research, claim that sociological theory and research should not be distorted through efforts to apply their findings. Social scientists grant that they can use the professions as objects of study, but find it difficult to indicate how they can contribute to the technical skills or cultivation of the professions.[6]

Several forces have militated against full application of these disciplines. It takes time to integrate new concepts into established social institutions such as the professions, and for people of different backgrounds to work together long enough for joint accomplishment. Yet the needed time has not been available, nor were there funds within institutions to purchase it. Also, behavioral scientists and professional educators have had different expectations of cooperative relationships. The practitioner hopes for a behavioral generalization applicable to professions, while the scientist can only produce an

[5] Dwight L. Ladd, *Changes in Educational Policy* (New York: McGraw-Hill, 1970), p. 215.

[6] Bernard Berelson, *The Behavioral Sciences Today* (New York: Basic Books, 1963), p. 225.

actuarial finding. There is a tendency during the early stages of cooperation to ask for or to promise too much. While some fields have evolved satisfactory working relationships (for example, medicine and military science), relationships between most professional faculty and social scientists have been tentative and precariously structured.

This matter of relationships is complicated by problems of role and status. The clinical professions of law, medicine, and theology are well established within the university and their professors neither gain nor lose status through ties with the behavioral scientists. But the social scientists do fear loss of prestige with their colleagues if they "contaminate" their basic research with application.

Then there is the matter of technical language. Every profession has a technical language as well as a system of values and a preferred way of working. These facilitate work within the profession but handicap interdisciplinary communication. For example, a number of professions attach a different meaning to the word "case" or the term "social organization," and until these differences in meaning are clarified, there will be some confusion.[7]

A last serious obstacle is the matter of the validity of social and behavioral science findings and approaches for the professional fields. Not much attention has been given to the construction of a bridge between research findings and professional problems.

Presently there are no generally validated techniques for using the social and behavioral sciences effectively. However, some suggestions can be advanced. As a first step, adequate time must be provided and financed. Unless faculties from different fields have time to get to know each other well, explore each other's presuppositions, and understand each other's language, they cannot achieve true interdisciplinary work. Further, faculty members must be motivated to take time from their specialized interests to work together. Without faculty willingness to explore new concepts, no programs, however elegantly designed, will work.

In the future people in the specialized disciplines may be willing to take time to serve the professional field, but the pull of disciplinary and departmental interests is still too great to expect widespread crossover. For a time, professional schools would prob-

[7] Berelson, pp. 222–231.

ably be wiser to hire social and behavioral scientists and ask them
to construct special courses to serve professional need. In creating
such courses, social scientists should be told precisely what competencies they are expected to develop in professional students. Simply
asking an anthropologist to create a course in a law school is not
sufficient. But there should be a chance of achieving a course of
relevant content if he were told to aim for specific changes in
behavior.

Clinical or Field Experience. Clinical or field experience is
judged so important that most professional schools seek to provide
it. But with the exceptions of medicine, dentistry, and nursing, there
is little actual field work for the majority of students. Practice
teaching for public school teachers is, of course, customary, but
critiques of its conduct reveal serious flaws. Assuming that clinical
work is essential, it is proper to inquire into the necessary conditions
for its success in a professional program.

First, it must be accepted that clinical experience is expensive
and that unless a school is willing to accept the cost, it might be
better advised to leave clinical training alone. Ideally, there should
be a place for clinical work and clinical material close enough to the
professional school for easy transportation and communication. The
hospital or university laboratory school is, of course, the best model.
There should be sustained and formal efforts to integrate clinical
experiences with theoretical studies. Obviously both academic and
practitioner supervisors should be available to consult with students
and to provide security in the uncertainties of inexperience.

Students should have time enough to steep themselves in
clinical work until they actually feel like practitioners. The brief day
or two of actual teaching that practice teachers are often provided is
probably worse than no teaching experience at all. The moot court
experience of senior law students is probably too brief and too artificial to be of much value. The optimum time in clinical practice
varies from field to field, with medicine requiring the longest; but a
three-month period should be the minimum for most fields.

Competent and willing supervisors are essential. While there
is value in the internship, which is an on-the-job experience with
little or no supervision, or in the paid employment of an aspirant
professional during student years, the essence of clinical experience
should be close supervision, criticism of practice, and relating of

practice to theory. Someone must be constantly responsible. A criticism that practice teachers level against university-based supervisors is that their visits seldom come at the time the cadet teachers really need consultation. One major experiment found that making active classroom teachers into supervisors, and paying for part of their time from university funds, solved the problem. When cadet teachers needed to talk over a problem, the supervisor was just a few doors away.

There have, of course, been attempts to approximate class supervision when experienced faculty were unavailable. At Michigan State University, teaching assistants and videotape provide supervised teaching experience. Once each week the cadet teacher's entire teaching performance is recorded. The cadet teacher reviews the film of himself and selects a portion for replay to a group of other teaching assistants in the same course. Students devote about three hours each week to watching and criticizing each other's film clips. Results, in the form of cadet teacher satisfaction and demonstrated improvement in teaching performance, suggest the system works, but it is still a substitute for personal supervision.

Two other conditions should be mentioned. Supervisors, whether assigned to the professional school or the host institution, should be adequately paid for their supervisory services. Tokenism may produce results for a time, but in the long run, if supervision is to be professional, it must be well paid. Formal evaluation of clinical work should be made quickly available to the student. This last is all-important, yet impossible to accomplish unless the other conditions are met.

Relevance. No book written in the 1970s dealing with curricular problems can ignore relevance. Student activists and their apologists have made the term a shorthand criticism of the entire educational system. But to help in serious curricular revision, whether in the undergraduate college or professional school, we must assign precise meaning to the word. Willingham has argued that there are at least four types of relevance for higher education: personal, social, educational, and economic.[8]

"Higher education has personal relevance," he says, "to the extent that it helps individuals find their roles in society." This

[8] Warren W. Willingham, *Accessibility of Higher Education* (Palo Alto: College Entrance Examination Board, 1970).

means that there must be equal opportunities for people to gain access to professional schools appropriate to their interests and desires. It also means that an effective and humane guidance system and admissions process must facilitate expressions of choice. The major professional schools have been particularly remiss in not providing guidance or information which could help students, especially those from minority groups, to aspire to professional careers. But personal relevance also has a qualitative element. Professional education should contribute to the growth of mature, competent, adult professionals able to serve society and understand and defend its values. Professional schools and their curricula must therefore give close attention to students' personal interests and their views of the world. Greater freedom of selection, more small group instruction, and serious efforts to convey the essence of the humanities can make the curriculum more personally relevant.

The professional curriculum has social relevance to the student in defining social roles and responsibilities, and as a pressure release mechanism. The pressure release mechanism works at one time to marshal and apply natural resources where they are needed and at another to assist in readjusting roles across society. At the present time, an imperative is the enormous task of bringing minority groups into the professional field and supplying neglected areas with the professional services the people need. Education and theology have begun programs to interest students and train them for work in ghettos and remote rural areas. Student protests have suggested, however, that much education has not been socially relevant, that much theoretical, discipline-oriented course work is too far removed from real life. Then, too, as professional schools have tried, especially since the death of Martin Luther King, Jr., to attract minority group students, they have faced but not solved curricular modifications to meet the needs of these new students. In graduate programs the need is expressed in pleas for black studies, but in professional schools there may not be the appropriate response.

Educational relevance consists in teaching effective modes of action, and this necessity points straight to the heart of the problem of the professional curriculum: Should the curriculum be broadly theoretical and liberal, or highly applied and practical? It may be that this historic dichotomy has become largely immaterial for the speed of technological change demands that education keep pace but insures that it never really can. Consequently, the professional school must give more attention to retraining and continuing education. This entails a radically different relationship between education and work; the once stable pattern of a single preparation for a profession followed by a lifetime of practice is no longer feasible. The professional schools should realize this and act accordingly.

Professional education has economic relevance in that it produces individual modes of action which are beneficial to society. It must therefore be concerned with the development of human resources for the good of society. Faculty planning in the 1970s has not met this need, as is evident in the potential oversupply of Ph.D.'s and undersupply of medical doctors. For the future, professions and professional schools must be more precise in estimating manpower needs and must set longer-range goals. This in turn means that training in each professional school must be correlated with development of other schools.

Balance. Equally important to relevance is curricular balance. On the one hand, too much theory leaves the graduate unemployable; on the other, too long a period of preparation or too much applied experience reduces his potential for long-range development. To maintain balance we must constantly examine the curriculum and mechanisms for rapid change. There is no easy formula for balance, but there are certain criteria which may be applied.

One of them is logic. Looking at a total professional curriculum, we can ask whether a reasonable person would judge it to be balanced to achieve its objective? If courses in a professional school of education based on experimental psychology outnumber all others, this would be an imbalance. If a school of nursing demands much basic science and offers only a few courses in nursing training, a similar judgment can be made. A combined panel of practitioners and theorists in a profession might be expected to have a sense of balance or fitness by which they can judge the curriculum as it appears on the pages of a catalogue.

Realism is an important criterion. Is there enough time allowed for a given course or activity? Can a course in statistics offered three hours each week for ten weeks develop the skills necessary for a consumer of statistical data? Are ten hours of required lectures on psychosomatic disease enough to make the future internist sensitive to other than biochemical procedures? Is a survey course on principles of economics adequate for a law curriculum? This criteria can effectively be applied in a common sense way.

Economic balance is also essential. Schools faced with finite resources must eventually put dollar values on what they do and must weigh in financial terms anticipated gains from alternative activities. This process is implicit in the newly popular interest in cost-benefit analysis. All reforms in the various professional fields will cost money and compete for money with older elements in the curriculum. Field work or clinical work is expensive, as is inter-disciplinary teaching, internationalism, and computer-based instruction.

Before adopting an innovation, serious questions should be asked about both immediate and long-term cost. During the 1960s, expansion of professional education was facilitated by expectations of continued extramural support. When those assumptions proved unwarranted, especially in medical schools, entire programs and even schools were jeopardized. A number of questions should have been asked and answered as precisely as possible. What are the relative costs of various program elements? What are the relative benefits? Is there reasonable assurance that the institution can maintain a program once it is initiated? What assumptions about future financing are made and how valid are they?

Curricula must also maintain a psychological balance between the theoretical or academic parameters of the curriculum and the psychological and physiological needs and aspirations of students. We can argue that part of the student protest during the 1960s came from imbalance of curricula and student wants. Undergraduate curricula had become so discipline oriented that student needs were neglected. The professional faculty can, and frequently have, put together curricula which are elegant in the disciplinary logic they displayed, but if students do not perceive that logic as relevant to what they would need in practice, the curriculum is subverted. Becker shows how this actually happened in medical education.[9]

[9] Howard S. Becker and others, *Boys in White* (Chicago: University of Chicago Press, 1961).

A final criterion is the relationship between curricular demands and the rewards and life style of the profession. Beyond a doubt, a richer curriculum for nurses or engineers could be created; but would students tolerate a larger, more expensive program in view of the rewards practice actually provides? Nursing education has been particularly plagued by this problem. Its leaders have seen that longer, more rigorous professional training is desirable. But as long as nurses are ill-paid and regarded by doctors as second-class citizens, such reform can not be made.

The situation is similar in professional retraining. Sensitive to the fact that even people in professional fields may change careers several times in a lifetime, a few professional schools have created retraining programs—education and business are good examples. But if the length and cost of a retraining program outweigh the anticipated gains to the individual, the program will be neglected or will require extramural financial aid to students. For example, a retired Air Force officer aged forty-five with a master's degree must expect to spend about $40,000, including forgone income, to obtain a doctorate that will enable him to enter college administration. There is serious question as to the worth of the program to such a person.

In general terms, if the professional curriculum and the life-style and rewards of the profession are too divergent, the professional school will not be able to provide the number of practitioners that are really needed.

V

Graduate Education

Whereas the various professional fields reveal a fairly consistent set of changes, innovations, and proposed reforms, graduate education in the arts and sciences does not. Although there may be some confusion regarding purpose of preparation in professional fields (practitioner or academician), effective practice is a major goal and ineffective practice becomes visible relatively quickly. Thus social workers themselves could sense that a training program preoccupied with psychological bases of behavior was too limited a preparation for contemporary social work practice, and employers of engineers who were prepared during the period of heavy emphasis on basic engineering science were quick to demand that more applied work be added to engineering education. No such immediate assessment of the relationship between preparation and performance happens with respect to master's or doctoral work in the arts and sciences, especially in the humanities and social sciences. For example, since the large majority of recipients of the Ph.D. in history are employed as historians and spend the bulk of their time teaching history, serious gaps in training

91

historians in research methodology can continue unnoted decade after decade. Even more fundamental to the lack of consistent reform movement in graduate education in the arts and sciences is the vast uncertainty that has characterized graduate education since its emergence in the American university. Only when agreement on purpose crystalizes (if it ever does) is there likely to be consistent innovation and evolution in graduate educational practice. Such agreement will necessarily have to reconcile seemingly irreconcilable purposes.

Changing Purposes

Character Formation. One purpose, which has rarely controlled the main course of development of graduate education but has been sufficiently determinative to affect peripheral practice and to contaminate questing for other purposes, is that graduate education is intended to produce broadly learned men. This point of view has its roots in the beliefs of nineteenth century educators, such as Woodrow Wilson, who believed that the college was responsible for purveying a liberal and humanistic culture to students—and graduate education even more intensively so. Although it can be argued that graduate studies designed to produce broadly learned individuals never really had much of a chance to become characteristic in view of the powerful forces of science and technology, a yearning for that more pristine ideal continues to crop up in discussions of reform in graduate education. For example, Mark Mancall in an analytical essay concerning the nature of graduate education has observed that

> The graduate curriculum provides little or no time for broad education experiences which have been largely relegated to undergraduate education where, in turn, the product of the graduate curriculum executes his task but poorly. The decline of political theory, social thought, fear on the part of many graduate students to engage in speculation, the desire for intellectual security as opposed to the willingness to challenge accepted conclusions, the formation of the thesis into a research project—all these witness the decline of originality and the rise of mediocrity among our students. Except in rare cases the system tends to perpetuate mediocrity and honor the per-

formance of tasks rather than to encourage speculation. The growth of knowledge is too often measured by the addition of new facts rather than by increased wisdom. Furthermore, these characteristics are perpetuated increasingly at the faculty level as the habits of graduate education become ingrained in students who become faculty members. In short, the primary objective of graduate education as presently constituted is the direct performance of tasks, and William James' criticism of graduate students as "meek in the eyes of their examiners" is as true today as it was in 1903. The cult of specialization and professionalization is tending to destroy the concept of a community of learning, and those tentative efforts now being made to cross disciplinary lines as a means of reintegrating knowledge, both among faculty and students, must be encouraged by changes in the structure of graduate education itself, if we are to develop the university as a truly intellectual center.[1]

Preparation of College Teachers. Historically the most important purpose of graduate education has been and is the preparation of teachers—originally the preparation of college teachers but more recently the preparation of both secondary school and college teachers. While the proportion of Ph.D. recipients who become college professors, especially in the natural sciences, has dropped and may continue to drop, this purpose is still central. The paradox of this goal is that the traditional training program of graduate study does nothing to prepare individuals for the practice of college teaching. The most serious debates concerning graduate education have been over this matter. On the one hand, most graduate faculty members believe that graduate training in a broad comprehension of a single discipline, coupled with intensive study of a small segment, is the best preparation for teaching. Critics of this stance, including a substantial number of university presidents, contend that since teaching undergraduates is likely to be the professional destination of a majority or substantial plurality of graduate students, programs should be designed to embrace several disciplines and should provide explicit preparation for the task of pedagogy.

[1] Mark Mancall, "A Proposal for the Reformation of Graduate Education at Stanford University," in *The Study of Education at Stanford,* vol. 7, *Graduate Education* (Stanford: Stanford University, 1969), p. 63.

Research. The third purpose of graduate education, to pre-pare people for research and scholarship in a specialized field, seems to have largely determined program content. Certainly, the con-tention that the Ph.D. degree is a research degree has perpetuated such matters as faith in the thesis as the apex of a graduate program and research productivity as the proper hallmark for the successful graduate. However, below the surface, paradoxes appear. Within the natural sciences the programs have been contrived to produce technically competent research workers, but in the social sciences and humanities the clear relationship between the program and the practice of research becomes clouded. Virgil K. Whitaker made this point as he reflected on his experiences as dean of the graduate division at Stanford.

> [He] had to learn sometimes in the hard way how different are the problems in the sciences or even in the social sciences and how different are the basic attitudes involved among students. . . . One fundamental difference is that stu-dents in the sciences are primarily motivated toward research, those in the humanities toward teaching. Students in the social sciences probably vary between these poles from department to department. . . . There is a major difference in the concept of the Ph.D. itself, once again with the sciences at one pole and the humanities at the other. In the sciences, broadly speak-ing, the Ph.D. program is thought of as training in methodology and the dissertation often becomes merely a major research exercise demonstrating the candidate's mastery of the meth-odology of his subject. In the humanities, on the other hand, professors are relatively indifferent to methodology or have even lost sight of it altogether and the older notion that the dissertation should be a major contribution to knowledge per-sists. Once again the social sciences lie somewhere in between. This basic concept of the Ph.D. dissertation is one of several reasons why the post-doctoral Fellowship has become an im-portant part of training in the sciences and in many areas pre-requisite to a career of teaching and research in a major university, whereas it is relatively unknown in the humanities and far less common in the social sciences. The same difference in attitude toward Ph. D. training and Ph.D. dissertation is an important reason for the somewhat greater average time taken by graduate students in the humanities to achieve the Ph.D.

. . . The question of differences between the various disciplines is fundamentally important and needs to be checked out thoroughly. If real diversity exists, then a high degree of departmental autonomy is necessary and desirable, even though it inevitably results in some inconvenience for students and more for administrators. If the diversity is only apparent and results, in reality, from the rivalries and idiosyncrasies of autonomous departments, then the resulting inconvenience to students at least should not be tolerated.[2]

Preparation of Practitioners. A fourth and emerging goal of graduate education in arts and sciences is the preparation of practitioners in a number of fields outside higher education. One aspect of this matter has been accommodated through the establishment of graduate programs within professional fields such as business administration and education. However, if, as seems likely, a smaller proportion of graduate degree holders are entering college and university teaching and more are entering the professional labor force in applied occupations, the purpose and the kind of program needed must command attention. Some take a relatively sanguine view that there really is no problem for graduate education in arts and sciences. "In view of the fact that the Ph.D. has been established in such professional fields as Business Administration, Public Administration and the like, the panel expressed no feeling that the research-oriented Ph.D. should be substantially changed for persons not intending to enter the field of higher education. The main problem with the Ph.D. product in Chemistry and certain other fields appears to be one of attitude and lack of appreciation of the importance and interest of industrial employment."[3] But others accepting the validity and inevitability of increasingly varied vocational destinations of graduate degree recipients urge serious attention be given to program diversifications. W. Gordon Whaley, one of the most consistent observers of graduate education in the United States, recommended: "Each graduate degree awarding institution should study the relations between the character of its

[2] Memorandum of Virgil K. Whitaker in *The Study of Education at Stanford*, vol. 7, p. 110.

[3] *Report on the Conference on Pre-doctoral Education in the United States* (Washington: Washington Research Council, 1969), p. 72.

degree programs and the probable life careers of the individuals who will pursue these degrees. A set of alternative types of programs should be developed by each graduate school and information about them made available to incoming students so that they may choose those programs most in their interest at the outset. Up-to-date information on options available might avoid much blind choice and subsequent frustration."[4]

Custodial Function. A different, and for the most part unarticulated, purpose of graduate education is that it is a substitute for work or in our recent past for military service. Within American society a developmental pattern has evolved which has delayed achievement of full adulthood in its physiological, sociological, political, psychological, and economic dimensions until the late twenties or early thirties. Thus there has emerged a period between adolescence and full adulthood of fifteen to twenty years in contrast to an earlier life style which saw adolescence and full adult status achieved within two or three years. Given this extended period of youth which the work force is unable to absorb, the society must contrive activities for youth which are reasonably satisfying and are not too destructive socially. It is possible to envision graduate education in just such a way. Indeed, the phenomenal increase in graduate enrollments during the late 1950s and 1960s may have represented in part decisions by youth to occupy themselves in graduate work with no particular presumptions of a positive relationship between it and subsequent vocational work. Were this particular issue to be widely and seriously debated, the results might speak forcefully to such matters as the potential oversupply of graduate degree recipients. If graduate education is designed primarily to fulfill a professional preparation, then it can be argued that sharp decreases in graduate enrollments should be contrived. However, if graduate programs are conceived of as healthy ways to occupy large numbers of youth, then one could envision no limit to the numbers of students who should be encouraged to work for master's and doctor's degrees. And, if that mission were accepted, it would mean a reconsideration of program with the goal of producing humanely and liberally ed-

[4] W. Gordon Whaley, *Problems in Graduate Education* (Washington: The National Association of State Universities and Land-Grant Colleges, 1971), p. 8.

ucated men and women who could live productive lives regardless of ultimate vocational careers. Much of the literature espousing a counterculture, such as Charles Reich's *The Greening of America,* has seriously urged this newer and quite atypical posture toward advanced education.

Critics and Criticism

Graduate education in the United States is a paradox. A characteristic mode of graduate education evolved early and has persisted; yet that same mode has been subjected to almost continuous criticism expressing strident calls for reform. Much of the controversy has centered on the purposes of the Doctor of Philosophy programs. If they are to prepare college teachers, why the heavy emphasis on research? If they are to train research scholars, why should the Ph.D. be a union card for college teaching? Since so many dissertations appear excessively long and preoccupied with esoteric minutiae, why maintain the fiction of an original contribution to knowledge, and why not substitute some more relevant requirement in place of the thesis? If the foreign language requirement, tenaciously maintained by faculties, is not an essential tool for research and scholarship, why not eliminate it or determine a more appropriate language requirement?

The intensity and the focus of criticisms of the characteristic mode of graduate education in the United States have varied, of course, according to the concerns of the critics. The nature of the tensions, the parameters of graduate study, and the conventional wisdom of the present time can best be explored through the comments of two typical critics and of graduate students themselves.

Berelson's Defense. Bernard Berelson examined much of the literature about graduate education, made some independent studies himself, and, in the main, found graduate education to be good, viable, and needful only of minor modifications.[5] He argues that the purpose of doctoral training is to prepare teachers and scholars; that the research training culminating in a thesis has not been over-

---

[5] The following information and evaluation substantially follow Bernard Berelson's *Graduate Education in the United States* (New York: McGraw-Hill, 1960).

emphasized, and indeed could be emphasized still more strongly. Although frequent demands are made to broaden the intellectual preparation of doctoral students, intense specialization is a positive good without which the Ph.D. degree would lose its distinctiveness. Experiments with interdisciplinary sorts of doctoral programs have generally proven unsuccessful because academic disciplines cannot be joined in any contrived manner, and because the market expresses wisdom in preferring the holder of a specialized Ph.D. to one having had broader sorts of experience.

While Berelson has no objections to graduate schools providing teaching experience for all Ph.D. candidates, he does not feel that to do so is imperative. First, an increasingly large proportion of doctoral degree holders enter non-academic positions after graduation and hence do not need preparation in teaching; second, employing institutions properly should provide guidance and in-service training for new degree holders in their first teaching position. Writing in 1960 with considerable prescience, Berelson rejected special degrees for college teachers, such as a strengthened master's or a Doctor of Arts degree, on two grounds: first, he foresaw that graduate schools would be able to produce all the needed Ph.D.'s, and second he felt that the sheer prestige of the Ph.D. degree would minimize the value of another degree which would be regarded as having inferior status.

Berelson is equally sure of other aspects of graduate education. A relatively few very strong institutions produce most of the Ph.D.'s and will continue to do so. This elitism is good. It insures standardization of product and is a means by which quality control can be exercised with respect to new institutions seeking to create programs. The existing techniques of graduate student selection are essentially sound, emphasizing as they do qualities of intellectual power revealed in previous academic work and in measured academic aptitude. Because such intensive screening of candidates is carried out during the first two years of graduate study, the much maligned high attrition rate of these students does not seem excessive. Nor does he find that graduate students spend an excessively long time receiving their degrees when the time they spend in other activities is properly weighted. The Ph.D. candidate who interrupts his graduate study in English or history to teach his subject is probably deepening his understanding. Hence, in the long run, he may be better off for having required ten years before receiving his degree.

Berelson approves of the rigorous and demanding examinations throughout doctoral study. Where the oral examination in defense of the dissertation has degenerated into a ritual, there is no objection to eliminating the formality. A better course of action would be to strengthen both the preliminary examination system at the end of the coursework and the oral examination. The dissertation rests at the heart of Ph.D. work and will always be retained. A number of dissertations do not make particularly original contributions to knowledge, but the goal of making such a contribution should be held high. The growing tendencies for faculty to regard the dissertation as a training instrument and to shorten somewhat the length of theses to allow more careful reading by several different faculty members are wise.

The tendency for the master's degree to become an all-purpose sort of certificate does not give cause for concern, since the master's degree no longer implies any particular research competency, but is increasingly becoming an extension of undergraduate programs. Nor is a post-doctoral degree needed, although post-doctoral fellowships will certainly remain in graduate education. Maintaining the high quality of the Ph.D. will insure its continued acceptance as an index of scholarly capability.

Berelson's pride in graduate education is reflected in his overall assessment:

> On the whole, over the years, the graduate school has done a great deal for society:
>
> It has grown from a few fields training a few students in institutions to a large and impressive national system of advanced training.
>
> It has trained a large body of professional people for American higher education and trained them in subject matter.
>
> It has increasingly trained staff for the secondary and elementary school system, especially at the level of leadership.
>
> It has increasingly trained personnel for administrative as well as research posts in government and industry.
>
> In addition to providing personnel for enriched grad-

uate work on its own campus, it has led a number of educational experiments at the college level and it produces a number of leading texts used throughout the system of higher education.

It has now taken the lead in the reconstructing parts of the curriculum at the high school level and in the further training of high school teachers.

In all these ways it has served as the source in which a large part of the educational system is renewed and refreshes itself.

In both educational and non-educational spheres the graduate school's stamp is accepted as a qualifying mark of competence, often the qualifying mark so that the graduate school has become the chief screen of the scientific and scholarly talent in society.

Its leading personnel have increasingly served as advisors and consultants on the largest issues of our national life—foreign relations, economic affairs, scientific policy, civil rights and liberties, health and welfare. . . .

To anyone who sees life steadily and sees it whole, this is quite an accomplishment for a relatively few decades.[6]

McGrath's Attacks. Other critics are considerably more skeptical. McGrath believes that graduate education has fastened a stranglehold on all collegiate instruction and is likely to cause the demise of liberal learning in the United States.[7] Because academic departments control both undergraduate and graduate curricula, and because departments tend to value most highly those sequences of courses leading to intense specialization in a discipline, other courses of more general or liberal concern are eliminated. Graduate students proceed through a program of intense disciplinary specialization and in subsequent faculty roles impose the curricular model of the graduate department on undergraduate institutions, even though that model may be alien to the best interests of the undergraduate institution and its students. Because graduate education has so stressed research, the significance of and respect for teaching

---

[6] Berelson, pp. 258–259.

[7] Earl J. McGrath, *The Graduate School and the Decline of Liberal Education* (New York: Teacher's College, Columbia University, 1959).

has seriously declined. This is especially tragic since the evidence indicates that relatively few Ph.D.'s engage in active research after receiving their degrees. Thus, the anachronism is producted of graduate schools stressing research but sending the majority of their graduates into careers of teaching for which they have provided no preparation.

If liberal education is to survive and appropriate reforms are to be made in the graduate school, certain essentials must be achieved. There should be separate programs for the large majority of graduate students who will enter college teaching. Those programs would stress the nature, methods, and techniques of education, and would provide closely supervised apprenticeships or internships in college teaching. Different sorts of dissertations would be required of these students, dissertations which encourage synthesizing or conceptualizing studies rather than seeking to establish new facts through rigorously controlled experimentation.

It is interesting to note that a recently completed study of graduate education at Stanford reflects many of McGrath's views. It suggests that training of a student in a doctoral program should normally include teaching experience, supervised by a faculty member, and evaluated by that student and faculty member in mutual consultation.[8]

The restoration of liberal learning demands that the meaning of scholarship and of research be so clarified that graduate programs for those preparing to devote their lives primarily to undergraduate teaching and to factual research, respectively, can be differentiated. As a first step, there could be agreement that, although all must be scholars, teachers need not be engaged in research in the sense of making original contributions to knowledge.[9] The Committee on Graduate Education at Stanford recognized the wisdom of this approach when it recommended explicit recognition that the fundamental goals of a dissertation project are to serve as a student's supervised apprenticeship in his chosen field, to allow him to demonstrate mastery of the tools of the trade, and to give him a

[8] *The Study of Graduate Education at Stanford, A Report to the Senate of the Academic Council* (Stanford: Stanford University Press, 1972).
[9] McGrath, *The Graduate School and the Decline of Liberal Education,* p. 38.

taste of scholarly accomplishment. The committee considered that these goals can be fulfilled even if the dissertation does not meet the traditional ideal of being a major contribution to knowledge based on independently designed and executed research.[10]

With respect to providing broad experience and increased interdisciplinary work, the differences between McGrath and Berelson are poignant. Berelson comments that the interdisciplinary Doctor of Social Science degree at Syracuse University, one of the largest interdisciplinary efforts, actually sent most of its graduates into secondary work. McGrath, viewing the same program, sees it as one of the most promising attempts to make graduate education relevant for the college teacher,[11] and quotes approvingly an outside assessment of the program: "The broad factual background that serves as a base for a teacher's professional role can be best obtained if the narrow lines of traditional academic specialization are avoided. This emphasis on breadth of understanding in the several social sciences does not preclude depth. Along with breadth of perspective, the college teacher should have content depth in a particular area but such an "area of depth" should be defined only partially in terms of traditional concepts. For example, although a college teacher needs considerable background in political science if his area of depth is that of American political systems, he must also have extensive knowledge of American history, economics, geography, sociology, and social psychology."[12]

Berelson and McGrath differ radically on the effects of graduate education. Whereas Berelson sees enormous contributions that graduate study has made to society, McGrath sees just the opposite.

> The decline of liberal education in this country parallels almost exactly the ascendancy of the graduate school. A review of the rise of the latter will show unmistakably that this relationship is not advantageous. On the contrary, it will disclose

[10] *The Study of Graduate Education at Stanford,* p. 203.

[11] The Director of the program, Ray Price, agreed with McGrath and claimed Berelson never examined the program or its products.

[12] McGrath, *The Graduate School and the Decline of Liberal Education,* p. 54, citing Syracuse University, "The Doctor of Social Science Program at Syracuse University," December 1958, pp. 1–2.

that this newer branch of higher education has had a direct and profound, and on balance a harmful, effect on higher education and the institutions society believes it has established to provide such an education. It will show that during the expansion of graduate education the liberal arts colleges began to surrender their independence. Gradually they relinquished the function which for centuries in British and later in American higher education had been their heritage and their glory, to wit, the function of instructing young people in the Western European intellectual and spiritual traditions.[13]

Student Criticism. In several recent studies, attempts were made to elicit graduate student response concerning their graduate education experiences.[14] Although the students concerned expressed much satisfaction with their graduate work, they also agreed considerably on a number of weaknesses. Taken in the aggregate, these serve as additional indicators of needed change.

Too frequently courses were organized and scheduled apparently with the professors' interests in mind and without reference to experience needed by students to help master a field. All too often seminars were poorly organized, seemingly shedding no light on either the professor's work or the student's emerging research interests. Many of the courses seemed repetitive of work taken in undergraduate college and taught by a similar lecture method, even when groups were small enough that another mode would be possible. While graduate professors generally received high marks for knowledge of a subject, their teaching left much to be desired.

A second group of criticisms involved guidance. While some graduate students felt that their relationships with their professors were good, a large number complained that professors were unavailable when needed, provided poor guidance, or were themselves ignorant of the pitfalls of which students should be warned. Lack of

[13] McGrath, p. 14.

[14] Ann M. Heiss, *Challenges to Graduate Schools* (San Francisco: Jossey-Bass, 1970); Allan Tucker and others, *Attrition of Graduate Students* (East Lansing, Michigan: The Graduate School, 1964); Don Cameron Allen, *The Ph.D. in English and American Literature* (New York: Holt Rinehart and Winston, 1968); John L. Snell, *The Education of Historians in the United States* (New York: McGraw-Hill, 1963).

guidance seemed especially significant in the selection of dissertation projects, and too often professors were unconscionably long in returning drafts of a thesis or of a proposal. Consistent with this criticism about faculty unavailability was the widely held belief that faculty members spent too much time building research and consultation empires and were thus distracted from their primary responsibility to their graduate students.

Examinations, particularly the preliminary examination, did force students to work fairly extensively on their own and to synthesize previous experiences. However, questions too frequently were capricious; no guidelines of appropriate answers had been established; and questions did not adequately sample a full doctoral program. The oral examination was regarded by a few students as entertaining, by some as a symbol of "finally arriving" at a professional level, but for large numbers, it was an occasion for professorial sadism or demonstration of internecine warfare among the examiners.

In a related vein, students experienced too many formal hurdles (applications for candidacy, multiple examinations, distribution requirements, and the like) which made graduate study a survival course rather than an enriching educational experience. Because of the bureaucratic system and the idiosyncratic desires of professors, much graduate training seemed to reward conformity and ability to comply with the demands of others rather than creativity and independence of spirit. For example, theses must follow established models or encounter difficulty, examination answers must reflect professors' attitudes, and students must conform to prevalent departmental beliefs.

A large proportion of the graduate students in all four samples indicated that there was not adequate training for college teaching, and they expressed a desire that graduate programs should give explicit attention to preparation for the role of teacher.

Behaviorism vs. Humanism. Possibly influencing the call for relevant courses and work experience is the incipient revolt of some younger scholars against excessive preoccupation with behaviorism, scientism, and disciplinary elegance, although the long-term significance is difficult to gauge. Thus far, demands of dissident young Ph.D.'s for substantial change in curriculum or style of graduate education have not been effective. But the fact that annual meetings of learned societies have within the last several years been scenes of confrontation between younger and older professors suggests some attention to the phenomenon should be given. Illustrative are some of the issues raised in psychology and in political science. Some of the younger psychologists see graduate work in psychology as being socially irrelevant, with research problems successfully ignoring the big issues of poverty, race relations, and the like. So preoccupied has orthodox psychology become, they maintain, that it ignores essentially human concerns such as love, or moral and ethical values. Younger scholars in political science also criticize graduate programs for being parochially academic and avoiding real-life problems. Caricaturing orthodox scholars, a young critic has described the "ideal" type of first-year graduate student in political science:

> He should fulfill his language requirement with French or German, have math through calculus, an additional year of statistics involving some exposure to the computer; he should undertake some independent research project to demonstrate that he is the very model of a modern methodologist. He should maintain a high "B" average; he should, of course, be a Phi Beta Kappa and of some character and maturity. He need not waste time travelling abroad or consorting with politicians, administrators and other dubious types. He can learn about such matters in courses without leaving the campus. He may safely give up athletics, music, literature and campus activities. Above all, he should avoid community involvement or civic participation. It is not too important that he have the endorsement of his professors so long as he does well on their quizzes. He can manage this if he is careful to pick a college that is generous with A's and B's and does not give comprehensive examinations. He doesn't really need to learn much about politics and government for very few graduate departments screen applicants for substantive knowledge.

It may very well be that the demands for reform on the part of young professors will quickly fade and that their pleas for humanism and social relevance will be forgotten. However, Martin Trow, after comparing attitudes and values of graduate students, younger faculty, and older faculty, stated: "It appears . . . that the academic profession is selectively recruiting those most hostile to its current practices: those graduate students who would give greater power to students, both graduate and undergraduate; those who feel that their field is too research-oriented; those who feel that big research centers are a threat to scholarship; those who feel that strikes are legitimate for faculty; those who do not feel that disrupters should be expelled in every case. These are the graduate students most likely to enter college and university teaching."[15]

Changed Forces and Pressures

During the early 1960s, the matter of whether or not graduate education should change, or was likely to do so, was somewhat at an impasse. A cogent rationale suggested that graduate education was fundamentally sound and needed only minor changes. This point of view was generally reflected in practice during most of the euphoric 1960s. Prestige universities, crowned by their graduate and research activities, prospered and became models to be followed by virtually all other institutions of higher education including liberal arts colleges. They were richly supported by an impressive public and seemed likely to retain essentially the forms existent in 1960. But in many respects, the 1970s are radically different from the 1960s and some of these differences may be sufficiently profound to instigate real changes in higher education generally, and graduate education in particular.

Expectations of Society. Fundamentally, institutions of higher education are social institutions which must be responsive to the expressed needs of society or else lose viability. From 1964 onward increasingly intense waves of public dissatisfaction with higher education crested with demands for change. Research, especially in some of the seemingly non-productive but esoteric fields of the social and behavioral sciences, became suspect. The steady lowering of teaching loads, especially on the part of graduate faculties, attracted first the attention and then the ire of legislators. Undergraduate students began to complain about university lack of attention to their needs, and the public became incensed when student dissatisfactions

[15] Martin Trow and Travis Hirschi, "Age, Status and Academic Values: A Comparison of Graduate Students and Faculty" (n.p., n.d.).

manifested themselves in dissent, protest, riot, and threats to grind the university to a halt.

General public dissatisfaction has already been effective in producing vindictive legislation designed to contain campus protest, some decline in voluntary support for higher education, and an even greater decline in state appropriations. There have also been well-articulated demands for elimination of professorial prerogatives such as security of tenure and unlimited academic freedom. A recent strident attack alleged: "There is one and one only honest justification of tenure: it is there! It has been there a long time. Tenure, not freedom, is academic man's most cherished idol."[16]

The graduate school first became the most visible symbol of prestige and high public regard; it is now vulnerable as the most visible symbol of academic abuse. Failure to reform will lead to the serious consequences of loss of students, revenue, and influence.

Size. First among many new and potent social and educational forces which may dictate change in the nature of graduate education is the sheer size and rapidity with which graduate enrollments have increased. When Berelson was idealizing graduate education in 1960, although he did admit growth, he was still visualizing a relatively small student population and an appropriate ratio of professors to students so that seminars, examinations, and thesis work could be tailored to individual student needs. However, the vast numbers of students currently enrolled in graduate study, and the potential for further increases, suggest a definite qualitative difference. Taking estimates on the announced plans of institutions, we can predict an increase in annual doctoral production from 26,100 in 1968–1969 to between 60,000 and 70,000 in 1980.[17] Similarly, master's degrees could, if present plans are realized, increase from 188,600 in 1968–1969 to between 250,000 and 400,000 in 1980. Much of this expansion will take place in institutions rapidly expanding in size from less than 10,000 students to between 20,000 and 30,000 students. If expectations are realized, graduate study will take place in institutions of 20,000 students or more, with almost half upper division, graduate, and professional students.

16 Robert Nisbet, "The Future of Tenure," *Change,* April 1973, p. 31.
17 Lewis B. Mayhew, *Graduate and Professional Education, 1980* (New York: McGraw-Hill, 1970), p. 1.

As a result of such increases in graduate programs, several developments seem likely. First, master's programs will probably regress even more sharply to being a fifth-year extension of undergraduate preparation with no pretensions to research. Second, especially in view of increasingly serious financial problems, some modification of the mentor-apprentice relationship between the professor and the graduate student will be required. Already in some institutions the graduate student seminar, in the sense of a small group of six to eight students and a professor, has evolved into a large discussion class. Third, especially in the light of student criticisms of graduate work, increased size will demand different techniques for advising and guiding graduate student progress. In this respect, size might dictate either more formal patterning of programs into which groups of students can be enrolled or much greater reliance on independent study with infrequent student-faculty contacts.

Cost-Price Squeeze. A second force, which may have even more effect in bringing about changes in graduate education, is the growing financial crisis in higher education. After examining a carefully selected sample of institutions, Cheit has made a general assessment of the crisis:

> The essence of the problem is that costs and income are both rising, but costs are rising at a steady or slowly growing rate depending on the period and the measure used, whereas income is growing at a declining rate. The rate of growth of expenditures may decline in any given year—as it has at some schools for 1970–71—but the longer range trend has been toward a growing rate of costs. For most colleges and universities, the main consequences of the resulting divergence of cost and income began to appear in the academic year 1967–68 or in 1968–69. This financial problem arose immediately after a decade of unprecedented growth in higher education. But contrary to what might be expected, that growth has not protected the schools but may well have made them more vulnerable to a downturn. Many were undercapitalized, overextended, moving into enlarged areas of responsibility without permanent financing, or still raising quality standards. Because the increasing demand on the schools (both from without and from within, for research, for services, for access, and for

socially current programs) are an important part of the reason for cost increases. The cost-income problem is far more than the consequence of inflation, over-extension and an external economic downturn.[18]

How this financial situation will affect graduate education cannot be foreseen. Some believe that the financial condition will ease by the mid-1970s, in which event, changes may be relatively minor; but even minor changes may have significant results. For example, there is likely to be an overall decline in the funds available for fellowship and scholarship aid to graduate students; hence the graduate school may more closely resemble medical and law schools in that students and their families would be expected to pay a large proportion of the total cost. That fact alone might bring about a stabilization of time and expectations concerning graduate study, so that most students could know when they enrolled that at the end of a given period of time they would emerge with a degree—as now is the case in medicine. Particularly in public institutions, the expanding cost of graduate education may lead legislators to demand higher faculty productivity in the form of more contact hours per week and larger classes. Already legislation to this effect has been passed in Michigan, and also in California where budget increases for the state university were denied. Quite obviously the realization of such demands would directly affect individual research of faculty members. Further, it is entirely possible that the whole nature of a dissertation could be changed because financial stringencies simply would not allow the intensive one-to-one sort of thesis work which in theory at least has prevailed in the past.

If financial limitations persist, even more profound changes in graduate education could transpire. Comprehensive universities, reluctant to concentrate on a relatively few graduate and professional programs, may be forced into cooperation and division of labor with other institutions. Further, a number of institutions may have to eliminate some of their larger contract research installations. This, in turn, would affect how graduate students are prepared, since, particularly in the sciences, the growth of post-doctoral study

[18] Earl F. Cheit, *The New Depression in Higher Education* (New York: McGraw-Hill, 1971), pp. 15–16.

and of teams of doctoral students working on related thesis topics has been a correlate of large-scale contract research.

Graduate Supply and Demand. Another matter suggesting that graduate education is entering a new era is the probable excess of supply of Ph.D.'s over any conceivable demand. The potentiality of this phenomenon has been implied by Allan M. Cartter who was one of the first in the mid-1960s to predict that an oversupply of Ph.D.'s might be imminent:

> In the last decade many innovations have been discussed, but there has been little consensus and less implementation for we were all living in a prosperous world of seemingly constant development and expansion. The 1970s, however, portend budgetary constraints, since both the traditional and the new external sources of support will decline. They will see, in addition, an oversupply of Ph.D.'s since the demand for new faculty depends on three basic factors—replacement, expansion, and improvement, of which the first remains relatively constant and the third is tied to the other two. The second is the key, however. Growth in the college-age group is declining, and although the ratio of college enrollment to the college-age population continues to rise, it will soon reach its effective peak. . . . Thus the need for new college teachers will decline.[19]

One can only speculate at the beginning of a period of retrenchment on what changes may transpire, but several developments can be envisaged. An oversupply of rather narrowly trained Ph.D. recipients may suggest that a broader based education would allow for greater career flexibility. At the same time, demands by recently trained Ph.D.'s for career orientation may force graduate schools into some variant of continuing education. If, as seems likely, a number of Ph.D.'s, who originally aspired to university work, are diverted into junior college teaching, junior college leaders may succeed in convincing graduate schools to alter the training patterns,

---

[19] Allan M. Cartter, "Graduate Education in a Decade of Radical Change," in *Proceedings of Conference on Changing Patterns in Graduate Education* (Berkeley: Center of Research and Development in Higher Education, 1970), p. 20.

especially in view of recent widely publicized junior college reluctance to hire Ph.D.'s. Graduate schools and graduate professors do feel responsibility for placing their graduates, and should graduate training become incongruent with the requirements of a large consumer, the discipline of the marketplace might bring about change. These pressures are already having effect in some institutions that during the 1960s either abolished the master's degree or used it primarily as a consolation prize. Faculties have resuscitated the degree for some of their students in response to junior college desires for teaching-oriented faculty members.

Changes in Undergraduate Education. Higher education is a complex set of interacting processes and elements, and significant changes at one point bring about changes elsewhere. As a result of student pressures and public expressions of discontent with the educational system, undergraduate education has begun to change. Some of these modifications may not directly affect the nature of graduate study, but a few have enormous potential for creating change.

Between 1960 and 1970 there was a decline of general education which had become the means by which colleges and universities provided the common knowledge needed by college students. Also during that period institutions became disenchanted with the orthodox academic calendar divided into semesters or quarters, and the last years of the 1960s saw a plethora of new academic calendars. There has, too, been interest and experimentation in the new media and educational technology, which will doubtless increase during the 1970s. Another reform of considerable significance for graduate education is the variety of attempts to group faculty and students in new ways. The assumed homogeneity and compatibility of departmental groupings finally proved inadequate for undergraduate purposes and new styles such as group colleges began to attract attention. Also potentially powerful in bringing changes to graduate study is the move to create ad hoc issue oriented courses and courses of varying time lengths. Should, for example, undergraduate institutions simultaneously adopt a completely free elective system and fill the curriculum with non-disciplinary courses, corresponding changes in the structure of graduate education would become inevitable. In undergraduate colleges, the movement against preoccupation with academic studies divorced from the real world has resulted in a sustained search for ways of providing off-campus experiences for which academic credit would be given. The prime example is the cooperative work-study, which Asa Knowles of Northeastern University considers will be increasingly recognized in the future.

Each of these reforms in undergraduate education should, and probably will, result in modification of graduate work, or else suggest similar changes that can be made in graduate programs. If general education no longer provides a common universe of discourse, the graduate school may be forced into providing one. If departments no longer provide the small group experience people require for wholesome development, departmental influence could become weakened; and if off-campus experience proves a healthy way to alleviate preoccupation with on-campus academic life, a similar need may become apparent at the graduate level.

Recommendations from Current Literature

Most of the recommendations found in contemporary literature either reiterate criticisms of the past or offer no real help to those concerned with program development. For example, Heiss makes a series of recommendations of this kind. "It is imperative in this 'age of discontinuity' that universities re-examine their goals or set their priorities," or "curriculum revision, reform, or innovation should be systematic, involve the useful deliberation of the best minds, and be pursued under conditions which remove the constraints imposed by time schedules, fatigue, or other interfering commitments."[20]

Somewhat more specific, but again of no great help, are the suggestions made by Snell:

(1) Provide better orientation and guidance of graduate students, especially in work on the dissertation.

(2) Set guidelines for various stages of progress.

(3) Put less emphasis on formal courses, especially lecture courses.

[20] Heiss, *Challenges to Graduate Schools.*

(4) Restrict the dissertation somewhat in scope of topic, amount of research expected, or length.

(5) Raise general standards for admissions; require fulfillment of the language requirement prior to admission.

(6) Encourage Ph.D. candidates to by-pass the master's degree; waive the requirement of a master's thesis.

(7) Eliminate the final oral examination for the Ph.D.

(8) Relax or eliminate the foreign language requirement.

(9) Reduce the number or size of the fields that are covered on the examination for the Ph.D.[21]

However, a few definite recommendations can be culled from the critical literature which do point to specific reforms. First and most frequently mentioned is a concern for the preparation of college teachers and the steps that might be taken to insure better results. So significant is this matter that Chapter Eight is devoted exclusively to it.

The entire concept of a comprehensive university has been called into question as a viable model, and a refrain that pervades conference reports, individual critiques, and the like is that there should be much greater division of labor within the graduate field. If the University of California at Berkeley possesses a great strength in a field, that probably is sufficient reason why Stanford should not. Similarly, if a state already maintains a comprehensive university with reasonable strength in a number of fields, there is good reason why the state should not attempt to replicate it in another institution. Self-denial may be impossible given the orientation toward prestige which characterizes American graduate education, yet long-term viability seems to make the effort imperative.

The problems of various minority groups have been met in a relatively superficial, numerical way. After the death of Martin Luther King, Jr., universities did launch major efforts to increase black enrollments and subsequently other minority enrollments as well. Fellowship funds were provided and the proportion of minority group students on campuses did increase significantly. However, criteria for admissions have been vague to the point of: "admitting outside the competition, but with some assurance of academic sur-

[21] Snell, *The Education of Historians in the United States*, p. 181.

vival." Attempts at remedial work for minority group students whose backgrounds were seriously deficient appear to have been neither systematic nor particularly imaginative. Further, no evidence has been accumulated as to the efficacy of the commonly-accepted device of a year of postbaccalaureate but pre-graduate work. Criticisms continue to mount that the socializing or acculturative elements of graduate education have not really been worked out to apply to minority group graduate students.

Then, a particularly troublesome problem that has yet to be resolved is the matter of academic standards. The prevailing attitude is absurd when it argues that minority group students coming from educationally disadvantaged backgrounds may be admitted as marginal students, but that at the point of graduation they should be held to exactly the same standards as the more privileged students. This does nothing to answer the problem of how to bring culturally disadvantaged graduate students up to the same level of performance demonstrated by highly privileged graduate students within a reasonable time. At present, there is simply no evidence available that it can be done, yet there is a fundamental social imperative that it should.

Finally, with respect to minority members, especially those searching for a new identity, is the matter of what role ethnic studies should play in a graduate program. There is considerable student demand for such studies which could be either heavily cognate or elective fields or even major fields for a substantial number of students. But the rationale for such balance needs serious attention.

A related criticism is that graduate work in the arts and sciences has been, for the most part, discipline oriented, whereas the emerging needs of society and interests of students are problem oriented. This issue is most clearly illustrated in the relationship between professional fields such as engineering and education and the most prestigious graduate fields in arts and sciences. If the Ph.D., oriented as it currently is toward disciplinary rigor, is held as a model toward which the doctoral degrees in professional fields should move, the needs of future practitioners will very likely be ignored or overlooked. The point is elaborated eloquently by two distinguished commentators. Bowen, after praising graduate education, has argued:

Many of the recent criticisms of the Academy are, in
my opinion, justified. The Academy is narrowly specialized and
discipline oriented. It is scientistic. It is rather exclusively
concerned with the quantitative and the empirical and neglects
values, ideologies, and emotions, and is too closely tied to the
narrow values and aims of the military industrial establishment. . . . I do not mean that the scientific method and
scholarly detachment as we have known them are to disappear
or that specialization is to give way to some miraculous re-
integration of knowledge. The scientific outlook still has a
firm place in the Academy, but the university will be giving
more attention to values and meanings. It will be increasingly
concerned with areas not amenable to scientific exploration
and qualification.[22]

In a similar vein Gould contended:

There will always be a need for speculative inquiry
without regard for current problems, of course, but the degree
of pride in and emphasis upon remote pure research that has
been evident in graduate schools can no longer be socially
justified. . . . We shall not only have to strip away much of
the snobbery about pure research, untainted by mundane
practical applications, but we shall also have to seek new academic linkages and integrations at the graduate level. . .
As society's tasks have become more specialized and society
itself has become more fragmented and compartmentalized,
there has arisen a new need for generalists, for systems analysis,
network planning, policy science, for educated persons who can
see the far-flung and cascading consequences of seemingly
isolated acts like spraying fruit trees against insects, building
roads through a city, or helping one beleaguered nation abroad.
Graduate education can no longer train only effective specialists,
but must confront the rapidly swelling need for socially active
broad-thinking generalists. Without excellent coordinators,
administrators and comprehensive thinkers, our pluralistic
society so dazzling and efficient in many of its parts faces the
danger of serious social disintegration.[23]

[22] Howard R. Bowen, "Stresses and Strains," *The Graduate Journal,*
1968, *8* (2), 343.
[23] Samuel B. Gould, "A New Social Role," *The Graduate Journal,*
1968, *8* (2), 355.

VI

Graduate Curriculum and Instruction

Graduate education generally has not been innovative. It would appear that the real desire is to improve on the present system rather than to make any marked change. Changes do take place from time to time in individual departments, but no universal program of reform is considered possible or desirable. Hence this analysis can only outline the changes taking place at different institutions and the suggestions for change urged by learned societies and professional organizations. From these we can try to determine whether an overall pattern of changing practice can be suggested.

Prior Considerations

Two factors that either directly or indirectly affect changes in curriculum and instruction are admissions standards and the time required to develop competency in a given field. Of the two, the questioning of admissions standards is the more recent, and arose largely because of minority group charges of discrimination.

Admissions Standards. As noted earlier, Berelson has argued in defense of the fact that admissions requirements are tightening and that the quality of students accepted by graduate schools is steadily increasing. In view of the intellectual nature of graduate work, he saw no reason to search for admissions criteria other than those indicating sheer intellectual potential. He expressed only one caveat to this stance: "Across the system as a whole, just about everyone who applies to a graduate school gets into one. The only way to get more good people trained at the doctoral level for industrial employment or university research or college teaching, or professional practice, or any other specific outcome, is to get more good people trained. The only way to get more good people trained is to get more good applicants. The only way to get more good applicants is to get more applicants."[1] He then recommended a specific reform: recruitment for doctoral study should be conducted more systematically and more energetically.

In the way this admission process operates, final decision rests with an academic department or, even more restrictively, with an individual professor who has the option of accepting or rejecting any applicant. Undergraduate gradepoint average, the college from which a student graduated, the undergraduate major, and measured academic aptitude are the typical criteria. The better known graduate institutions tend to accept more students (perhaps by as much as a third) than they expect to graduate, on the assumption that considerable screening will be done by formal course work and the preliminary examinations. Graduate facilities in well-known institutions have been naively sanguine about the attrition thus engendered; there is no evidence that further screening of students already ranked high in intellectual ability will result in an even higher level of ability on the part of degree recipients. Indeed, MacKinnon contends there is "an increasing body of research data which suggests that highly creative youths as well as youths with creative potential are not always those whose academic records

---

[1] Berelson, *Graduate Education in the United States*, p. 227.

insure their admission to college."[2] Highly creative persons in a variety of fields were in general not distinguished for the grades they received or for their level of measured academic aptitude or intelligence above a minimum level of ability to manipulate abstractions. For example, "The college gradepoint average of a group of research scientists correlated low and negatively (−.19) with their later-rated creativity as scientists." And, "taking scores on the Terman Concept Mastery Test (Terman, 1956) as measures of intelligence the researchers found that the correlation of intelligence with creativity in a sample of architects was between minus .08 and minus .07 in a sample of research scientists."[3]

There are three major approaches to changes in admissions policies. The first, which has not as yet attracted much following from graduate schools with respect to Caucasian students, is to minimize the role of gradepoint averages and other measured evidences of intelligence. MacKinnon has argued for this sort of reform. He believes that markedly lowering the level of intelligence required for admissions would not result in fewer students of outstanding creative ability. "We must supplement intelligence and aptitude tests with independent measures of extracurricular achievement and originality, and if additional checks are to be used, with tests that tap those traits and motivational dispositions which have been shown to be positively related to creative striving and creative achievement."[4] Holland and Richard, basing their conclusions on a sample from a population of 612,000, similarly contend that: "Measures of academic potential are among the chief methods used to determine admission of students to college. Our present findings, however, suggest that the emphasis in colleges and universities on academic potential, a relatively independent dimension of talent, has led to neglect of other equally important talents. If academic talent has a substantial relation with vocational and other non-classroom achievement, then this intense pervasive concern with academic

    [2] Donald W. MacKinnon, "Selecting Students With Creative Potential," in Paul Heist (Ed.), *The Creative College Student: An Unmet Challenge* (San Francisco: Jossey-Bass, 1968).

    [3] MacKinnon, pp. 104, 108.

    [4] MacKinnon, p. 108.

potential would be less disturbing. Unfortunately, college grades are generally poor predictors of real life success and are at best only inefficient predictors. Since a college education should largely be a preparation for life, both in the community and in a vocation, we need to examine grading practices."[5]

In contrast to the first approach, disciplinary studies of graduate education admissions almost invariably recommend increased selectivity. For example, the panel for sociology of the Behavioral and Social Sciences Survey saw that: "The market for trained sociologists will probably be very tight in the next decade. We are apprehensive that the resultant pressure to produce Ph.D.'s in great numbers may lead simply to headlong expansion and this expansion may pose a threat to the quality in graduate admissions. . . . Because the rate of expansion of graduate training will be higher in those institutions now regarded as relatively less distinguished, the importance of maintaining higher standards is all the more important . . . [Therefore,] it is recommended that universities and departments strive to maintain high standards for graduate admissions where they are high, and raise standards where they are low."[6]

The third and the only substantially innovative approach is that of a significant number of graduate schools which are attempting to recruit minority group members who do not meet the formal admissions criteria generally imposed. This has placed graduate education in an ambivalent position and has raised the question of whether or not graduate schools should maintain their policy of selectivity. On the one hand, there is a general awareness that the proportion of minority group members in graduate schools should be increased beyond the deplorable levels prevailing through the late 1960s. On the other, it is recognized that students from the Black, Mexican-American, and Indian populations normally do not possess strong gradepoint averages (especially if they have attended highly selective undergraduate institutions) or a high level of academic

---

[5] John Holland and James M. Richard, Jr., *Academic and Non-Academic Accomplishment* (Iowa City: American College Testing Program, 1966), p. 16.

[6] Neil J. Smelser and others, *Sociology* (Englewood Cliffs, N.J.: Prentice-Hall, 1969), p. 160.

aptitude. This has recently led institutions into a variety of experiments with admissions criteria, but no substantial body of evidence has yet been accumulated to indicate their success or failure.

The admissions process at the University of California, Los Angeles, seems indicative of how departments are coming to accept a wider variety of criteria. "Instead of using the high gradepoint average and test results as the main criteria for admission, departments were more amenable to giving consideration to potential motivation and personal history. Many students who had attained acceptable undergraduate records while being employed thirty to forty hours per week were considered for admission as were other students who had achieved well in their major but had spotty records in other areas. Recommendations from professors were heavily weighed, as were written statements by students. In many instances, personal interviews were conducted by departments. Departments were greatly reassured by the knowledge that academic assistance and financial assistance were available, and that there was strong support given students participating in the program."[7]

Cornell University has a policy that "if a student is known to be black, and he has a marginal record in terms of standard admissions criteria, he will be given the benefit of the doubt." This seems to imply some sort of quota of students who will be accepted outside normal competition. The University of Illinois welcomes applications for admission to graduate study from black students and refers the credentials of each applicant to faculty members in the relevant department. There judgments are made on the basis of specific minimum entrance requirements and "on potential for success in the program." Since the University of Illinois is making a massive effort to increase the number of black students, evidence of potential other than academic indexes is being used. The University of Iowa, also interested in increasing its enrollment of black students, states that a student, who has a gradepoint average below the minimum required "but who can supply other evidence of high potential for graduate study," can be processed through a special graduate admissions apparatus. Michigan State University maintains a center for

---

[7] *Graduate Education and Ethnic Minorities* (Boulder: Western Interstate Commission for Higher Education, 1970), p. 50.

urban affairs which is the operating unit for supporting disadvantaged students. The university's policy, however, clearly reveals its ambivalent position: "To minimize the risk of encouraging mediocrity admission is still based upon the individual's past performance and future promise. There remains, however, a definite opportunity for persons who would not ordinarily qualify for financial assistance. To be eligible for support, the applicant must qualify for admission to the Graduate School, possibly on a non-degree or provisional basis initially." The University of Michigan maintains an opportunity program designed to provide support for black students and instructs candidates to indicate on the application form that they are also applying for this program.[8]

Related to this concern for minorities is a growing awareness that women have been discriminated against in admissions policies, particularly in large and prestigious graduate schools. Although women's academic records tend to be higher than men's, women are proportionately underrepresented in graduate enrollments, especially in mathematics and the sciences. Suggested changes in policy are: first, to provide for what in effect would be a quota of women students; and second to allow women to enter graduate study on a part-time basis or to interrupt graduate study for marriage or childbearing with the privilege of reentry without loss of credit. As is true of changes in admissions policies for blacks and other disadvantaged minority students, changes are so recent that evidence of their effectiveness is simply not available. It does seem to be true, however, that minority group efforts to enter the mainstream of American society and women's demands for more equal treatment are forcing graduate schools to modify admissions standards.

Length of Programs. An area of reform which has long been debated is the appropriate length of time a program should take. Much of the debate derives from differing conceptions of the nature of doctoral work. Berelson reached the conclusion that, when one excludes non-academic time, the actual time spent in doctoral study compared favorably with the time spent by students in law or medical schools. Further, he was prepared to defend what many would

---

[8] Julie Paynter, "Graduate Opportunities for Black Students, 1969–70" (unpublished study, 1969).

consider an excessive time for students to obtain degrees on the ground that much of their non-academic activities during this period contributed to their maturation as scholars and teachers. In spite of his contention, criticism as to length of time continues unabated. The Carnegie Commission on Higher Education in its policy statement, *Less Time—More Options* (January 1971), urged that the Doctor of Philosophy degree should customarily be awarded after a four-year course of study following the bachelor's degree. The Assembly on University Goals and Governance argued: "Many disciplines would be well advised to consider what has become commonplace in the natural sciences, where students frequently receive their advanced degrees in a relatively short time, having demonstrated their capacity for independent research. In too many fields the use of stilted nineteenth century scholarly formulae results in the production of huge pretentious documents that mock the presumed intention of dissertation requirements."[9] The Newman Report[10] implied the same point of view by noting the shifting of students, especially in the humanities and social sciences, from one field to another, with an attendant stretch-out program or high attrition rate.

In 1972, the Study of Graduate Education at Stanford recommended that each department demonstrate a clear timetable for the expected progress of its students toward the Ph.D. within four years. Timetables requiring longer than four years would require specific approval.[11] The Senate of the Academic Council has now officially accepted this recommendation.

While the general trends favor a four-year doctorate there are serious barriers to attaining such a goal. One barrier is the attitude of a number of professors who believe that it is almost unseemly to hurry what is conceived to be preparation for a life of scholarship and contemplation. Such professors would agree that "the question is not how quickly but how slowly we could get the candidates through." The way doctoral study is conducted, with

[9] *The Assembly on University Goals and Governance, A First Report* (Boston: American Academy of Arts and Sciences, 1971), p. 20.
[10] Frank Newman and others, *Report on Higher Education* (Washington: U.S. Government Printing Office, 1971).
[11] *The Study of Graduate Education at Stanford.*

extreme prerogatives given graduate professors, is affected by this attitude. No one will ever know how many candidates have been retarded unmercifully because professors insisted upon "just this one more item of preparation" before certifying a candidate for his oral examination. Clearly, another barrier relates to financial conditions: graduate students in those fields not receiving substantive fellowship support must drop out to teach or do other work periodically to obtain enough money to continue their education. Wilson[12] has listed a number of factors of varying importance which serve to lengthen graduate work: discontinuity of attendance (caused by marriage, military service, and the like); work as a teaching or research assistant; the nature of the dissertation (off-campus dissertation, for example); financial problems; inadequate foreign language preparation; lack of coordination between early and advanced stages of work; family obligations; inadequate undergraduate preparation in the field; transferring from one field to another; changing dissertation topics; changes in the composition of a dissertation committee; and personal or family health problems.

If the goal of a four-year Ph.D. degree is a worthy one, the question is: How may this be accomplished? Wilson made several cogent suggestions:

(1) develop at disciplinary and departmental levels distinct patterns of expectations regarding the understandings, knowledge, skills and competencies which recipients of a Ph.D. degree should be expected to exhibit

(2) specify the amounts, types, combinations of curricular and other forms of experience (e.g., as in teaching, research, clinical practice) which are thought to be central to the development and/or cultivation of the desired attributes

(3) incorporate these elements into a programmatic model which reflects the judgment of the appropriate graduate faculties regarding the educationally and professionally optimal sequencing and organization of the relevant experiences and which projects normal patterns of progression through (and time schedules for completing) the sequence as programmed and, finally

[12] Kenneth M. Wilson, *Of Time and the Doctorate* (Atlanta: Southern Regional Education Board, 1965).

(4) develop and implement a basic strategy for translating programmatically projected expectations into actual patterns of student progress—i.e., for facilitating the movement of students into and through the preparation system "on schedule," with due regard for individual differences. Such a strategy must include as a necessary but not sufficient element a plan for continued financial support *throughout the projected duration* of the program contingent upon a candidate's meeting clearly defined criteria of satisfactory progress.[13]

Working on very similar lines to Wilson's suggestions was a project at Fordham University to provide paid supervised teaching experience and some instruction in pedagogy for doctoral candidates. The concern was prompted partly by problems endemic to higher education, partly by factors indigenous to Fordham and the greater New York area. The institution recognized that students were taking too long to complete the doctoral degree partly because of the need to earn a living. It also recognized that many who completed the Ph.D. degree did not have any teaching experience before they became full-time faculty members. Paid teaching experience under supervision was therefore arranged, in an attempt to solve both of these problems. It was hoped this solution might also serve to regularize a phenomenon in graduate institutions in the New York metropolitan area. Typically, as students moved toward the end of their doctoral work and sought jobs, they did so in the metropolitan area but thereby lost contact with their graduate institution. Further, the location, the work, and the concerns of the employing institution frequently conflicted with graduate school goals. A regularized internship program, applications for which would flow through the graduate institution which would supervise the matching of the student to the host institution, could help bring some order out of the seeming chaos.

Fordham University selected a limited number of doctoral students each year and placed them in appropriate liberal arts colleges where the candidates could teach part-time and spend the rest of their time either preparing for their comprehensive examinations or working on their dissertations. For this they would be paid a

13 Wilson, p. 177.

stipend. In connection with the program, each candidate participated in a seminar on college teaching offered for all interns and was subject to supervision both by a professor from Fordham and by the mentor teacher at the host institution. According to plan, students spent the first two years of doctoral study in course work. The paid internship occurred during the third year, at the end of which the dissertation proposal should have been completed. This was followed by a fourth year during which the thesis was expected to be completed.

Course Proliferation

Possibly the most profound development in graduate education has occurred in the sheer magnitude and variety of courses available to graduate students. The reality of this can be tested by simply leafing through graduate catalogues of some of the major, and even quite a few of the minor, graduate institutions. So specialized are large numbers of courses listed in the various fields that it is difficult to reach any conclusion other than that courses are included in graduate programs chiefly as means by which professors express their current research interests. The variety is so great that it is impossible to conceive of any two graduate students in the same department coming out with a common set of experiences and a common point of view toward the subject. Now it may be that such intense variety and high degree of specialization is the essence and glory of graduate education. On the other hand, simply by applying some curricular principles evolved in connection with undergraduate education, one might reach the conclusion that proliferation of courses is responsible for escalating costs of education, but without any demonstrable educational validity. McGrath[14] established that there was no positive correlation between undergraduate curricular extent and departmental success or reputation. If the same could be demonstrated with respect to graduate curricula, and a serious effort made to limit the number of courses,

[14] Earl J. McGrath, *Memo to a College Faculty Member* (New York: Institute of Higher Education, Columbia University, 1961); and *Cooperative Long-Range Planning in Liberal Arts Colleges* (New York: Institute of Higher Education, Columbia University, 1964).

then time and resources for some of the other suggested reforms might be made available.

Program Flexibility

Graduate education is becoming increasingly concerned with the matter of flexibility. Its concern is paradoxical, however, in that forces and factors are pressing for both greater and lesser flexibility of program. Graduate catalogs normally indicate a few specific course requirements followed by more general regulations specifying a total number of course and seminar credits which must be accumulated before preliminary examinations. However, Heiss argued from her data that "most of the psychological stress and educational disillusionment resulting from too little independence seems to occur during the first year of graduate study when many students are locked into a rigid succession of courses and examinations."[15]

Much of the literature on reform stresses greater freedom. Again, Heiss is indicative. She urged that "at the Ph.D. level programs of study should be individualized to the particular needs of the student, and the student as an investor should be responsibly involved in its design."[16] Rather idealistically, she visualized the first-year graduate student articulating his ultimate goals and then planning a program which would make use of the full resources of the university to help him achieve those goals in a reasonable time. Recognizing that many students may have overstated the amount of effort required in their degree program, she nevertheless felt that facilitating a feeling of greater freedom would be wise. "The structure of Ph.D. programs should liberate the student from a preoccupation with grades, credits, course examinations and similar constraints which replicate his undergraduate role and experiences." And she gave, to illustrate her argument, a description of the Ph.D. student at Stanford: "Having worked toward the degree by taking a requisite number of units, fulfilling specified requirements, achieving a certain grade average, passing qualifying examinations, and

[15] Ann M. Heiss, *Changing Patterns in Graduate Education* (Berkeley: Center for Research and Development in Higher Education, 1970), p. 5.
[16] Heiss, *Challenges to Graduate Schools,* pp. 283, 284.

writing an often crushingly boring dissertation that passes as an original contribution to knowledge, the graduate student, his imagination probably restricted and dulled, his mind perhaps withered and exhausted, his soul jaded, dreamless and unwondering, his enthusiasm gone with his youth, is suddenly transformed by the magic of a degree into an educator charged with the responsibility of imparting to those who come after him the excitement of learning and a sense of the high adventure in ideas. Often he leads them no further than into the intricacies of the footnote."[17]

However, the issue is complicated by a number of factors. First of all, changes in undergraduate curricula now enable students to select quite widely from existing courses and even in some institutions to create their own courses. While the virtues of independent study and selection have yet to be completely validated,[18] institutions continue to make provisions for variation; hence a student could very well present himself to a graduate school with a curriculum vitae created primarily by himself. Graduate departments might then find such heterogeneity in the backgrounds of first-year graduate students that they would need to provide some greater uniformity of first-year courses. Currently, whether warranted or not, graduate departments in arts and sciences act as though they assume basic preparation in a discipline produced by a strong academic major. Typical of this assumption is the statement for the botany department of the University of North Carolina at Chapel Hill: "Although students applying for admission to graduate study in Botany should ideally have an undergraduate major in Botany or in Biology, including a substantial number of Botany courses, capable students with a Bachelor's degree may be accepted with the following minimal undergraduate background: General Botany and General Zoology (or an acceptable year course in General Biology) and a year of General Chemistry. A student with a limited undergraduate background in Botany and related Sciences should expect to spend more than the usual time on graduate degree work."[19]

[17] Heiss, *Challenges to Graduate Schools,* p. 284.
[18] Lewis B. Mayhew, "Can Undergraduate Independent Study Courses Succeed?" *College Board Review,* Spring 1971, (79), 26–30.
[19] *University of North Carolina Bulletin.* Chapel Hill, 1971.

Now, if the character of undergraduate education changed radically, as some urge, those assumptions of background would be called into question.

Other reforms being suggested for graduate education must also be taken into account. If heavier emphasis on mathematics and computer science is to become part of the doctoral program of students in the social sciences, for example, and if doctoral work generally is to be restricted to a four-year period, pressures for more specific requirements will result. This would be especially true if (as presently seems unlikely) postdoctoral work were to become institutionalized and established as a common mode by which research professors gained the sophistication now presumed to be provided by the Ph.D. The generally recognized postdoctoral program would suggest a more tightly prescribed Ph.D. program to insure the breadth of coverage claimed desirable for college teachers. Then, too, the size of graduate enrollments must be considered. Already in some of the largest graduate institutions, the number of graduate students in a department is so large that the requisite individual counselling does not take place, except perhaps in those sciences engaged in contract research. Curricular requirements have always been a surrogate for sustained faculty counselling and guidance. If graduate enrollments continue to expand at the rate anticipated, requirements may become necessary if only to insure adequacy of program for most students.

How much program flexibility there should be, of course, will vary according to disciplines. If the ideal of a four-year doctorate were to be realized, one-fourth of the total program in some form of core requirements would seem warranted. "While this may sometimes delay the entry of the student into original research and thus delay his realization of independence and self-confidence, it also insures a Ph.D. with some measure of breadth, some exposure to the conceptual structure of his field at its frontier, outside the framework of a specialized research project. This tends to produce an individual of greater versatility, comfortable in moving outside the area of his greatest competence achieved in the course of the thesis. This flexibility is likely to become of increasing importance as national priorities change and the range of occupations entered by the Ph.D.'s increases.[20] An overall distribution of one-fourth prescribed courses, one-third dissertation work, and the remainder electives with provisions for teaching experiences thus would seem defensible.

Interdisciplinary Work

One common approach to changes in graduate curriculum and instruction is significantly apparent: virtually all American universities are considering greater use of interdisciplinary programs. While such fields as psychology, sociology and economics have developed increasingly close relationships with other disciplines, relatively few institutions have worked out the mechanics of how to do this, nor is there any overall rationale for interdisciplinary studies, or criteria on what they should include. Generally it is believed that interdisciplinary programs should occur at some of the interstices of established fields (for example, genetics) or as the result of some particularly challenging social problem (such as bioengineering). However, interdisciplinary courses and programs are also seen as a possible way of broadening graduate education or of meeting student demands that their course work be more relevant to contemporary conditions.

Interdisciplinary attempts can be made in several ways. The expansion of a discipline in a new direction with respect to research, or the drawing together of research interests in several different disciplines are among the most productive. Thus, research on decision-making in economics and political science, with major contributions from mathematics, produces a new variant of an older field of political economy. As research concepts are elaborated and knowledge increased, a new field of teaching appears with courses offered first for graduate, and then for undergraduate, students. Sometimes this process is facilitated by a sudden awareness of a critical problem which serves to force research and theoretical interests in several fields to move closer together. Urban planning is a case in point: it brings people from civil engineering, economics, political science, and sociology together with people from architecture and design. As these disciplines pool their insights, possibilities for

[20] Harvey Brooks, "Thoughts on Graduate Education," *The Graduate Journal*, 1968, *8* (2), 321, 322.

new courses emerge. When this happens, a team-teaching technique is usually employed for at least a limited period of time. For example, at Stanford, representatives of civil engineering, economics, and architecture teach a large course, open to both graduate and undergraduate students, on urban planning. At the same institution, senior faculty from the Stanford Linear Accelerator facility, the school of law, and the departments of history, political science, and economics were encouraged to create a series of courses in international relations to be taught by teams of senior faculty members.

A simpler and less expensive method is to encourage students to register for courses in different fields on the assumption that the student himself will be able to provide a synthesis. A third course is to establish a center or institute when there does not appear to be any existing mechanism to undertake specific interdisciplinary studies. Dressel and associates discovered a proliferation of centers and institutes generally seeking to achieve any or all of several purposes: Development of interdisciplinary studies and research not readily accommodated in the departments (Latin-American Studies); development of new fields of study or research (Electronic Acceleration Laboratory); a combination of research training and service (Institute of Higher Education); and training for graduate students, faculty field experience, research and methodological training (Social Science Training and Research Laboratory).[21]

Several institutions have followed these approaches. At Duke University, the graduate school offers an interdisciplinary program in biomedical engineering intended to combine engineering and biomedical course work with an interdisciplinary research topic. Also at Duke, there is a program in comparative studies on Southern Asia. An initial grant from the Ford Foundation, augmented by support for South Asian language training from the U.S. Office of Education, enabled the graduate school to create a two-purpose undertaking: to facilitate research on the political, historical, economic, and sociocultural development of Commonwealth countries in Southern Asia (India, Pakistan, Ceylon, Malaysia, and Singapore); and to provide for the systematic training of graduate students in economics, education, history, political science, religion,

[21] Dressel and others, *The Confidence Crisis* (San Francisco: Jossey-Bass, 1970), p. 122.

sociology, and anthropology. Students matriculate in one of the orthodox departments but must satisfy, in addition to departmental requirements, a language competency and cognate courses in other related departments. Duke also operates the Center for the Study of Aging and Human Development for those who want to pursue research training in some aspect of the behavioral sciences and the psychophysiology of human aging and development. The center apparently does not offer courses itself but serves as a referral agency to bring students into contact with professors in the many relevant subjects.

Ohio State University offers a variety of interdisciplinary opportunities through centers which, for the most part, require that a student satisfy the requirements in a single department as well as undertaking collateral work recommended by an interdisciplinary committee. For example, the Institute of Polar Studies comatriculates students in agronomy, anthropology, botany, city and regional planning, civil engineering, geodetic science, geography, geology, physics, zoology, microbiology, and entomology. Students follow the program of their principal study and add such other courses as an institute-appointed committee recommends. Serving a more open-ended function at the same institution is the Mershon Center for Education in National Security which offers seminars to graduate students who are from a number of different disciplines and are interested in policy analysis and policy formation with respect to national security.

Little is published either by individual institutions or in the form of normative studies with respect to how large enrollments are in interdisciplinary work or how far students are successfully placed after completing their degrees. It is clear, however, that several issues must be resolved if an interdisciplinary effort is to be maintained. In the first place, how much of the core requirements of a traditional discipline should be demanded of a student pursuing an interdisciplinary degree? During the late 1940s and early 1950s, the University of Minnesota and Michigan State University experimented with divisional Ph.D. programs which were expected to provide interdisciplinary experience. These, for the most part, went unused because a divisional program in physical science, for example, required the candidate to satisfy core requirements in both physics and chemistry, although he would finish with a degree less respectable and salable than a degree in one field alone. More recently, the same phenomenon seems to operate in the increasingly popular programs in American studies. Here, the candidate actually undertakes the equivalent of the course work for a Ph.D. in American history, and for one in American literature, although the thesis will be concerned with only one of these fields. This leads on to the question of what skills of inquiry, and at what level, are required for an interdisciplinary degree. The problem seems especially acute in fields such as history or sociology in which virtually all substantive courses contribute to methodological competence. To require a student in American studies to develop full historiographic competence equal to that of historians forces the old problem of a doubling or tripling of course work. But not to insist on these requirements may leave the candidate without the skills needed for a thesis to be reviewed by historical scholars. Another issue arises over the danger that an interdisciplinary graduate student can so easily become a pawn caught between conflicting demands, insights, and aspirations of advisors representing several different fields. And then there is the problem of placing students in a market which still values a disciplinary degree over an interdisciplinary one.

Other issues are also involved. There is the matter of how to maintain loyalties of faculty members to interdisciplinary programs when their basic funding and institutional security rest with a department. This seems especially acute for younger faculty members who are not yet on tenure: they might be interested in offering interdisciplinary work, but they must face the rigors of scrutiny by departmentalists if they are to be promoted or granted tenure. On a larger scale, there is the problem of financing interdisciplinary programs. Prime instructional cost continues to be budgeted through academic departments, and faculty time devoted to interdisciplinary work must either be contributed by departments or paid for by some other agency. Interdisciplinary work flourished moderately during the late 1960s when foundation and federal support was available, and centers, institutes, and the like could purchase faculty time from departments. Now, when outside funds are not available, the situation is becoming critical.

Finally, there is the question of quality. A number of graduate schools have created special graduate degrees for candidates whose interests are defensible but not congruent with any existing school or department. The normal procedure is for such students to form a faculty committee that represents different fields and can determine appropriate patterns of courses and thesis requirements. One danger in this procedure is that the program will not reflect an underlying logic which is insured in more orthodox programs. A second danger is that if a single committee not responsible to a larger faculty both devises a program and assesses the outcome, high quality may not be maintained. Yet to impose all-university review committees may make the interdisciplinary degree so bureaucratically complex as to discourage students from selecting that option.

Work and Field Experience

Within the professional schools there is now a pronounced trend to require more clinical and field experience and to introduce it earlier in students' academic programs. As a general rule, graduate schools of arts and sciences have not emphasized such a development, with the two exceptions of attempts to provide teaching experience as part of a graduate program and, especially in the sciences, to provide realistic research experience. However, critics of graduate education have increasingly called for the production of more scholarly practitioners, which indicates an awareness of the need for work experience or field work during an academic program. There is also a general belief that master's degree programs, now being rapidly expanded, should focus on practical aspects of emerging problem areas. Graduate schools, particularly developing ones, anticipate that problem-centered master's degrees will be either one- or two-year interdisciplinary programs designed to equip a person to enter a specialized branch of the work force. Studies on urban problems, international affairs, water resources conservation, marine engineering, criminal justice, criminal rehabilitation, and health care for the aged are illustrative of such programs. If such developments do indeed transpire, one can expect field work, clinical experience, or work experience to become central in the academic program.

The likelihood that this may happen is enhanced by the growing popularity of cooperative education. "Under a cooperative program the educational institution designs an academic calendar which allows the insertion of work periods at appropriate intervals in the curriculum. The institution assumes the responsibility for finding positions which are related to the student's professional objectives and which thus provide work experience that enhances knowledge associated with educational aims. These jobs are regular paying positions producing income by which students can finance their education.[22] Justification for cooperative education rests on the premise that every field for which students are preparing contains certain knowledge which cannot be taught in the classroom and must therefore be learned through on-the-job experience with professionals. A second premise, made especially poignant by the decline in graduate fellowship programs, is that most students must find employment, at least on a part-time basis, while they are in school; yet the jobs at which students work frequently have no relationship to their career aims or to their academic program. Cooperative work-study education, then, satisfies the dual desire to provide income-producing jobs and at the same time to extend and amplify the learning process of students.

While few examples currently exist, the general thrust of work experience is reflected in the policies of the University of Michigan. Required for certain graduate degree programs, the work experience consists of training and teaching or of doing research with considerably more of an applied flavor than is represented by the dissertation. It is presumed that all work experience requirements are established solely on the basis of their educational merit and are normally stated as a certain number of units of work experience. When part of a doctoral program, the requirement must be completed as a condition for candidacy. Departments wishing to make such a requirement must secure approval from the graduate school to insure that the program stresses educational significance.

Ethnic and Urban Studies

Ethnic Studies. The demand for ethnic studies in graduate education is so significant as to require separate discussion. At the

[22] Asa Knowles, *Handbook of College and University Administration* (New York: McGraw-Hill, 1970), vol. 2, pp. 2–224.

same time, their future is so uncertain that their chances of long survival and incorporation into the main intellectual current in higher education cannot be assessed. Black studies were the first of the genre to have a noticeable impact. Justification for black studies is based on several arguments. First, there is the contention that many of the courses taught in colleges and universities have been restricted to the Western European experience and have not given adequate attention to Africa, the Far East, or even the experience and contributions of Blacks in American civilization. Second, black studies are hailed as a means of assisting American Blacks to solve their identity crisis. Third, a program of black studies is seen as an important tie between black students and faculty and the larger Black community, a tie which, in the long run, it is hoped, will generate enough political and economic power to enable Blacks to compete satisfactorily in American society.

Consistent with American curricular history, the expansion of undergraduate programs in black and other ethnic studies is forcing the creation of graduate programs at both the master's and doctoral levels. Examples of these undergraduate programs are instructive and are indicative of potential developments in graduate education. As is true of other interdisciplinary fields, the overall model for ethnic studies is probably the area studies developed during World War II to provide military personnel a broad overview of the regions in which they would likely be serving. Thus most of the programs in existence for black, Chicano, or other ethnic studies draw heavily on some of the humanities and on the descriptive social and behavioral sciences.

The rationale for black studies and their content is exemplified by the program at the University of Washington at Seattle. There an approved interdisciplinary major in black studies explores a substantial segment of human experience previously neglected by the university. The major draws on many departments in the social sciences and humanities, and is not considered an isolating educational experience for those who enter it either as teachers or students. The program is for all students and seeks to achieve several objectives. The substance of the black experience is assumed to be intellectually valid and the study of it its own justification. In addition, planners of the program hope it will increase the self-awareness of black students concerning their own history and culture. The major should prepare students subsequently to teach in primary and secondary schools, or to serve in governmental and private agencies with minority concerns. A bachelor's degree in black studies could serve as a background for persons wishing to do graduate work in the social sciences, the humanities, or law and other professional schools. The program consists of the orthodox core courses, intermediate level courses, and upper division courses and seminars. Generally, students are expected to take courses in a number of different departments rather than concentrate in one. The nature and purpose of this interdisciplinary black studies major are suggested by the courses offered: The Literature of Black America, History of Jazz, Philosophy and Racial Conflict, Afro-American Culture, Mental Health for Minority Groups, The American Black Community, Human Biology of Sub-Saharan Africa, West African Societies, Basic Swahili, Bantu Linguistics, History of South Africa, Music of South Africa, Government and Politics in Sub-Saharan Africa, Comparative Social Systems: Africa. In addition to these specific courses the organizers of the program encouraged other university departments, especially those in the college of education, to integrate black materials into their course offerings.

A similar pattern is found in other ethnic studies programs. At the University of California at Davis, a program in native American studies is being developed with the following major components:

(1) Native American literature, including ancient Mayan texts, oral literature and the considerable body of literature written by non-Indians about Indians.

(2) American Indian legal political studies, stressing such things as the Constitution of the Iroquois, the legal-political experience of the Cherokee Republic, and American Indian law

(3) Native American arts, underscoring Indian contributions in basketry, ceramics, weaving, painting, woodcarving, and sculpture.

(4) Native American religion and philosophy, which would at least consist of three broad geographic areas: Meso-American, South America, and North America.

(5) Native American education which would explore the wide range of problems of schooling for Indians.

(6) American Indian languages.

(7) American Indian tribal and community develop-ment.[23]

Similarly, Chicano studies are rooted in the social sciences and humanities. At the University of California at Santa Barbara a two-year program in Chicano studies is based on history and language studies, with such courses as English for Chicano students and Spanish for Chicano students being the tool subjects. History was deliberately chosen because it could provide the most comprehensive approach to the totality of the Chicano experience.[24]

In order to prepare teachers for these burgeoning programs of ethnic studies, and to produce the research and scholarship needed ultimately to enrich curricular offerings, graduate programs are beginning to appear. For the most part, these programs culminate in the master's degree, but in a few places they serve as preparation for doctoral degrees. Those programs that are either planned or in existence bear a striking resemblance to undergraduate ethnic studies. Atlanta University offers a cross-disciplinary M.A. program in Afro-American studies, administered by its Center for African and Afro-American studies. The requirements are those normal for the school of letters and science: a minimum of 24 hours of course and seminar work, a general examination, and a master's thesis. All students are required to take introductory courses on African societies and Afro-American culture, seminars on Afro-American culture, and a course entitled "The Black Man in the New World." The California State College at Fresno offers a professionally oriented M.A. degree in La Raza studies. In this program, essential courses are "Graduate Survey of Trends in Ethnic Studies," "Research Methods in Bibliography and in Field Work," "Parameters of Chicano Urban Demography," "Farm Labor Migration," "Labor Organizations,"

[23] Jack D. Forbes, "Native American Studies," in Robert A. Altman and Patricia O. Snyder (Eds.), *The Minority Student on the Campus* (Boulder: Western Interstate Commission for Higher Education, 1970), pp. 168–169.

[24] Jesus Chavarria, "Chicano Studies," in Altman and Snyder, p. 177.

"Historiography and the Chicano," and "Concepts of La Raza." Colorado State College offers an M.A. in cultural studies. The University of California at Riverside offers a Ph.D. program in "The History of Black People and Race Relations in the United States," and both San Jose State College and San Fernando Valley State College are offering master's programs in Chicano studies.

As master's programs have become operational, they have revealed deficiencies which can only be rectified through doctoral work in ethnic studies. There is an urgent need for the training of increased numbers of minority faculty to staff undergraduate ethnic studies programs. Further, there is a vital need to conduct research and analysis at the graduate level, the findings of which can be used in the development of course content and teaching materials. Hence, two major forms of doctoral work are being suggested:

> (1) [One structure] includes approximately two years of advanced study in graduate courses in the subject field comparable to those for the Ph.D., but allowing for breadth rather than specialization. Approximately a third year is devoted, though not necessarily sequentially, to selected options designed to broaden background and relate to college teaching. Examples include: study of adjacent subject areas; special problems in curriculum in the subject field; background courses in learning, educational psychology and sociology, and higher education; research techniques in education; a practicum in traditional and new teaching techniques and educational administration. About half of the fourth year is devoted to preparing a dissertation that may consist of an analysis or synthesis of a significant phase of the subject field, or to a project in applied research, such as the development of curricular materials and their testing in a classroom situation. In the remaining half of the fourth year, the candidate participates in a full-time college teaching internship and a related teaching seminar. This program culminates in the Doctor of Arts.

> (2) [The second variant of a doctorate in ethnic studies will be that found in more research oriented universities. This will follow the] established pattern of the Ph.D. in a traditional discipline with concentration upon U.S. Ethnic Studies in advanced courses and seminars and dissertation research. . . .

This is not to say that the new focal or interdisciplinary doctorates should not be considered for U.S. Ethnic Studies. New
programs of doctoral study are being introduced each year, but
typically only after growth of the field to the dimension of a
disciplinary identity.[25]

For the immediate future it seems likely that the number of Ph.D.'s
in ethnic studies will be somewhat limited and that the emphasis will
be placed on degrees to prepare teachers.

Urban Studies. Similar to the social origins of demands for
ethnic studies is the rapidly expanding concern for urban studies.
Interest took an upward turn when violence in the ghetto reinforced
the point that urban centers were degenerating to an almost unliv-
able condition. Once the crucial characteristics of a group of urban
problems have been revealed, universities have taken one of several
different stands. A few have created urban research centers to deal
with urban problems or to supplement city planning programs
which, until recently, were generally housed in schools of architecture.
Others have encouraged traditional departments to add some course
work and research emphasis to urban manifestations of traditional
subjects. Both these approaches are somewhat fragmented (reflecting
in fact the fragmentation in the university or in society). More and
more institutions have therefore begun to search for interdisciplinary
approaches to urban problems, a curriculum which concentrates on
the city in its totality and which can draw on the content and
methodology of many different disciplines. For such an interdisciplinary effort to succeed, field work must be an essential ingredient
not only as a learning experience but also as a means of exposing
problems susceptible to research.

Unlike ethnic studies, which were developed mainly in
courses for undergraduate study, urban studies are much more prevalent as graduate programs. The most significant trend in graduate
urban studies programs is a clear movement away from the city
planning focus, with its strong emphasis on physical factors, toward
a multidisciplinary approach which can accommodate social and

[25] H. W. Magoun, "The Preparation of Faculty in U.S. Ethnic Studies
Fields," in *Graduate Education and Ethnic Minorities* (privately published),
p. 83.

behavioral sciences perspectives. As with so many recent developments, it is impossible to evaluate the various approaches because their effectiveness, or lack of it, has not yet been demonstrated. However, the range of what is being attempted is revealed in a number of different institutions.

The University of Pittsburgh master's program in urban and regional planning, part of the Graduate School of Public and International Affairs, allows students to elect a professional emphasis in urban planning or regional development planning, or to elect a broad, more theoretical program emphasizing systems analysis, research methods, and community political systems. Students select course work from among eight core courses in the Graduate School of Public and International Affairs, and the entire program requires four semesters of course work and a thesis. Other related graduate programs are available in public administration, which focuses on urban ecological conditions; in urban community development administration, which stresses action research; and in urban executive administration, which is intended to prepare students for central administrative positions in urban-related agencies and bureaus.

The program in metropolitan studies at Syracuse University is located in the Maxwell Graduate School of Citizenship and Public Affairs and is very similar to the basic program at the University of Pittsburgh. However, the Syracuse program does not grant degrees, thereby leaving the actual conferment of degrees to the more traditional departments.

Reflecting much current thinking about graduate work in urban affairs is the program in city planning at the Massachusetts Institute of Technology:

> The evolution of the Department of City and Regional Planning at the Massachusetts Institute of Technology illustrates the broadened outlook on physical planning that the increasingly social and cultural nature of city problems is forcing upon many of the nation's professional schools of planning. The graduate department of city and regional planning is thirty-five years old. Its initial enrollment was restricted to architects. One-third of the present enrollment is now made up of architects and engineers, the remainder from other fields. The traditional concerns of physical planning have been sup-

plemented by the issues of unemployment, race and sociological and political alienation. The research arm of the department, the Laboratory for Environmental Studies, embraces four divisions which correspond to the directions in which the department has evolved: race and poverty, quality of physical environment, underdeveloped countries and regions, and information systems for decision making.

The Department has abolished all course requirements. Each candidate for a Master's or Docorate in City Planning plans his own program with the help of a faculty adviser. The course requirement now states that each student is expected to develop (1) a general understanding of contemporary urban society and its major components, social, economic, spatial and political, (2) skill in the techniques for analyzing urban and regional communities, their social and economic characteristics, spatial patterns, political structure, behavioral impact and processes of change and (3) skill in the synthesis of development policy, including the statement of the problem, the formulation of objectives, the generation and evaluation of alternative plans and policies; implementation and the monitoring and adjustment of action.[26]

The University of Wisconsin at Milwaukee established a graduate department of urban affairs in 1963, which has manifested a steady growth since then. As a separate department tied to the College of Letters and Sciences and to the graduate school, it is more able than are traditional departments to provide graduate students a base for urban-focused work. The program tries to train urban affairs generalists who are able to relate theory to practice and to proceed with wise pragmatism when theory is lacking. The program is interdisciplinary, stressing social, economic, and political aspects of urbanization, and policy decision-making. All students are required to take a core of courses; however, there is some thought that most of these prescriptions should be eliminated.

Also in 1963, the University of Chicago established a center for urban studies to coordinate existing research at the university, to conduct classes, and to initiate field studies and applied research. The center intended to resolve contradictions between specialization

[26] Joseph G. Colman and Barbara A. Wheeler, *Human Uses of the University* (New York: Praeger, 1970), p. 128.

and generalization by recognizing both interdisciplinary and disciplinary needs. The general point of view of the center rests on the conviction that neither city planning nor the mastery of one particular discipline can provide the skills needed to solve contemporary urban problems.

In contrast with ethnic studies, urban studies research has flourished and in many ways has produced subsequent teaching missions. The joint center for urban studies at the Massachusetts Institute of Technology undertakes both basic and applied research projects, including such matters as historical roots of civil disorders and insurrections, school desegregation, urban delinquency, and welfare. The Boston College Institute of Human Sciences and the Washington University Institute for Urban and Regional Sciences not only conduct research but maintain a teaching component as well.

At Boston College the research, educational and demonstration projects of the Institute of Human Sciences are thought of conceptually as falling under one of the five programs now in operation. The rationale for this procedure is two-fold. First, the programs form a conceptual umbrella to link the output of several individual projects akin to each other and thus amplify results. Second, the administrative responsibility and authority is thus decentralized in order to achieve more efficient collective use of Institute of Human Sciences resources and talent. The five programs under which the research, educational and demonstration projects fall are: Deprivation and Social Transition; Intercultural Conflict and Cooperation; the Individual and His Adaptations in Society; Urban Change and Development; and Voluntary Participation and Leisure Activities in the Urban World. Most of the research projects are basic. Several deal with prevalence, activity, and participation of volunteer organizations. Only two formal courses have been organized thus far. A "Seminar in Urban Change and Development," for advanced students in universities in the Greater Boston area, and for general practitioners in the field of Urban Studies, and a seminar in "Urban Development Research and Policy" for Boston College graduate students. The former course deals with actual contemporary urban problems. The latter is structured for extensive use of case records, team work in applied research, independent research, discussion and presentation in group work.[27]

If these and other specialized fields are to expand in the total graduate educational complex, several issues must be resolved. First, no coherent logic so far has been presented comparable to the logic of history, for example, which would allow programs to be institutionalized and maintained without constant defensiveness. Much of the justification of these specialized courses is polemical, exhortative, and frequently militant. Second, the problem of job opportunities for students who have received advanced degrees in specialized studies is far from assured. Even well established programs in American studies, producing substantial numbers of Ph.D.'s, have not solved this problem. Third, there is the matter alluded to time and again in reports of the lack of adequate library holdings and substantive research results which can sustain special studies. Last, none of the graduate programs has solved the problem of providing the broad exposures desired in the social sciences and humanities and the sophisticated research skills needed for persons to pursue scholarly careers. Schools of education have, of course, struggled with this matter for generations, and one can anticipate a long-term effort within the interdisciplinary specialized studies as well.

The sheer variety of course offerings in departments and the tentative, informal arrangements to effect synthesis of courses in common areas of concern would seem to deny or make impossible any cohesive program of changes and reforms in graduate curriculum and instruction which would be generally true in sciences, social sciences, and humanities. However, suggested or tried changes imply a potential new profile for graduate work in the arts and sciences. Obviously there will be differences among departments and among major fields of knowledge, but there seems to be a surge toward shortening graduate programs for both the master's and the doctoral degrees with somewhat more prescribed core work in the doctoral programs than has been true in the past. Institutions are struggling with the nature and problems of interdisciplinary work, but

[27] Colman and Wheeler, pp. 131–132.

so great is the interest that some variant of interdisciplinary work is likely to be found in most programs. Graduate schools somewhat reluctantly have begun to review and revise admissions practices and seem likely to be forced to extend the consideration of broader qualifications for admissions, employed first with disadvantaged students, then with graduate students generally. Lastly, and with quite faltering steps, graduate departments are trying to accommodate the needs of future practitioners, either by making dissertation requirements broader to conform to applied criteria or by providing some applied experience.

VII

Structure and Organization

Much of the success, but also the rigidity, of graduate education in the arts and sciences derives directly from the departmental structure. It is the department which provides a focus of loyalty and identification for professors, and which has made possible many of the great advances in research. But at the same time, it has created barriers between fields, has jeopardized institutional goals for more limited and frequently selfish departmental ends, and has established the values of a discipline as superordinate to the human values of students seeking an education that contributes to their individual development.

Departmentalism

Departmental Structure and Its Critics. One cannot deny that academic departments have made substantial contributions to American higher education. They are a relatively simple way of organizing people of like mind and interests—a way that allows considerable freedom for professors to pursue individual research and teaching interests. Departments are a logical method for creating and administering university operating budgets: the departmental budget is the module that combines with program planning and budgeting to form the institutional budget. As the source of faculty recruitment and as the base upon which tenure and professorial appointments have rested, the department has become an effective means of personnel management. The department has also proved a reasonably effective device for combining the seemingly irreconcilable elements of undergraduate and graduate studies within the same institution. This point can perhaps be best illustrated by noting the generally accepted goals or missions of departments: instructing undergraduate and graduate students, conducting basic applied research, advancing the discipline and profession nationally, advising undergraduate majors, assisting junior staff in career development, and serving business and industry. The department, thus far, has been flexible enough to allow some effort to be expended on all of these goals. A different organization would, beyond doubt, be more complicated and could be quite redundant, as was exhibited during the high point of the general education movement, when a number of institutions organized a separate general education faculty possessing many of the attributes of the faculties offering advanced undergraduate and graduate work.

However, departments have exhibited considerable weaknesses as well—so much so that some observers believe only the abolition of departments will allow genuine reform in both undergraduate and graduate education. This attitude is implied by the statement of the graduate dean at one of the major institutions in the country:

> As for curricular requirements, they remain departmental matters and little shifts and changes occur all over the lot all the time. The graduate school itself has only two requirements: First, beginning with those entering for the first time next year, we shall require three years at the full tuition rate; and second, we require a thesis approved by two officers of instruction. Everything else, e.g., language requirements, written and oral exams, etc., are entirely up to the departments. I wish I could report any change in the nature of theses, but I can't. They seem to remain as bulky and pompous as ever. As for using newer media, while we know that

some kind of oral and viedo circuits recently have been put in at high cost, I hear only that very little use is made of them as yet educationally. Further, as for now at least, we are not examining the graduate school save as to how we can raise and save money.[1]

One of the major weaknesses of departmentalism is that departments have grown farther and farther away from institutional goals and objectives. Dressel and his associates have identified three phases of departmental development through which, they suggest, departments evolve logically as institutions increase in size and complexity. To begin with there is a natural tendency to stress undergraduate education and to depend on university funds for support of departmental activities. This means that departments normally will conform quite closely to university-wide priorities enforced through the efforts of strong and deeply entrenched deans and central administrative officers. As the institution enlarges and develops more specialization, a departmental orientation emerges which fosters a concern with research and graduate programs. But, while departments will now seek and receive some extramural funding to insure departmental autonomy, they are still sufficiently reliant on university support not to depart too radically from university goals and objectives. However, as the evolutionary process continues, the departments establish their research characters and a disciplinary orientation emerges as a crowning glory. Dressel indicates how disastrous the results can be:

> Individualism becomes rampant as professors by virtue of their reputations and funds obtained through their own efforts develop sections and fiefdoms within their department which are virtually immune to any intervention by chairman, dean, or other administrative levels. Where the disciplinary orientation holds sway and research productivity and publication establish a ready means of transfer from one institution to the other, a department for many of the professors becomes only a convenient, perhaps necessary, but very likely a temporary attachment. Undergraduate instruction, even the service instruction to non-majors may continue to be prized in such

[1] Unpublished record of interview.

a department as long as it is a necessary vehicle for the employment of graduate assistants, assistant instructors and teaching fellows to relieve the professors of undergraduate instruction and to assist them in research activity as well as to increase graduate school enrollment. If fellowship and research support become adequate to provide the assistance required, the faculty have no compunction about turning the teaching of undergraduates over to graduate assistants admitted on a marginal basis or even on a waiver of usual graduate admission requirements. A still further step desired by some faculty with disciplinary orientation would be the elimination of all responsibility for undergraduate education, except possibly for a few very carefully selected Honors undergraduates who are able to move into graduate education and research at an accelerated pace.[2]

A second weakness of departmentalism is that the stress placed on the individual interest of faculty members can prevent the development of any overall curricular patterns for either undergraduate or graduate training. It is quite conceivable for major departments to leave completely uncovered broad curricular and research areas needed for the preparation of future college teachers because these areas do not coincide with the idiosyncratic interests of any member of the department. Once departments have developed beyond the stage of university orientation, they are able to exert continuing control over faculty positions and funds to such an extent that these imbalances can be perpetuated, with the university administration powerless to rectify conditions. Further, departmental control over appointive and funding powers, with no effective means available for university monitoring, can lead to distortions in staffing policy. Academic traditions are such that, especially in discipline-oriented departments, the central administration of the university seems almost afraid to contradict a departmental judgment as to what is and what is not appropriate scholarship in the field.

It is this evolution of departments to a position that is beyond monitoring and control that has led to some of the more serious abuses. Some highly research-oriented departments will not only refuse to offer service courses but indeed refuse to produce

[2] Dressel and others, *The Confidence Crisis*, p. 218.

master's or even Ph.D. recipients. In other departments the pre-occupation with disciplinary evolution is so great that the educational needs of undergraduate and graduate students are scarcely considered. Well-established departments having a high proportion of professors on permanent tenure can, and frequently do, refuse to make adjustments and compromises needed to assist institutions to respond to new conditions. For example, at one land-grant institution the needs of a rapidly industrializing economy required people trained in computer science with both sound theoretical grounding and experience with equipment. Neither the mathematically oriented department of computer science in the college of arts and sciences nor the department of computer technology in the college of engineering would cooperate in developing a joint doctoral program, and the central administration, although recognizing the educational need, was unwilling to force the issue.

The most recent and most comprehensive study of departments in American higher education reached this conclusion: "The universities and the departments within them are out of control. Administrators and faculties too readily interpret their own aspirations as meeting or transcending the educational needs of the clientele which they serve. In seeking support to fulfill these aspirations, they engage in half-truths and reluctantly acquiesce to requests for data which are so selected, manipulated and presented as to support their case. . . . Departments and other units within the university must be brought under control so that their resources are allocated and used in accord with priorities set for the university by the university in cooperation with those who support it."[3]

Alternatives and Signs of Change. The first impression that arises from examining university catalogs and from visiting universities with a strong graduate orientation is that departmentalism still prevails and that departments have sufficient power to resist demands for change. The prevailing comment from graduate deans queried as to what changes were taking place in graduate education in the arts and sciences was that since departments were for the most part autonomous, any changes would have to originate in departments, but that generally those units did not appear particularly

[3] Dressel and others, p. 232.

eager to undertake change. However, there does seem to be some ferment which might ultimately produce a different structure for higher education in the United States.

Dressel and his associates saw several new developments essential for reform. First, they urged the imposition of a rigorous management system which would make all subordinate units responsible and accountable for the expenditure of resources for specified and approved missions. Then they urged that a greater variety of organizational structures be encouraged, with reasonably well-defined and appropriately differentiated missions. Thus, there should be separate organizations concerned with the applied and service activities, such as centers for continuing education and cooperative extension programs. Since the educational needs of undergraduate students are quite distinct from those of graduates, universities may need to introduce a number of undergraduate colleges with nondepartmental organization and separate facilities. This would leave the discipline-oriented department free to concentrate in the two related areas for which it is best suited—graduate study and pure research. In a sense, Dressel and his associates restated in contemporary idiom the goals sought by William Rainey Harper at Chicago and David Starr Jordan at Stanford. Having envisioned the mission of the university as the production of research and the training of research-oriented scholars, Harper and Jordan sought to create feeder institutions that would assume responsibility for undergraduate education. Historical, sociological, and economic forces made those dreams unattainable. Whether conditions have now changed sufficiently to make that particular model viable is a matter of conjecture.

The organization of the University of Wisconsin at Green Bay presents a model which, although untested with respect to graduate education, may suggest the possible direction of change. This institution, given the mission of becoming a distinctive university, has focused its entire educational service and research emphasis on the environment. The basic academic units are four colleges, each of which is highly interdisciplinary with respect to faculty appointments. These four colleges offer seventeen interdisciplinary programs, called "concentrations." Each concentration is responsible to a chairman and an interdisciplinary faculty whose appointive and budgetary support reside in the concentration rather than in a department. The need for some disciplinary course work and research is met through units called "options." These options are essentially departments, but without the perquisites and prerogatives which have made for departmental autonomy. They must seek permission from the concentrations to offer disciplinary courses. They must recruit faculty through the concentrations, thus satisfying interdisciplinary needs as well as departmental needs. And they must receive all budgetary support, whether for equipment, travel or teaching assistance, through the concentrations. The institution in its present form is five years old and has awarded thus far only bachelor's degrees. However, planning for graduate work is proceeding in the expectation that graduate programs at the master's level will follow almost exactly the format characteristic of the undergraduate program. Thus, master's degrees generally will be interdisciplinary in nature, will focus on problems rather than disciplinary concerns, and will tend to be action or service oriented. The chancellor and some of his chief assistants believe that the model is ultimately adaptable at the doctoral level.

Another attempt to solve the problem of departments has been made at the University of California at Santa Cruz. This institution has the mission of becoming a comprehensive university (of approximately 20,000 students) stressing both undergraduate education and graduate education and research. The scheme consists in the creation of a number of colleges (of 700 to 1,000 students each) responsible for undergraduate education. Each of these colleges has developed a particular theme or emphasis. In addition, there is the orthodox array of departments, largely responsible for the graduate program and specialized research. Faculty members are appointed to both college fellowships and departmental posts, dividing their time more or less equally between the two. Support of faculty members is provided by the colleges and departments on a half-and-half basis. The evidence thus far is that, under the able and dedicated leadership of the first chancellor, the reconciliation of the seemingly irreconcilable seems to have taken place with a minimum of difficulty. The likelihood of success may be also related to the fact that this was a completely new institution with a physical plant specifically designed to accommodate the two separate functions.

Each college has its own group of buildings which provide congenial locations for faculty offices and laboratories, thus cementing faculty loyalties which otherwise might have been concentrated in an isolated department.

By far the most widespread attempt to modify departmental structure is the creation of centers or institutes. While complete evidence is unavailable, as many as five thousand institutes may be operating in major universities. These seemingly have come into existence in response to several forces: the inability of the academic department to adapt to new functional demands; new sources of financial support; new constituencies; different faculty aspirations and role expectations; increased urging from external sponsors; and rising individual and institutional needs for status and prestige. Although some centers or institutes did exist prior to World War II, the greatest expansion—to between six and twenty institutes per university—occurred during the 1950s and 1960s. These centers or institutes relate to many areas of human concern: labor and industrial relations, ethnic research, ethno-musicology, pacification, linguistics, community development, environmental health, medieval Spanish, and psychopharmacology. However, approximately two-thirds fall into the category of the basic and applied sciences. The remainder are spread over the social sciences, business, government, education, and related areas. While many of the earlier institutes were located within schools or colleges, a majority of the more recently created institutes are administered from an all-university structure.[4]

A number of centers perform functions different from those of an academic department, but in a very real sense most have been established as substitutes for academic departments. Dressel and his collaborators remarked: "Yet the institute proliferates in great part because of the fallibility of traditional academic departments whose instructional and research activities are tied tightly to the disciplines which justify their existence. Academic departments typically have neither the resources nor the interest to attack problems transcending their disciplines. Faculty members are uncomfortable when

[4] This résumé is based on Stanley O. Ikenberry, *A Profile of Proliferating Institutes* (University Park: Center for the Study of Higher Education, 1970).

asked to operate outside the theoretical constructs with which they are most familiar. Thus, when funds become available in problem areas not previously established as being of university concern, often the university is plotted into new concerns. The institute provides a natural vehicle for assembling staff, attracting more funds, indicating institutional commitment and determining responsibility and accountability of resources."[5]

However, the creation of centers and institutes is still far from a perfect solution for problems of departmentalism. One important drawback relates to the matter of funding. Centers and institutes have frequently come into existence supported by extramural financing that is committed for a relatively short period of time. As long as an institute relies exclusively on outside financing, retaining senior faculty and their loyalties is somewhat precarious. If the center employs full-time professional people, there is the difficulty of providing them tenure and other faculty perquisites. If the center uses professors who spend part of their time in the center and part in a department, the problem of departmental loyalties intrudes. On the other hand, as centers and institutes become securely lodged and obtain guaranteed institutional support as well as the prerogative of appointing tenured faculty, they begin to take on many of the characteristics of a department and manifest many of its inflexibilities. The dynamics of some of these problems are captured by Dressel and his associates who stumbled onto the rising significance of institutes in their comprehensive study of academic departments.

> The character and problems of institute staffing are closely related to it budgetary sources. A director of Latin-American Studies Institute who co-ordinates for several departments a doctoral program using staff and courses from these departments may actually have no staff or budget of his own. He may be privileged by the goodwill of the chairman and/or the dean to have a say in new appointments, tenure, curriculum development and degree requirements. His influence on the curriculum and degree requirements is enhanced by

[5] Paul L. Dressel and others, "The Proliferating Institutes," *Change*, July–August 1969, p. 23.

his influence with those faculty members in the several departments who teach courses designated as part of the Latin-American Studies program. If the Director is a scholar of some repute and the initiator of the program, he may have extensive influence. If he is an untenured faculty member, he will be fortunate if his own department reduces his teaching load by one course and the dean provides him with a part-time secretary. Nevertheless, the title, the sign on the door and the privilege usually accorded of sitting with chairmen at meetings called by the dean, offer some recognition which an enterprising operator can, by grants or politics, promote to something more impressive in a few years.

However, seldom does the institute director achieve significant stature and power until he gets a budget and a staff of his own. The easiest and quickest route is to obtain funds from external sources. The director who accomplishes this can then appoint staff members, secretaries and graduate assistants whose jobs emanate from him and whose loyalties are, therefore, clearly to him. If funds are sufficient to import some scholars whose stature commands departmental recognition, courses can be developed, even though offered through departments; graduate students can write dissertations under institute direction; and, ultimately, the institute may achieve departmental, school, or college academic prerogatives. And surely the instructional contribution deserves a permanent lien on the general fund budget.[6]

Degrees and Their Significance

The concept of academic degrees is validated for contemporary use through the responsibility of institutions of higher education to certify people who have demonstrated a specified level of competence in some academic, technical, or professional field. However, the excessive number of named degrees in the United States calls for some substantial indication of their precise meaning. But the movement toward consensus within the academic community as to how numbers should be limited and meaning specified is tediously slow; any discussion of nomenclature leads straight to some of the most perplexing substantive issues facing graduate education,

[6] Dressel and others, *The Confidence Crisis*, pp. 124–125.

Chief among these is the fact that the Ph.D. degree is regarded as the proper credential for college teaching, yet the degree itself symbolizes no particular preparation for teaching but rather preparation for independent research in a relatively narrow field of learning. Resolution of this issue could be attempted in one of several different ways, none of which is generally accepted. One way is to retain the Ph.D. degree as the principal doctoral certificate but to create within that degree structure several tracks to accommodate student career goals of undergraduate teaching, research, or working in business or industry. Another approach is to reject any substantial modification of the nature of Ph.D. training and at the same time to create new titles for those who need a doctoral degree but not necessarily a research-oriented one. A third approach argues essentially for a devaluation of the Ph.D. so that it is more generally available to larger numbers of graduate students and is somewhat more flexibly structured. For the limited number of individuals who have the talent and interests to devote themselves to original scholarship, devaluation of the Ph.D. would eventually lead to the creation of a new superdoctoral degree to be granted at the end of some stipulated time of postdoctoral study.

A second issue is the fact that master's degrees have assimilated such a variety of meanings. Dean Peter Elder of Harvard University epitomized this situation most aptly when he suggested that the master's was a bit like a streetwalker, one for every taste and every pocketbook. This variation in the significance of master's degrees is illustrated by the fact that master's degrees in certain professional fields (education, business, and social work) signify professional capability, while in many of the arts and sciences they certify to no particular professional or vocational competence. In a similar vein, master's degrees in arts and sciences and in some of the professional fields merely certify to a year of work beyond the bachelor's degree, whereas in others (medicine, dentistry, and law) a master's degree may be more advanced certification than the doctorate itself and indicative of very definite research training.

A third critical issue is that the articulation between various levels of degrees is rarely explicit. This produces considerable uncertainty about the implications of any given degree as a preparation for future academic work or as an appropriate terminal certification.

Thus the Associate of Arts degree granted by junior colleges may or may not indicate capacity to enter into a baccalaureate program. The bachelor's degree is so frequently of a general or liberal education sort, that it is not particularly predictive as to whether students should or should not enter into a master's program. Uncertainties become even greater with respect to the function of the master's degree as preparation for subsequent graduate work. Most of the recommended or attempted reforms of the American degree structure are intended to resolve these three issues.

Master's Degree. During the past forty years, there have been regular attempts to redefine the nature and purpose of the master's degree. Two important efforts in this direction were recently made by the Council of Graduate Schools. In 1963 the Council attempted standardization by arguing for several different but interrelated functions of a master's degree: an introduction to graduate study; a remedial period to cover deficiencies in undergraduate education; and a terminal professional program. Again, in 1966, the Council urged reform and argued for: first, development of a reasonably strong faculty before a school could award the master's degree; and second, a coherent sequential program of lectures, seminars, discussions, and independent studies, designed to give the student an introduction to the mastery of knowledge, to creative scholarship, and to research in his field. Especially vocal was Oliver C. Carmichael, who sought to create a master's degree that would serve as a qualification for college teaching in junior colleges or in the first two years of four-year colleges. According to Carmichael's scheme, students would progress through an articulated three-year program (the junior and senior years of the baccalaureate degree plus one more year) to attain the title "Master of Philosophy." But despite these and other efforts at reform, the master's degree is remarkably similar to what it was at the turn of the century. It is still a recognition of at least one year's work past the baccalaureate, but it reveals very little concerning the program elected, the nature of courses, or even the performance of students.

After reviewing in detail the fluctuating history of the master's, Spurr has presented a series of plausible and rational recommendations, but without much hope that they will be accepted any more than were earlier recommendations.[7] He feels that the fatal flaw in present usage is that the master's degree may be bypassed on the route to the doctorate; hence, it tends to be regarded as a second-class degree or a consolation prize. If it could be recognized as the first graduate degree and signify a definitely higher stage of accomplishment than the baccalaureate, it could achieve academic respectability. For this to happen, however, the degree must be required of all graduate students. Properly conceived, taking a master's degree en route to the doctorate should not retard the progress of the doctoral candidate and could at the same time be of significance to students who do not move on to doctoral study. Thus Spurr urges that all students entering graduate school be admitted solely as candidates for the master's degree. They should be admitted into doctoral work only after successful completion of the master's. As a corroborating recommendation, a year—certainly not more than eighteen months—would be the time limit to complete the master's program. Each student could then make the decision whether to terminate academic training at that point, to move into a professional doctoral program, or to continue with a doctoral program in liberal arts and sciences.

Others are even less sanguine than Spurr that the Master of Arts or Master of Science can be so refurbished. A majority of Yale University faculty in 1966–1967 voted to eliminate the master's degrees except in certain very definite terminal professional programs. The master's degree in arts or sciences was replaced with the Master of Philosophy, ostensibly to raise the standards required for the master's degree which had lost distinct meaning at Yale, as it had in the nation at large. The primary purpose of the change, however, was to provide a new intermediate degree which would represent mastery of a discipline in the full scope and depth required for the Ph.D., except for the demonstrated ability to organize and complete a major research project. The competence anticipated for the Master of Philosophy would be adequate foundation for careers in teaching and in other fields not requiring a highly developed research competency.

[7] Spurr, *Academic Degree Structures: Innovative Approaches.*

The Master of Philosophy thus was Yale's answer to the endemic criticism of the inadequacies of Ph.D. programs for the preparation of college teachers. Yale preferred the creation of this intermediate degree to the option of modifying the existing Ph.D. requirements on the ground that serious modification would lead almost inexorably to a debasing of the Ph.D. degree. Recognizing that the creation of the Master of Philosophy itself would not be insurance that the degree would not follow in the footsteps of the Master of Arts or Master of Science, the Yale faculty also adopted a policy that recipients of the Master of Philosophy degree would have first option for entrance into Ph.D. programs at Yale and first call on available fellowship or scholarship funds. The aspirations of the Yale faculty were well summarized by the graduate dean, who argued:

> Academic innovation is not easy and the prestige of the Ph.D. as a union card for college teaching is high; but it is my hope that other universities will join Yale in offering this new degree, since I believe it is an appropriate answer to a clear and growing need. I also hope that many institutions will offer holders of this degree teaching positions, especially for teaching in the first two years of college, that may lead eventually to tenure. Our major universities and colleges will properly continue to insist upon persons who have completed the Ph.D. or its equivalent. For many and perhaps most of their teaching positions, experience in research, i.e., experience in the verification of old knowledge and the search for new, is a necessary although not a sufficient condition for imaginative and effective teaching in many courses at all levels and especially at the advanced undergraduate level. But there are many positions, especially those concerned with general education in the first two years of college, which can be filled by persons who combine the achievement represented by this new degree with commitment to and skill in the art of teaching.[8]

Although an auspicious start was made for this intermediate degree at Yale, a footnote to the story should be added. A letter

[8] John Perry Miller, "The Master of Philosophy: A New Degree Is Born," in *Under the Tower* (New Haven: Yale University Press, 1968), p. 3.

of July 3, 1971 from the present dean of the graduate school at Yale University contains this paragraph: "You may be amused to know that within the past year eight departments have voted to recommend that we re-establish the M.A. and M.S. Indeed, the Executive Committee has agreed that in October a meeting of the full Faculty will be called to dicsuss this issue at length, the Executive Committee being in disagreement about this possibility."

Other institutions have attempted intermediate degrees. In 1967, Rutgers University adopted a Master of Philosophy as an intermediate degree in twenty-seven out of fifty-three departments that offer the doctorate. It signifies that the student has completed his graduate studies and has demonstrated a comprehensive mastery of his general field of concentration. The Master of Philosophy degree makes the recipient automatically eligible to proceed with the doctoral program within four years of receiving the degree. At the University of Kansas the Master of Philosophy is offered in several fields and at the University of Southern Mississippi the Master of Philosophy degree is designed to prepare junior college teachers in a number of subjects. Several institutions in the Western Intercollegiate Conference (the Big Ten) have adopted certificates or the phrase "Candidate in ————." The University of California has adopted the title "Candidate in Philosophy" for its intermediate degree. Spurr believes that "Candidate in Philosophy" is the most widely adopted designation for the successful completion of the general studies stage of the doctorate.[9]

Doctor of Arts. At the same time as experimentation and discussion of intermediate degrees, there has come broad investigation of a substitute doctorate intended to prepare college teachers who have no particular need for the heavy research emphasis of the Ph.D. It is difficult to discover the origin of recent consideration of the Doctor of Arts degree, which is the most frequently suggested alternative, but certainly the Doctor of Arts program at Carnegie-Mellon University was one of the earliest attempts and is still the most frequently cited experiment. The present rationale for such a degree has been cogently elaborated by the Carnegie Commission on Higher Education. It observes that although the Ph.D. is a highly

[9] Spurr, *Academic Degree Structures: Innovative Approaches,* p. 93.

respected degree, useful for advanced research and for the training of future research workers, it is not particularly useful for persons who teach and generally do no research. Even more serious is the fact that a Ph.D. program may enforce such a narrow training that adequate preparation for undergraduate teaching may be precluded. The commission favors a Doctor of Arts degree which would require four years of study beyond the bachelor's (in theory the same as the Ph.D.), but in place of a dissertation students would be asked to do within a chosen field an independent piece of work that was not necessarily an original contribution to knowledge. Curriculum would involve a broader base of subjects and an explicit opportunity to study and practice methods of teaching. As envisioned, the Doctor of Arts would not be just an attenuated Ph.D. program but rather a specifically designed program stressing elements essential to the task of teaching. The commission seems persuaded that reform of the Ph.D. would not be a particularly happy solution to the problem of better preparation for college teachers. The new degree, adequately organized through the efforts not of one department but of the entire university and given adequate recognition by the major graduate schools, should take a respected place alongside of the Ph.D.

Perhaps the most vigorous exponent of the Doctor of Arts degree is E. Alden Dunham,[10] who uses his analysis of state colleges as a springboard for his radical proposal for reform. He feels that the predicted oversupply of Ph.D.'s in the 1970s would provide a reason for channeling large numbers of aspiring graduate students toward degrees more relevant to teaching than to research. In view of the faculty needs of two- and four-year institutions, which would be educating 50 percent or more of all students in higher education, there would be employment opportunities for people appropriately prepared. Since the major producers of Ph.D.'s would not be likely to change their efforts substantially, Dunham believes that the state colleges and regional universities could very well take the lead in developing these new programs. Dunham is not at all persuaded that an intermediate degree or a revitalized master's degree could ever be very effective as an alternate, nor does he see the possibility

[10] E. Alden Dunham, *Colleges of the Forgotten Americans* (New York: McGraw-Hill, 1970).

for reform of the Ph.D. Thus he argues that "there should be a new and different doctoral program and degree for the preparation of college teachers in the Arts and Sciences." To prevent the almost immediate downward drift in status which is one of the prevailing criticisms of the Doctor of Arts degree, he urges: "that no institution should mount a program unless it is fully committed to it. Aside from the provision of sufficient resources, the specific test of commitment is the willingness of the institution not only to hire graduates of its own program but to promote them and give them tenure as well." As an additional safeguard he posits that, where full-blown Ph.D. programs exist, the institution might very well refrain from attempting a parallel Doctor of Arts program. The program as envisioned:

> represents a maximum of three years of solid graduate work. It is a degree awarded by the faculty of arts and sciences, not by the faculty of education. Heavy involvement by arts and sciences people is essential, not just for prestige but because at least 75 percent of the program is in academic areas. While there is heavy emphasis on scholarship, the thrust of work is applied scholarship, and the dissertation relates to curriculum and instruction at the college level. There is in-depth study of a discipline but also interdisciplinary and problem-centered approaches to general education for which at present it is almost impossible to find enthusiastic faculty. As at Carnegie-Mellon University, the educational component of the program, about 25 percent, might consist of a course in learning theory, methodology, cognition, dissertation seminar, and internship, whether in a two- or four-year college. Future faculty members should know something about teaching the students they will teach, and the history and problems of higher education. A final and important point: the doctor of arts is a terminal degree; it is not a consolation prize for losers en route to the Ph.D., nor is it a beginning step for people aiming at the Ph.D.[11]

A variant of the concept of the Doctor of Arts degree is the Diplomate in College Teaching awarded by the University of

[11] Dunham, p. 161.

Miami. This is a program specifically designed to prepare junior college teachers and is a two-year program beyond the bachelor's degree. The first year consists of intensive study in one field equivalent to the level required for a Master of Arts degree. The second calendar year consists of approximately three equal parts. Two-thirds is distributed between two relevant cognate fields; the remaining third is devoted to formal study of teaching and the problems of education, and a carefully supervised internship. The program, which in 1973 is in its fifth year, has recruited students primarily from teaching posts in southern Florida junior colleges. Substantively, the students feel the program is well contrived and helpful to them in their role as junior college teachers. However the title of the degree is somewhat confusing, and a number of the junior colleges have been unwilling to grant salary increments based on the possession of the Diplomate in College Teaching. Thus there is serious discussion at the University of Miami regarding the possibility of converting the diplomate into a Doctor of Arts program and using Dunham's criteria for program development.

The University of Miami may be a natural place for the flowering of a Doctor of Arts program. Its diplomate program could be adjusted and expanded to form the basis of the Doctor of Arts program. No other Florida institution offers or plans to offer the Doctor of Arts degree, hence there would be no regional competition. Miami University itself is not heavily involved in Ph.D. work and is not likely to become so for a variety of reasons, especially financial ones. In addition, the rapid expansion of the branches of Miami-Dade Junior College provides a rich source of potential graduate students for the Doctor of Arts program as well as a market to absorb the products for at least a decade and a half in the future. There is one minor drawback, which is that some of the sources for extramural funding, which have supported the Diplomate in College Teaching, seem more entranced with the unusual title than with the idea of supporting another Doctor of Arts program.

It is difficult to judge the future prospects of the Doctor of Arts degree. The major associations concerned with graduate education have endorsed the idea, and candidates are eligible for various sorts of fellowship support. The Carnegie Commission on Higher

Education has clearly espoused the concept, and the Carnegie Corporation has provided substantial funds for institutions to experiment with the new program. However, the haunting fear remains that the combination of high prestige generally accorded the Ph.D., together with a very real and expanding oversupply of Ph.D. recipients, will preclude any real development of the Doctor of Arts degree. Here an analogy may be instructive. The Doctor of Social Science degree at Syracuse University appeared to be a well-contrived program producing people generally in demand as college teachers. However, when recipients of the degree were given the opportunity to exchange their degrees for the Ph.D., something in the order of 90 percent jumped at the opportunity. Similarly, the history of the Doctor of Education degree can be instructive. This was originally intended to be a practitioner's certificate and theoretically was conceived of as equal in rigor but different in substance from the Ph.D. degree. Generally, one of two developments has transpired: either the Doctor of Education has been consistently regarded as a second-class degree with less rigorous requirements—for example, no language requirements—or the demands have been so modified that there is no perceptible difference between the Ed.D. and the Ph.D. degrees. When schools of education have reached that point the obvious question arises: If there is no difference, why not concentrate on the more prestigious degree? Although the need for better preparation of college teachers persists, careful assessment of the Doctor of Arts degree suggests that it will not emerge as the major facilitating device.

Although the chances of resolving any of the issues of degrees are difficult to gauge, a general direction of resolution can be inferred from these actual examples and from a set of principles elaborated by Spurr.

> First, the number of different degree titles should be kept as low as possible, allowing for substantial variation within each as regards subject matter, emphasis, quantity, and even quality of effort.
> Second, degree structure should be flexible in time required for the completion of the academic program in order to encourage acceleration, but should have rather specific

over-all time limits in order to discourage too attenuated an effort.

Third, each degree should mark the successful completion of one stage of academic progress, without implication or prejudgment as to a student's capacity to embark on following stages.

Fourth, degree structure should be so interrelated that the maximum opportunity exists for redirection as the student's motivation, interest and intellectual achievements permit.

Fifth, the various components of the educational experience are not optimally separable into different time periods. While there is general acceptance that the student trained both in the liberal arts and in a specific field of concentration, or in a specific profession is more desirably educated than either the pure generalist or the pure specialist, it is by no means clear that one phase of education should be separated in time from the other or, if so, which should precede which. To be specific, it is not desirable to confine general liberal arts education to the first two years and subject matter specialization to the last years of undergraduate study.[12]

Postdoctoral Study. Until recently, postdoctoral work was little understood, partly because of problems of definition. In some respects, the young instructor or assistant professor on a term appointment functioned in the same way as the postdoctoral fellow. Similarly, it was difficult to distinguish between a postdoctoral student and a non-tenured research associate with the university. In an effort to define the role of postdoctoral students, the National Academy of Sciences Study of Postdoctoral Education in the United States drew up a list of exclusions and inclusions for categories of postdoctoral students.

Exclusions. (1) Although appointments to instructor and assistant professor are temporary, they are excluded because they are understood to be part of the regular series of academic appointments and lead, if all goes well, to a permanent position.

[12] Spurr, *Academic Degree Structures: Innovative Approaches,* pp. 26, 27.

(2) Visiting professor appointments are excluded if they fill regular places on the host institution's academic staff.

(3) Service research appointments which are not intended to provide an opportunity for continued education in research are excluded.

(4) Internships and residencies are excluded because research training under supervision of a senior mentor is the prime purpose of the appointment.

(5) Holders of Doctor's degrees who are studying for another doctorate that does not involve research as a primary activity are excluded.

Inclusions. (1) Postdoctoral appointments, supported by whatever funds, that provide an opportunity for continued education and experience in research are included.

(2) Scholars on leave from other institutions are included if they come primarily to further their research experience.

(3) Appointments of holders of professional doctoral degrees who are pursuing research experience are included, even though they may be candidates for a second doctoral degree.

(4) Appointments in government and industrial laboratories that resemble in their character and objectives postdoctoral appointments in universities are included.

(5) Persons holding fractional postdoctoral appointments are included. For example a postdoctoral Fellow with a part-time assistant professorship is included.

(6) Appointments for a short duration if they are of sufficient duration to provide an opportunity for research and a formal appointment can be made.[13]

Using the definition inferred from these inclusions and exclusions, the National Academy of Sciences through a questionnaire study arrived at some of the dimensions of postdoctoral study in the United States. It was estimated that in the spring of 1967 there were approximately 16,000 postdoctorals, including both citizens of the United States and foreign nationals. The vast majority concen-

[13] National Academy of Sciences, *The Invisible University* (Washington: National Academy of Sciences, 1969), p. 45.

trated in engineering, mathematics, physics, and the biological
sciences, including medicine. The institutions where they studied
were usually members of the Association of American Universities.
In fact, approximately one-fifth of all the institutions granting doctoral degrees accounted for approximately 70 percent of all postdoctoral work.

The reasons people undertake postdoctoral study are varied.
For the most part, the Ph.D. taking on postdoctoral study aspires to
a lifetime career of research and teaching in some field in which he
is not yet prepared to become a professor, especially if his doctoral
research was a part of a larger team effort. Some Ph.D.'s feel that
the transition from graduate student to professor is too abrupt and
that the three-pronged responsibilities of being a professor (teaching,
research, and service) should be taken on gradually. Quite a few
realistically consider status. To achieve stature in the eyes of their
students, some would like to have their first research paper published before beginning to teach. Others feel that the prestige of a
university in which they do postdoctoral work will enhance their
chances for desirable employment; and some recent doctoral students are convinced that "the establishment" requires that they have
postdoctoral experience if they are to land desirable posts in recognized institutions. Doctoral students from relatively small universities also want to experience the academic world at a larger institution and to see how research is conducted at developed institutions,
for it is at that sort of university that younger Ph.D.'s aspire to serve.

Departments and institutions also reflect a variety of reasons
for conducting postdoctoral study. In some it is strictly an accidental
concomitant of having an outstanding faculty which attracts postdoctoral students. Then postdoctoral students represent an important
resource by which contract research projects can be staffed.
Especially in institutions where students move directly from doctoral
student capacity to a postdoctoral capacity, a postdoctoral fellowship represents a way of maintaining continuity of work in ongoing
research projects. While postdoctoral study is basically research
oriented, these advanced students also make an important contribution to the teaching staff and will frequently be asked to handle
intermediate level or even advanced courses as part of their overall
postgraduate experience. While there is considerable variance with

respect to how long students remain in this postgraduate capacity (a relatively few seem to remain permanent postdoctoral students), generally the experience extends from six or eight months to two years. There seems to be a general feeling among professors who have directed postgraduate study that a year is the optimum time and that to extend postgraduate work for a second year yields diminishing returns.

Suprainstitutional Coordination and Control

The responsibility for creating and adopting a rational degree structure may ultimately rest with suprainstitutional boards of coordination or control. Various states created such boards during the 1960s to meet higher education needs emerging in the post-World War II period. At that time American social policy was stated in a number of postulates: (1) Based on the belief that as much as 85 percent of college-age groups could profit from some formal education beyond high school, universal access to higher education is considered desirable. (2) A highly developed and industrialized nation needs a continuous and expanding flow of technically and professionally trained individuals to provide the skills and services required. (3) Higher education should increasingly assume responsibility for using research to help solve vexing problems. (4) The economic vitality of states, regions, and the nation rests in large part on expanding systems of higher education. Since each of these elements of social policy required planning and efforts transcending the capabilities of institutions, states began to create mechanisms to coordinate educational efforts.

But restrictive factors were also involved. As costs of higher education continued to mount, states had a clear imperative to insure the most economical conduct of higher education while still achieving broadly accepted educational outcomes. Some agency clearly needed to prevent unnecessary duplication of programs, particularly the extremely costly ones in the graduate and professional fields. State coordinating agencies or boards of control, therefore, early turned attention to how graduate and professional work could be accomplished within the financial limits of their states. But efforts to plan rationally have not always succeeded, and the financial burdens on the states have increased dramatically with the recession of the late sixties and early seventies. Illustrative of this situation are remarks by Linwood Holton of Virginia:

> As you know, the most expensive programs to establish and operate in higher education are the graduate programs. While there was a need at one time for more such programs in Virginia, I wonder how much of a need there still is today.
>
> I say this because the most rapid growth in Virginia's higher education over the past six years has been in the very expensive graduate program.
>
> For example, according to the 1971 *Fact Book on Higher Education* just published by the American Council on Education, the rate of growth of graduate education in Virginia between 1964 and 1969—five years—was 190 percent. I repeat: 190 percent. . . .
>
> Not only are these programs costly, some substantial people question whether many of them are worthwhile. All of us know that there are in some fields a number of Ph.D.'s that constitute a glut on the market today.
>
> So I would respectfully suggest that before our individual institutions start proposing new graduate programs that they look to see what already exists elsewhere in the state or in the South, or elsewhere in the nation. We could go into regional development with states North of us or West of us as well as South of us.
>
> Actually I think, and I believe you'll agree, that our basic higher educational need in Virginia is not more individual graduate programs but on the contrary it's a need to provide more accessibility for higher education at the undergraduate level, particularly for students of lower-income families.[14]

Generally, the states have adopted one of several different approaches to a more rational assignment of role and scope to the types of institutions comprising each state system. Perhaps the most widely publicized and most rigid is that adopted in the California master plan of 1960. That system describes three levels of public

[14] Linwood Holton, "The State's Commitment to Higher Education," *Momentum* (Commonwealth Conference on Higher Education), September 1, 1971.

higher education: the locally controlled junior colleges, the state colleges some of which have recently been redesignated state universities, and the several branches of the University of California. The master plan allows state colleges to offer master's work in the liberal arts and sciences and in some of the applied fields and professions, but the university has the sole authority in public higher education to award the doctoral degree in all fields of learning, except that it may agree with the state colleges to award joint doctoral degrees in selected fields. During the first decade in which the master plan was operative, the prohibition worked—only the University of California offered doctoral work. It did so in spite of mounting unrest and tension on the part of state college administrators and professors who desired full graduate status for their colleges. But that prohibition is no longer applicable.

A less inflexible system was embodied in the Illinois master plan which sought to allow each institution to develop freely those programs for which it had outstanding resources and competence, while still preventing unbridled and unnecessary growth of expensive graduate and professional programs. The technique used was to create systems of institutions as in California but to allow each system to make decisions subject to a statewide review regarding appropriate levels of program to be adopted. Even more flexible in regulating the development of new graduate work is the Florida organization in which all senior institutions are responsible to a board of regents. In principle, the board of regents would assign various roles to different institutions, but in practice, it has been fairly tolerant of all institutions aspiring to and working toward doctoral work. Similarly tolerant of expansion of graduate work into a number of state institutions is the Ohio master plan which also codifies a belief in competition: "Some competition in graduate study and research seems desirable. Monopoly in higher education may be as harmful to progress and freedom as monopoly in other social institutions: economic, social and religious. When only one institution undertakes graduate study and research, there may not be any basis for comparing its accomplishments and failures with those of other institutions. Competition, moreover, is a spur to effort."[15]

[15] Ohio Board of Regents, *Master Plan for State Policy in Higher Education* (Columbus, 1966), p. 88.

The critical elements of such systems of coordination and control for the nature and extent of graduate education are the methods by which requests for new programs are reviewed and the kind of economic sanctions which are applied. Several states (for example, Georgia, New Mexico, and Texas) rely on the professional staff of the coordinating or controlling board to review requested programs and to recommend whether or not they should be approved. Oregon has used a standing committee of lay board members to review the need for requested programs; Washington and Ohio use statewide committees composed of representatives from institutions. None of these has been perfectly satisfactory. Professional staffs tend to be regarded suspiciously by individual institutions; lay members are unsophisticated with respect to delicate academic nuances; and committees composed of institutional representatives run the danger of degenerating into political agencies engaging in a great deal of logrolling and back-scratching. Berdahl, after looking intensively at a number of different states, describes approvingly the system for program review that operates in Illinois. There, the Board of Higher Education selected a commission of nine individuals of national academic stature, the majority of whom were from outside the state, from lists submitted by each publicly supported institution. This board of scholars was expected to study and review needs for doctoral programs, to recommend how those needs could be met, and to review and evaluate applications from any state institution to offer advanced degree programs. In performing the latter service, the board would determine the need for such programs, assess faculty qualifications and physical resources, and finally make specific recommendations to the Board of Higher Education.

In addition to reviewing proposed new graduate programs, statewide coordinating and controlling agencies have attempted, with varying degrees of success, to concern themselves with several additional matters related to graduate work. The first of these is the matter of reviewing and approving new courses. Unless such review power is present, expansionist institutions by gradually creating individual courses can reach a point where all the work necessary for a new graduate program is already being offered. There would be no reason for an agency to deny formal adoption of what amounts to a fait accompli. Yet, for an agency to review the thousands of course changes that characterize any dynamic institution would place an almost unbearable burden on any reviewing mechanism. Thus agencies have typically not produced workable procedures for dealing with the matter of individual courses. A second element is the matter of asking institutions to terminate programs that appear to be unneeded or to effect a reallocation of programs from one institution to another. Statewide boards of control (for example, the Board of Regents in Ohio) have substantial power to do both but have rarely exercised that power. Coordinating councils (for example, the California Coordinating Council) do not have such power and indeed generally have not seriously examined the issue. Also clearly influential with respect to graduate programs is the amount of research and public service activity institutions undertake. Much of the expansion of graduate work during the 1960s resulted from federal grants and foundation support. Obviously, extrainstitutional support is limited in time, hence states are concerned about what sorts of continuing subsidy they are expected to provide. As yet, no very successful mechanism has appeared which satisfactorily both allows institutions independence to solicit outside subvention and safeguards future financial concerns of the state.

There is, then, continued exploration of ways by which agencies representative of the state at large can exert real control to insure rational and economical development of graduate and professional work. This exploration seems to be moving in the direction of statewide boards of control responsible for all public higher education in the state. Legislation in 1971 in Wisconsin and North Carolina to create single boards is illustrative. This quest is brought about by two substantial failures of mechanisms thus far attempted. First, although a principal reason for a standing statewide coordination and control agency is to limit in some rational way graduate and professional work, such limitation does not appear to have come about to any appreciable degree. In spite of the much publicized oversupply of doctorates, institutions (particularly developing institutions) continue to request and sooner or later to receive permission to add new graduate programs. Exponents of statewide coordination, such as Robert Berdahl or Lyman Glenny, argue that substantial limitation does take place within the structure, much of it before decisions need be made by a coordinating or controlling agency. However, it is difficult to visualize the kind of information that would support such a finding. Second, boards of coordination and control have had virtually no impact in producing innovative new programs in graduate work. Rather, when programs have been considered, analysis has been in terms of quite orthodox and conventional criteria. Berdahl, for example, lists the three major criteria used to assess requests for new programs: institutional readiness, state needs, and state ability to finance.[16] If coordinating and controlling agencies ever do approach the substance of graduate education, they have the potential to bring about profound modifications in practice.

Accreditation

Until quite recently, the six regional accrediting associations have not devoted specific attention to graduate programs. Reasons why this has been so range from the highly individualistic character of graduate programs, governed as they are by specific departments, to the fact that graduate work, especially at the doctoral level, is offered by a relatively small number of institutions of such power and prestige that the judgments of accrediting associations would have little real effect on institutional conduct. But as the number of institutions beginning to enter graduate work has increased, especially newer institutions of regional rather than national significance, regional associations have begun to consider more specifically the standards and criteria for adequate graduate programs. This distinction is well revealed in comments from the North Central Association of Colleges and Secondary Schools in its policy statement: "This policy requires member institutions planning to introduce graduate work which represents a significant change in the scope of their activities, to have such graduate work reviewed prior to its initiation. Certain colleges and universities which have shown through the demonstrated quality of their efforts that they are mature graduate institutions are exempt from this policy, however.

[16] Robert O. Berdahl, *Statewide Coordination of Higher Education* (Washington: American Council on Education, 1971).

Examples of these would include the Big Ten institutions, the University of Chicago, and The University of Notre Dame."[17]

Although regional associations are increasingly interested in graduate work, most of their statements and guidelines remain relatively broad and seemingly replicate the criteria applicable to undergraduate programs and institutions. However, the North Central Association has prepared a set of guidelines which at once indicates the movement of accreditation into this difficult field, states conventional wisdom regarding appropriate reforms, and provides a checklist of recommended practice within the broad field of graduate education.[18]

(1) Is the program consistent with institutional strengths, role, and purpose?

(2) Has the need for the program been demonstrated?

(3) Is there an adequate pool of students to justify the program?

(4) Have the additional needs and costs in faculty, facilities, equipment and library been determined?

(5) Are the available resources adequate for starting the program without depriving existing programs of needed support?

(6) Do existing programs have the quality to provide an adequate base for development of an advanced level program?

(7) Has the relationship of the proposed program to existing ones in the institution been fully explored?

(8) Is there available an adequate cadre of faculty of sufficient scholarly stature and experience?

(9) Are the admissions policies clear and appropriate to the program?

(10) Are adequate funds available for the support of graduate students?

(11) Does the administrative structure provide for coordination or direction of the graduate program with the assistance of a faculty committee or council?

[17] Unpublished letter.

[18] *Guides for Institutions Offering Advanced Degree Programs* (Chicago: Commission on Institutions of Higher Education, North Central Association, 1971), p. 15.

(12) Has the curriculum been carefully developed in reference to the specified objectives of the program?

(13) Are the opportunities for research, field experience, and internship adequate in quality and number?

(14) Does the program have sufficient structure to insure its distinctive character, while remaining sufficiently flexible to meet the particular needs of individuals with varying goals and backgrounds?

(15) Are the programs generally consonant with standards and models existing in other institutions of quality? Is the rationale for innovative patterns clear and are provisions for evaluations included in the plans?

(16) Has attention been given to the non-course needs of graduate students such as housing, food, and recreation?

(17) Do provisions exist for insuring that graduate students have a voice in the formulation of institutional policies?

New Organizational Forms

For the most part, colleges and universities offer or plan to offer graduate work through conventional departmental structures. However, a few institutions are seeking for various reasons to modify this conventional organization and mode of operation. Although no one modification is found sufficiently frequently to constitute a trend, three approaches appear promising alternatives for institutions facing particular circumstances. Of these approaches, cooperative arrangements are appropriate to groups of graduate schools in relatively close proximity to each other; upper division and graduate colleges have potential in the presence of a heavy concentration in junior colleges; and special-purpose colleges that deliberately reject the goal of becoming comprehensive universities seem feasible only for recently created or developing institutions.

Cooperative Arrangements. Prior to 1960 the prevailing mode in American higher education was the single-campus autonomous institution seeking self-sufficiency. But during the 1960s, as costs and available knowledge increased, institutions began to realize that comprehensiveness for any one campus was impossible. Some institutions began to experiment with various sorts of cooperative arrangements, ranging from allowing students in adjacent independent institutions to cross-register for courses, to merging two institutions whose emphases seemed complementary. Of several widely publicized efforts, Atlanta University, at the University Center for Graduate Studies formed by the predominantly Negro colleges in the Atlanta area, is unique in American higher education. The Claremont University Center and Graduate School is a somewhat similar structure, with the graduate school appointing some faculty of its own but, for the most part, serving as a device by which graduate work can be offered by the independent colleges in the Claremont group. Case Western Reserve University is the result of a federation of the former Case Institute of Technology and Western Reserve University which brought together the considerable strength in engineering science and management of Case Institute with the strong liberal arts and health-related sciences of Western Reserve. Another merger of this kind was that of the Carnegie Institute of Technology with the Mellon Institute to form Carnegie-Mellon University. Here, the aim clearly was to seek greater comprehensiveness by joining the research strengths, especially in chemistry, of the Mellon Institute with the more applied strengths in engineering and management of the Carnegie Institute.

Indicative of a range of possible cooperative ventures are the joint graduate consortium of five private institutions based in Washington, D.C.; the cooperative programs of four colleges and a large university in Massachusetts, all located in the Connecticut Valley; and the Graduate School of the Union of Experimental Colleges and Universities.

In 1964, the American University, Catholic University of America, George Washington University, Georgetown University, and Howard University signed a charter to establish procedures for the coordination of graduate study and research among their universities. Although some bilateral arrangements had previously existed within the group of Washington-based institutions, it gradually became apparent that a more formal arrangement would allow fuller exploitation of the several strengths of each of those institutions. An executive officer was appointed and was responsible to a policy board representative of the five institutions. The consortium decided quite early that it would attempt no broad program of operations but rather would develop modes of cooperation deriving from the solution of specific problems, such as reconciling differences in academic calendars, tuition, and course-numbering systems. In contrast to procedures at Atlanta University and Claremont Graduate School, matriculation of graduate students is within one of the cooperating institutions, with the graduate student advisor responsible for selecting the most appropriate resources from those available. Thus, one of the first effects was to enrich the curriculum offerings available to graduate students attending any of the five institutions. Similar departments in each university are expected to consult with one another about staffing and programming developments; however, ultimately each department is responsible to its own institution. The same general principle applies to libraries and other services.

A rather different level of cooperation is represented by the University of Massachusetts and Mount Holyoke, Amherst, Smith, and Hampshire colleges. These institutions offer a cooperative Ph.D. program, with the University of Massachusetts awarding the degree which carries the notation of the cooperating institutions. The requirements for the degree are identical with the requirements for the Ph.D. at the University of Massachusetts, except that residence is defined as the institution in which thesis work is done. The graduate council of the university is responsible for the cooperative Ph.D. program, but it does include a member from each of the participating colleges. Generally, whether or not given professors wish to participate in the arrangement is left to the departments themselves; hence there is no universal set of programs into which students at any of the institutions can move. When the cooperative Ph.D. program was developed, the University of Massachusetts was clearly a regional institution and the faculties of the cooperating colleges were clearly a scholarly asset. More recently, the University of Massachusetts has begun to expand and strengthen its graduate faculties so that the cooperative venture is in some respects a contribution of the university to the participating colleges. Nonetheless, the concept of cooperation appears sound and a five-college long-range planning committee has urged "increased cooperation in graduate programs with a view to devising a more systematic method for bringing faculty members at the private colleges into direct contact with the

University's graduate program, either by direct participation in the program or by finding opportunities to employ university graduate students in the educational activities of the colleges."[19]

Perhaps the most radical approach to cooperative effort in graduate education is the Union Graduate School of the Union of Experimenting Colleges and Universities. The parent organization came into existence to facilitate communication and program development of a group of self-styled experimenting colleges: Antioch, Bard, Goddard, Stephens, and the University of Wisconsin at Green Bay. Its leaders were persuaded that for many students existing graduate programs were too limited, prescribed, inflexible, and poorly adapted to a rapidly changing society. Thus a graduate school was formed to make use of adjunct professors located at other institutions, with a small core faculty affiliated with the parent organization. Only candidates who clearly cannot obtain their advanced training in conventional university doctoral programs are accepted. Once an individual is accepted, a program is created for him individually, with an emphasis on self-directed study. An advisory committee is selected to set all the conditions, subject only to review by the Union Graduate School, necessary for the completion of a degree. Rather than meeting the orthodox requirement of a thesis, candidates for degrees are required to demonstrate evidence of high achievement in a special project. The Union Graduate School came into existence in 1970, and thus is still too young to be adequately assessed. However, 123 students are actively working in the program and a series of colloquia have been held which are the devices used to approximate a residency requirement. These experimenting colleges have in the past developed some of the more promising innovations in undergraduate education, such as greater flexibility, greater use of off-campus experience, and increased and more sensitive advising. Obviously, what they aspire to do now is to serve a similar purpose for graduate education. Their contribution will perhaps continue to be exemplary rather than influence directly large numbers of graduate students.

Upper Division and Graduate Colleges. The second broad approach to the modification of existing structures represents in

[19] *Five-College Cooperation: Directions for the Future* (Amherst: University of Massachusetts Press, 1969), p. 85.

many ways an attempt to revise and update ideas that emerged during the formative period of graduate education in the United States. The aims of William Rainey Harper and David Starr Jordan to divert lower division undergraduate training into feeder institutions were never fulfilled, and the complex university, offering both undergraduate and graduate education with the same faculty, became the rule in American higher education. However, periodically attempts have been made to resuscitate—with uneven success—those ideas. The University of the Pacific in Stockton, California, made an attempt to rely on nearby Stockton Junior College for all lower division work, while the university itself offered upper division and graduate work in the liberal arts and sciences as well as some professional programs. The New School for Social Research (in New York City) began in the late 1950s as an upper division institution providing special programs for a limited number of students, and the University of Michigan in Flint established an upper division branch planned to offer not only the baccalaureate degree but master's work as well, particularly with respect to continuing education. None of these structures has persisted in their original upper division and/or graduate form. Almost as quickly as they came into existence, pressures began to mount for offering some lower division work, not only to insure disciplinary articulation but also to obtain a larger flow of students.

Despite those failures, a number of states are currently either planning or operating upper division and graduate institutions. Two upper division colleges, Florida Atlantic University and the University of West Florida, were established with Harper's ideas in mind and were seen as a way of strengthening and perpetuating a strong junior college movement within the state. In Illinois, New York, Pennsylvania, and Texas, new upper division colleges are being created. Since these are all quite new or have as yet not begun to operate, their contribution to graduate education cannot be known. The likely developments, as well as the perplexities that will be encountered, have been indicated by Altman, who has made the only comprehensive analysis of this sort of institution.

Existing upper division institutions—public as well as private—tend to offer some postbaccalaureate studies, although the existing pattern makes projection to the future difficult. In all except the Dearborn campus, where the institution is public, planners have envisioned at least master's programs, while several have anticipated offering doctorates. In some cases, such as Richmond College of the City University of New York, doctoral work is not a reasonable alternative since all doctoral work is offered centrally by a university graduate center. In other cases, such as the two Florida institutions, a struggle has developed between the upper division institutions and the established state universities, the former desiring the right to offer doctorates (for both educational and prestige reasons) and the latter claiming (with some degree of correctness) that the limited resources for doctoral programs should not be fragmented among institutions which do not now have the necessary expertise or facilities. The Dearborn experience, however, suggests that without a minimum of master's degree offerings, an institution may encounter difficulty in recruiting both faculty and students.

Future upper division institutions—such as those proposed for Miami, Jacksonville, Dallas, Houston, Minneapolis, and Chicago—will probably offer work through the master's degree, although this decision appears more dependent upon need and availability of resources at existing institutions than on any determination that the master's degree is more closely tied to the bachelor's degree than to doctoral studies. Whether the new institutions will eventually offer doctoral programs depends on the availability of resources within the system of which they are a part and on the political strength the new institutions can muster on their own behalf.[20]

Theme Institutions. A third possibility in reorganizing the structure for graduate work is for institutions to stress certain indigenous strengths or opportunities to the extent that they become theme universities. In the past, of course, there have been institutions that emphasized one kind of graduate work to the exclusion of others. The Massachusetts Institute of Technology and the California Technological Institute are cases in point. However, over the years

[20] Robert A. Altman, *The Upper Division College* (San Francisco: Jossey-Bass, 1970), p. 173.

they have both expanded the range of graduate work, and M.I.T. in particular can now be described as a comprehensive university polarized around science and technology. There have also been self-denying institutions, such as Princeton, that have restricted development to a limited number of fields in which the institution could present great strength. But within American higher education there have always been powerful forces pressuring institutions to regress toward a complex, multipurpose role and to seek comprehensiveness in one way or another.

However, leaders of a few schools are now seeking to reverse the tendency of institutions to regress toward the mean. As we have seen, the University of Wisconsin, Green Bay, is attempting to develop interdisciplinary graduate programs and to focus primarily on problems concerning the environment. The University of Hawaii declared in its academic master plan that scholarship would be "fostered with special diligence in areas in which the University has some inherent advantage" and/or "which promise to contribute significantly to the development of the State of Hawaii." In the eyes of its president, the university has a particular reason for seeking distinctiveness in its graduate education and research efforts: "Located near the center of the world's greatest ocean, at the intersection of trade and travel routes, tropical yet comfortable in climate, volcanic in origin, with high mountains and deep waters close at hand, these not-so-isolated Islands are the home of one of the world's few truly multi-racial, cross-cultural societies. . . . It is natural for a university in Hawaii to interest itself in the history, cultures, and languages of Hawaii's racial groups, both those that were here earlier and those which have come later. If any University can develop exciting, relevant ethnic studies programs, we should be able to do it." Other themes of the university—tropical botany, tropical agriculture, research in tropical diseases, and tropical meteorology—can be attributed in part to its location. And its location, coupled with the existence there of the East-West Center, dictates that research in all fields focusing on the Pacific Basin will be given special emphasis. While theme is more difficult to implement with respect to the professional fields, even these can and very likely should emphasize uniqueness. "We should build here the kind of Law School that could only be built at the University of Hawaii. This means, I think, that it might be associated with a strong graduate and research program in Comparative Law and perhaps in the Law of the Sea as well."[21]

Another theme of importance arises from the problems of how to serve the growing urban concentrations in the country. Several universities are currently struggling with the concept of becoming urban or urban-grant institutions. One such institution is Old Dominion University, a public institution that evolved out of an urban extension center of the College of William and Mary. After achieving the status of being able to grant an independent four-year baccalaureate degree, it was assigned the mission of becoming an urban university within the state system. In their attempt to define what that term means and to determine the implications for program development, the administration and faculty have grappled with a number of issues. It seems clear that the institution should try to redefine its purposes and to seek a reasonably clear delineation of its mission.

To meet the challenges of urbanism, Old Dominion and other universities located in urban or metropolitan areas should consider possible programmatic responses: (1) It has always been a major task of our universities to provide trained leadership to meet the requirements of a changing society. They should now enlarge their interest in the training of the professional and the technician to include the urban field, since the existing great shortage of well-qualified personnel will continue. (2) Knowledge about the city needs to be dramatically increased so that the quality of urban life can be improved. The university must push forward the frontiers of knowledge in the field of urban affairs. (3) The process of urbanization must be interpreted to the leadership in our metropolitan communities. The university has a long history of transmitting knowledge discovered in its laboratories and libraries into the mainstream of society. The outreach into the city of its understanding about the city should be no exception. Obviously, since Old Dominion is still struggling to discover how to deal with those issues, no predictions as to likely developments can be made. However, if it should succeed in

[21] The University of Hawaii, *Prospectus for the Seventies*, January 9, 1970.

defining operationally an urban university, it could become a model for others to follow.

Graduate Work at Liberal Arts Colleges

Although the phrase "graduate education" generally conjures up a vision of a complex university, single-purpose liberal arts colleges have begun to enter graduate work in substantial numbers and with some potential for effecting significant change in the nature of graduate study, at least to the master's level. No recent figures indicate the number of liberal arts colleges offering graduate work, but estimates range from 200 to 300 out of a total of between 650 and 700 institutions. The extent to which liberal arts colleges continue with graduate work, and the viability of their graduate programs will depend in large measure on the reasons why liberal arts colleges entered the field in the first place. By far the strongest motivation was the preparation of students, through the master's degree, for the fields of elementary and secondary teaching. Student preferences were also considered. A large number wanted to take their master's degrees in liberal arts colleges because of geographical proximity to places of work or residence. This matter of work and residency was also involved in liberal arts colleges establishing programs which would be of service to local industries. If a college offered advanced work, business and industry found this to be a decided advantage in local recruiting. Then, too, the demands of supporting denominations have tended to influence their related colleges to attempt graduate work.

But two much more internal forces have also been influential. During the 1960s when faculty members were in short supply, an institution that could allow new faculty members to teach graduate courses gained a competitive advantage in faculty recruitment. There was also a sensed need to have a cadre of more mature students to serve as laboratory and research assistants, counselors, dormitory aides, and the like. Graduate programs provided a method to recruit these, and a few institutions argued that the creation of specialized and demanding graduate courses would provide a resource to be used not only by graduate students but also by the most precocious undergraduate students at the institution.

Idealism also seems to have been involved: quite a few institutions agreed that perhaps the smaller liberal arts colleges could contribute to the broadly based social need for a master's degree by clearly redefining it, and give it once again a respectable status. A similar argument has been advanced by the relatively few liberal arts colleges that have also developed doctoral programs. General dissatisfaction with the existing doctoral programs in the larger institutions suggested that a smaller, more manageable place could exercise the requisite creativity to produce a better doctoral program. However, master's work for liberal arts colleges, if it is to be distinctively done, is considerably more expensive than undergraduate programs. If it is not more expensive—and a few institutions have testified that it need not be—there is strong presumptive evidence that the program has little significant impact.

The motivations of liberal arts colleges to enter graduate work and the range of approaches used to implement graduate work are revealed in institutional profiles. Antioch College offers a Master of Science Teaching to secondary science teachers participating in the National Science Foundation's in-service and summer institute programs. Colgate University not only offers Master of Arts degrees for those planning to enter public school teaching but also more specialized master's programs in guidance and administration. Goucher College has a master's program in elementary teaching; requirements can be completed in a presession four-week period and an academic year of two semesters. Hollins College, apparently not so influenced by the need for teachers, offers master's degrees in psychology, which are research oriented and experimental, and in creative writing, which are designed to conclude with the production of a volume of short stories or poems, or a novel. In an effort to overcome excessive departmentalization of graduate programs, Loyola University of Los Angeles offers the Master of Arts degree, which rests essentially on an interdisciplinary seminar in contemporary thought. A different sort of experience is provided by Middleburg College which has located graduate schools in foreign countries and which attempts to develop high foreign language facility. The University of Redlands not only has its own master's program but participates in an intercollegiate program of graduate studies which is an additional cooperative venture designed to produce Ph.D.'s. With the assistance of Ford Foundation money, Williams College created a master's degree in economics specifically designed to assist and certify students from underdeveloped nations. This particular program tries to relate intensive field experience with classroom experience.

Structural Changes

There are three remaining areas of real or potential structural change in graduate work. The first concerns the graduate faculty division of time between research and teaching, assuming that a distinction of this sort can really be made in graduate work. Generally, institutions, both developed and developing, anticipate that faculties will devote one-third to one-half of their time to research. While this research in the past has been grant- and contract-supported, increasingly institutions expect to support a substantial amount of faculty research through direct appropriations from state or from other internal sources of funds. (These are aspirations, however, and reactions on the part of state legislators create some skepticism that these dreams will be realized.) The amount of time spent on research is obviously related to the amount of time spent in formal teaching. Until the end of World War II, faculty teaching loads ranged from 15 to 18 or 21 hours a week. Even in complex universities, this would mean teaching three to six courses or sections of courses. Since the late 1950s this trend has been giving way, with loads in junior colleges being fifteen hours; in developing complex universities, nine hours; and in developed universities, six hours. The present trend would yield faculty loads of nine hours, or three courses a semester, if the professor taught only undergraduate courses; and three or six hours, or one or two courses, if he directed graduate study. There is some, but by no means a universal, sentiment that most faculties should teach one undergraduate and one graduate course; but in a fair number of institutions it is anticipated that the time is not far off when perhaps half of the faculty would teach only one course per semester. Some institutions have allowed and planned for purely research professors, but there seems to be even more general agreement that such positions are fundamentally inappropriate for educational institutions.

The other two areas of change involve the questions of the extent to which the position of Graduate Dean should be strengthened and whether there should be a separate graduate faculty. Surveys of opinions of graduate deans reveal overwhelming support in principle for strengthening their roles, but there is relatively little agreement as to how that should be done. Currently, graduate deans are somewhat of an anomaly. They are deans presiding over an important segment of a university's work; yet, for the most part, they are without faculty and have no real power over curricular developments. Operating through the graduate council, they can try to develop broad policy guidelines; and through various monitoring devices, such as reviewing applications, having graduate council members sit on oral examination committees, and spot-checking dissertations, they can seek to maintain some quality control over graduate programs. Increasingly, through the power to administer various fellowship programs they can influence the flow of students into the various departments, and through diverting overhead funds from contract research into the graduate office some can partially influence the nature of research to which the university is committed. Since graduate deans normally report directly to the provost or vice-president for academic affairs, and in some institutions to the president, they can through persuasion influence institutional policy. And in some institutions, where the roles of graduate dean and vice-president for research have been combined, the powers derived from reviewing research proposals and seeking extramural support for research allow additional influence to be exercised on institutional policy.

Although there are no clear trends for change, several developments are being attempted which might result ultimately in giving the graduate dean a more powerful voice. Some institutions have tried to create an administrative tie between deans of separate colleges and the vice-president for academic affairs by creating the two parallel positions of dean of undergraduate studies and dean of graduate studies. Neither of these has direct control over faculties, but each is assigned the function of reviewing faculty appointments and is provided a budget adequate enough to persuade departments to undertake new procedures or to create new courses and programs that are needed. A related device, which appears to be more prevalent in developing institutions than in those mature institutions long accustomed to intensive graduate work, is to assign to the graduate dean the responsibility for reviewing courses proposed for graduate credit and the credentials of faculty members recommended for the graduate faculty or for teaching graduate courses. Still another way of strengthening the office of graduate dean is to divert all, or a portion of, overhead funds from contract research to discretionary administration by that office. As the idea of accreditation of graduate programs has taken hold, some graduate deans have also achieved a measure of additional authority by virtue of the power to invite external visiting committees to review departments proposing to enter graduate work, or even to review periodically departments offering graduate degrees. Since the reports of such visitations are directed to the graduate dean, he has through this device alone an important means of effecting change.

In some institutions, such as Stanford, appointment to a professorial position (from assistant up to full professor) carries with it the privilege of teaching graduate courses; while in others, such as the University of Illinois or Virginia Polytechnic Institute and State University, faculty members after appointment must further qualify to be designated as members of the graduate faculty. As a general rule, the separation of professors into two faculties seems best designed as a quality control technique for developing institutions. For the mature and developed institution, such separation seems increasingly redundant and contributes only to irritation and discontent on the part of the faculties not privileged to direct graduate study.

Predominant Trends

Out of these various thoughts and attempts to make structural and organizational changes in graduate education come four general tendencies. The first is considerable dissatisfaction with departments, considerable experimentation with alternatives, yet little crystallization of opinion on a truly satisfactory alternative. Second, there are attempts to regularize degrees and to specify their meaning more clearly for the edification of both students and faculty. The third is to discover whether to place control of graduate education beyond the reaches of the graduate faculty itself through suprainstitutional boards, regional accreditation, or external visiting committees. Finally, various experiments are being designed to enrich available graduate work, sometimes through institutional cooperation, and to give more precise definition to graduate programs through sharpening the role of each institution. Here the matter of institutional distinctiveness has clearly become a significant concern.

VIII

Preparing College Teachers

Historically, the greatest and most vehement criticism of graduate education is that it does not provide training for the vocational choice of many Ph.D. recipients: college teaching. In the broadest sense, this failure is a consequence of the university's emphasis on scholarship and research and the accompanying indifference to teaching. At the 1966 annual meeting of the American Council on Education—devoted, amazingly enough, to improving college teaching—William Arrowsmith dramatically censured the university for renouncing its primary responsibility, to educate. In explaining how this has come about and why universities have given priority to research rather than teaching, he stated: "[College] faculties have come from the major graduate institutions and brought with them a style of life and valued goals of the university which are antithetical to the education goals of a college. These faculty teach the only thing they know, which is technical expertise gained in graduate schools. Thus, until universities reform themselves, their products cannot be expected to become vital educational forces. And universities seem unable to reform themselves because of the malignant, pervasive structure which establishes the department at the heart of university power." This departmental power, he declared, is "protected from above by the graduate deans and administrators who are more and more drawn from the research professoreate and therefore share its aims and ambitions" and is reinforced by the structures of national foundations, scholarly societies, and the American Council on Education. Furthermore, he expressed little hope for improving teaching as long as departments are permitted to promulgate "publish or perish" policies, reduce teaching loads, and demand early specialization. Although he himself is a scholar with impeccable credentials, Arrowsmith advocated "divorcing research from teaching, for the only likely alternative is to perpetuate teaching as a lackey of scholarship." To accomplish this, universities should "create powerful counter-vailing antidepartmental forces, having their own budgets, students, and normalized functions. One device might be the creation of many university professorships having such resources that they can with impunity ignore departmentalism."[1]

Direction of Change

If Arrowsmith's judgments are valid, improvement of instruction may not be possible. If, however, some changes are feasible, a logical approach would be to provide in graduate education some specific preparation for college teaching. Earl J. McGrath, whose entire career has been devoted to reforming higher education, has pointed out the need for such preparation. In his pool of 302 college presidents he found that three-quarters of them believed "that holders of the Doctor's degree were uninformed about the nature of undergraduate instruction . . . and were unprepared for the professional duties which they . . . at least tacitly agreed to perform." The opinion of these presidents, according to McGrath, "suggests that new college teachers, however well versed they may be in their limited specialized field, know little about such things as: (1) The types of students they will encounter in their classes. (2) The moti-

---

[1] William Arrowsmith, "The Future of College Teaching," in Calvin B. T. Lee (Ed.), *Improving College Teaching* (Washington: American Council on Education, 1967), pp. 57–71.

vations of these young people and their social, economic and even educational background. (3) The character of the present college curriculum and recent trends in its development. (4) The extraclass responsibilities the teacher in one of the smaller institutions must assume in the academic as well as the more inclusive social community, and a host of other matters included under the term undergraduate teaching used in its most comprehensive sense."[2]

The following questions, therefore, should be considered in planning changes in graduate education:

(1) Does the graduate program in any way help prospective teachers discover and develop a style of teaching which is likely to stimulate undergraduate students? The evidence suggests that graduate students are exposed to only a limited number of teaching styles. The young professor subsequently spends his life replicating those few models and is suspicious of exhortations to try new approaches.

(2) Does the graduate training program in any way expose students for a significant time to information about individual differences among undergraduate students and the range of motivations to which they respond? Evidence suggests that at no time are graduate students shown potential relationships between the modes and techniques of teaching and the differing interests and styles of undergraduate students.

(3) Does a typical doctoral program provide either the broad coverage or the selective elements of subject matter to create educationally potent courses and approaches to teaching? As McGrath indicated, products of graduate schools really have no conception of the nature or the means of providing a liberal education for undergraduates.

(4) Does the graduate program do anything to help prospective college teachers understand the nature of a college or to help them function freely and responsibly within a college? Evidence continues to mount that graduate students are not given insight into the nature of the college teaching profession, nor are they helped to develop a system of ethics appropriate to the profession.[3]

[2] Earl J. McGrath, *The Quantity and Quality of College Teachers* (New York: Teachers College, 1961).

[3] These questions are derived from W. Max Wise, "Who Teaches the Teachers?" in Lee, *Improving College Teaching,* pp. 78–80.

Some positive answers to these questions may result from recent efforts of a few universities to create specific programs to help doctoral students become more effective teachers. Based on a premise (which may itself be open to question) that a graduate school and its departments would be willing to contrive a structured graduate program of limited duration in which most graduate students would have some supervised teaching, a new set of principles for graduate education is emerging.[4]

(1) Graduate students should be provided a progressive sequence of teaching experience, advancing from directed observation of teaching and subsequent discussion of its dynamics to closely supervised episodes of teaching, and on to full responsibility for a course or a large segment of a course. Too frequently, teaching assistants have been thrown directly into conducting a section of a larger course and then in subsequent terms or semesters have repeated themselves with no opportunity to extend their teaching repertoires. How much better it would be if in his first year a graduate student visited classes taught by faculty members and was able to discuss his observations with the instructor. During the second year of graduate work he might teach a section of some generally required staff-taught course, and in the third year be allowed to teach a section or course close to his own developing specialized interest.

(2) Graduate student teaching experiences should focus on creative teaching and should not become preoccupied with the relatively meaningless and menial tasks of reading and grading examination papers, keeping attendance records, and computing final grades. These duties could properly be assigned to clerical people or could be arranged for under different contractual terms as a minor part of the life of graduate students.

(3) Graduate departments and specialized services in the university should inform graduate students on the full range of teaching methods and learning resources that could be used to improve education and encourage experimentation with them. Graduate students should not only be alerted to alternative successful teaching styles but should also be allowed considerable time to examine and experiment with visual, auditory, and programmed aids.

[4] These principles were generally derived from Vincent Nowlis and others, *The Graduate Student as Teacher* (Washington: American Council on Education, 1968), pp. 5–23.

(4) Too frequently, departmental manpower needs have determined little or no relationship to the graduate student's developing scholarly interests. Thus a deliberate effort should be made to relate teaching obligations to the central thrust of a candidate's program. A more imaginative approach would suggest many ways of accomplishing this: prescribing several lectures in an introductory course, contriving a pro-seminar as a part of an ongoing course, assigning a graduate student responsibility for one phase of an advanced course, or allowing him to direct independent study of an undergraduate or less advanced graduate student.

(5) Stress has already been placed on the value of sequential experience, but assignment to each sequence should be based on an evaluation of satisfactory performance of an earlier phase. For evaluation purposes, a growing array of tested techniques is becoming available, ranging from improved student evaluation forms to relatively inexpensive videotape equipment to record teaching performances for subsequent review. After evaluation, some graduate students should be terminated in a doctoral program if they demonstrate inability to cope with expanding teaching responsibilities.

(6) Complaints from teaching assistants emphasize their belief that they are really doing professional work and yet are often regarded as little more than menial laborers. An institution seriously interested in elevating the role of teaching and the significance of preparation for teaching should foster a climate of professional respect. Eliminating the practice by major professors of addressing graduate students by their first name while expecting to be addressed (often implicitly) by their own professorial title could be a first step. Obviously, graduate students also should be provided adequate physical space for their teaching and counseling duties, should be assigned work of truly professional caliber, and should be given full opportunity to discuss teaching problems in a professional way with senior faculty.

(7) An effective program for preparing college teachers requires considerable leadership on the part of administrators, especially departmental chairmen. Furthermore, successful programs have usually been associated with powerful and respected professors who were able to influence a total department to give more attention to the improvement of training and supervision of graduate student

teachers. With committed leadership many techniques become
possible: informal weekly meetings with a supervising professor,
specifically organized formal courses on college teaching, use and
discussion of new training devices (such as observation classrooms
equipped with one-way vision windows and professors in nearby
liberal arts colleges acting as mentors to graduate students teaching
in a graduate institution).

(8) Although Ph.D.'s spend from eight to ten years in colleges and universities, their interests are so narrow during their
graduate study years that they enter their first appointments understanding little about either the system of higher education into which
they are moving, or their prospective duties. Thus all graduate students should be given experiences that will facilitate a greater
understanding of the nature and problems of college teaching, the
relationship of specialities to the broad goals of undergraduate
education, the nature and importance of general academic duties,
and the ways in which young faculty members can exert educational
leadership both within the institution and in the larger structure of
American higher education. Fortunately, interested departments and
graduate schools now have considerable didactic material available
to them.[5]

Incorporating many of the ideas thus far advanced, Koen
has outlined the attributes of an ideal program for providing teacher
experience for graduate students. He bases his argument on the
assumption that the total institution rather than individual departments should assume responsibility both for the education of undergraduates and for the training of graduate students to teach.

The ideal training program has seven critical attributes.
In the first place it is complete in the sense that appropriate
mechanisms exist for the adequate development of graduate
students along each of the six dimensions of college teaching
(content mastery, course design, management of learning
skills, personal contact with students, self-evaluation, profes-

[5] See, for example, William H. Morris (Ed.), *Effective College Teaching* (Washington, D.C.: American Council on Education, 1970), which contains chapters on finding the levers to manipulate institutions and the total
organization of higher education.

sionalism and designing a training program). This assumes that the overall objective of the program is to prepare college teachers. If that is not the case, if T.A.'s [Teaching Assistants] are seen as overseers of laboratories and graders of papers, obviously such a system as the one suggested here is unnecessary.

Second, the program should be efficient in the sense that redundancies among training devices should be avoided, unless there is an indication that more than one kind of input is necessary to accomplish a desired end. It will be impossible, of course, to determine the degree of efficiency attained unless there is some method for evaluating outcomes. This in turn entails the process of stating objectives, designing and implementing training experiences and collecting appropriate evidence. Without proper evaluation procedures there is little hope of systematic progress.

Thirdly, the ideal training program must be practical. This means that the developing teachers must be given full opportunity to come to grips with real teaching, administrative and counselling problems, with help and guidance of the kind discussed earlier readily available to them. Formal courses about teaching without a chance to apply the concepts studied do not qualify on this score.

Fourth, a training program, if it is to be viable and productive, must be seen as legitimate by the academic community, that is, the devotion to scholarship and research that exists on virtually every campus, must be broadened so that the teaching enterprise is accepted as worthwhile and is professionally rewarding.

A fifth characteristic which a training program must have if it is to be maximally effective is continuity, by which is meant that despite changing generations of graduate students and the shifting administrative assignments of faculty members, training must be cumulative and transferable. It is typically the case that as each new faculty adviser to T.A.'s assumes the duties of his post, he tends to rely heavily on his personal opinion of the kind of training that is most useful and to set up a system that reflects his values. On the other hand, it is possible to work from an entirely different model. Decision could be made at the university or department level about kinds and degrees of college teacher competency that are considered desirable (and attainable). These would then constitute criteria of success. Each faculty member who serves as adviser to T.A.'s could then engage in a continuing quest for the most effective and efficient training schemes and he could do this as a member of a group which extends across departmental boundaries and across time.

As a sixth characteristic a useful training program must be flexible. If there is an overall university program, it must be possible for each college or department to introduce such variations as are necessary to meet its unique conditions. And within a departmental program it must be possible to provide each individual with the help he needs. This implies diagnostic capacities and available resources. In this connection it is particularly useful to differentiate between those graduate students who are strongly oriented toward a career in college teaching and those who intend to be primarily scholars. The former require a much broader range of teaching experiences than do the latter.

Lastly, a teacher training program should be aggressive. By this is meant that as the T.A. increases in skill and dedication to teaching, he be accorded steadily increased responsibility and autonomy so that by the time he completes his degree he has some familiarity with all the roles of the college teacher as they were analyzed. Keeping a T.A. instructor in a structured position where his duties are clearly prescribed for him and where the tasks have been highly over-learned for more than a few months (or perhaps weeks) can not be defended as training. It is acknowledged that there are many relatively dull, repetitive aspects to teaching. If we do not take advantage of the problem-solving capacities, the motivation to teach, and the creativity of our graduate students by involving them progressively in the full range of activities associated with the full role of college teacher, we are not meeting our responsibilities as trainers of new teachers.[6]

Experimental Programs

A number of these ideas and suggested principles are reflected in some current experimental programs designed for better prepara-

[6] Frank Koen, "The Preparation of College Teachers," in Donald S. Dean, editor, *Pre-Service Preparation of College Biology Teachers* (The Commission of Undergraduate Education in the Biological Sciences, 1970), pp. 30-33.

tion of potential college teachers. Those examples that were relatively successful were based on the twin premises of full financial support for graduate students and a definite temporal sequence culminating in a four-year graduate program.

University of Rochester. One of the first of these was an attempt to improve training of graduate students at the University of Rochester through developing those skills, traits, and insights necessary in college teaching. As an equal goal, Rochester also sought to improve the college teaching its undergraduate students experienced both with graduate students and with fully ranked teachers. This effort seems to have resulted from several factors. First, the dean of the liberal arts college had long been concerned about the improvement of college teaching and was constantly on the alert for devices which would force faculty attention toward problems of pedagogy. He sensed the need within his own office for personnel who could give attention to graduate students, especially to the problems they experienced as they undertook teaching in their respective departments. Second, a professor of psychology who, with his wife, had spent several years living in student residence halls, saw possibilities in a seminar on college teaching as a means of decreasing the discrepancy between what undergraduate students seemed to want and what they were actually receiving in their classes taught by graduate students. Third, the English department was attempting to revise its freshman English offerings and to use graduate students to teach courses judged as appropriate alternatives for the traditional rhetoric or composition course. Last, and enormously important, there was general awareness on the part of central administration of the growing national criticism of how graduate students were actually used as teachers and the fact that so few of these students were given any kind of formal preparation for the task.

The Rochester experiment included several discrete but interacting phases. First, an interview and questionnaire study was conducted on the attitudes and opinions of undergraduate students, graduate students, professors, and department chairmen as to what was good or bad in the use of graduate students as teachers. At the same time, a rather comprehensive survey was made of criticism of college teaching and of attempts to improve the preparation of college teachers. These data, when summarized, were used as background for a second phase, which was to convene a conference of representatives from a number of private institutions to share experiences of preparing graduate students for college teaching. After this, each department was solicited to find out whether or not it would be interested in attempting a major revision of the ways in which it used graduate students as teachers. Participation by the psychology and English departments is here reported.

The psychology department required all graduate students to teach in one of the psychology courses, generally an introductory course. In this course, a senior professor lectured and a graduate student taught discussion sections. Considerable attention was given to matching graduate students with courses appropriate to their interests and needs; additional effort was made to provide broader experience for those students who taught beyond the required one semester. As part of the teaching experience all students also participated in a seminar on college teaching conducted by the professor who delivered the lectures for the introductory course.

The English department carried out its intention to revise freshman English offerings and created a series of courses, any one of which could be used to satisfy the freshman English requirement. One of these, English III, was designed for students who might have some difficulty with college-level writing. This course, which was not remedial (it was in fact taken by about a third of all freshmen students), became the principal vehicle through which graduate students received experience in teaching. Integrated into the project was the accumulation of considerable information about freshmen from an inventory of reading tastes and from tests on both general academic attitude and English aptitudes. The department expected each graduate student to teach one section under supervision, observed him teaching on three different occasions, and organized an in-service seminar or colloquium in which students could discuss their problems and anxieties. Additionally, the director of the program rechecked at least one set of papers graded by the graduate student.

The results from these two departmental efforts were various. The senior professor in psychology was particularly satisfied with establishing the principle of teaching experience as part of the doctoral training for all students and with making this a nonremunerated (because graduate psychology students received other financial support), noncredit activity. The several heads of the freshman English program believed that the accumulation of information about students, the close supervision of graduate student teachers, and the substantial improvement in the freshman English course were all extremely worthwhile. On the matter of seminars opinions differed according to content. Although he continued to believe in the theory of a seminar on college teaching, the psychology professor felt that this was one of the least satisfactory activities, partly because graduate students, who were both teaching for the first time and completing their course work, did not have time to read from the growing literature on higher education. On the other hand, the graduate English students valued particularly their seminars, which tended to discuss quite practical problems such as developing tests and devising departmental examinations.

Both departments agreed on the importance of giving careful attention to placing graduate students in appropriate sections for teaching experience. Generally, graduate students who were selected more carefully for teaching responsibilities and were given orientation into the problems of teaching, appreciated this effort and felt they had grown considerably as teachers during the semester. Members of both departments also found that two or three years was all the time a professor should spend directing teaching assistants.

Michigan State University. At the University of Rochester it was assumed that senior professors would, at least for a few years at a time, take some responsibility for supervision of graduate students. A different set of assumptions was made at Michigan State University, which attempted to find new ways of improving the instructional quality of graduate teaching assistants in several different departments. The undertaking originated in several concerns and developments at the university. The first was widespread acceptance that the bulk of lower division instruction at the university was, and would likely continue to be, handled by graduate teaching assistants, who all too frequently entered the task of teaching with neither preparation nor direction for improvement. The university had been searching for ways to rectify this deficiency. Second, Michigan had long been institutionally committed to innovation in education. Evidence of this was the existence of the Educational Development

Program which was designed specifically to encourage innovation and experimentation within the university. And third, the Educational Development Program added to its staff a psychologist, experienced in training instructors for industry, who wanted to integrate some industrially developed concepts into academic operations.

The undertaking began with a period of exploration to develop key concepts which would subsequently be tested. During this period, a specialized seminar room was installed immediately adjacent to a television deck enclosed by one-way windows so class instruction could be both televised and observed directly without interference. A program was finally decided on which would meet several criteria. Since teaching is an essentially personal act, wide individual variation in teaching style would not only be tolerated but fostered; there would be no emphasis on a single style of teaching. The plan should be economical of faculty time since the Michigan faculty valued research more highly than teaching. This led to a consideration of ways in which graduate teaching assistants could be used as part of the teaching process. The design, when finally completed, called for teams of five to eight graduate teaching assistants from each of eight departments to be subjected to a one-quarter (ten weeks) treatment. The treatment would proceed from some introductory discussions with a mentor to experience in conducting a (televised) discussion group each week in the experimental classroom. Every Friday each team would meet for a debriefing session during which each member would present a television clip of his most recent teaching experience. His own action would be discussed and improvements suggested. Further, in the expectation that students would test their own emerging ideas with ideas contained in the literature, the design called for a reasonable, available library of materials on higher education and on teaching. This last, it should be pointed out, proved to be the weakest part of the entire effort.

The project was carried out much as it had been planned. During its first year, teams of teaching assistants from different departments were subjected to the treatment. During the second year, effort was concentrated on teaching assistants from the geography department. A systematic effort was made to evaluate the project by observing changes in teaching style of graduate assistants over a ten-week period and by collecting in-depth interview and questionnaire data from the trainees themselves. For the most part, the teaching assistants liked the experience and felt that they had grown a great deal as a result of the videotape recordings and the discussions of their performances. Not all departments yielded the same satisfying results. For example, in the foreign language department, the mode of instruction was so stylized and rigid that graduate teaching assistants had no room to change even if they wanted to. At least one department employed a Rogerian style of nondirective teaching, but that also appeared inappropriate for this particular method of in-service training since the role of the teacher was deemphasized.

The experiment at Michigan State seems to have produced several interesting results. The fact that teaching assistants in a number of departments have become conscious of the dynamics of teaching has made them somewhat critical of their own instructors, and this in turn has stimulated discussion of teaching within the departments. The dean of the College of Social and Behavioral Sciences has kept track of the project throughout, has interviewed graduate teaching assistants, and has indicated to the department heads his willingness to entertain budgetary requests for other departments to use the technique. The department of geography, which followed this model and concentrated on preparation of graduate teaching assistants, expected to adopt this procedure with all students in its graduate program.

Sarah Lawrence College. A much more expensive program, and one which probably has little possibility of direct application by large graduate schools, was an internship program conducted by Sarah Lawrence College for prospective college teachers. (A description is presented here because the program illustrates many of the principles already enumerated.) The program was an attempt to prepare college teachers for lower division undergraduate instruction. It originated from several factors indigenous to Sarah Lawrence College. Throughout, the background was the college's approach to education which insisted on intense personal interaction between teacher and student, limited numbers of courses, and great reliance on tutoring relationships. A principal motivation for this particular undertaking was the long-term concern for teaching held by the president of Sarah Lawrence. She believed that, if the college could be innovative, it might create models that would be adaptable else-where. (She also believed that the Ph.D. program was an inappro-priate preparation for teaching undergraduate students.) Under her leadership the college had pioneered in programs for mature women and had developed a center for continuing education which focused on these women's educational needs. In connection with the center and its program, the college almost by accident began developing special degrees at the master's level in such activities as the perform-ing arts.

The overall design of the Sarah Lawrence project was rela-tively straightforward. Women who generally resided in the West-chester County area and had bachelor's degrees were invited to participate in a three-year program to prepare themselves, on a part-time basis, for college teaching. At the end of the three years they would receive a master's degree and hopefully would be accepted not only in junior colleges but in lower divisions of four-year insti-tutions as well. During the first year these women would participate in a common seminar, "The American Idea," which would be taught by the leader of the project. Students would engage in reading a number of documents from American intellectual history and would discuss the ideas in the context of higher education. In addition, each student would take one other course, generally in the field in which she wanted to teach. Then, following the Sarah Lawrence pattern, she would be assigned to a faculty adviser for whom she would write a series of papers in her preferred field. Dur-ing the second year, students would take another interdisciplinary seminar and spend some time each week observing a class at one of the neighboring collegiate institutions. Once again, each student would be assigned an adviser, with whom she could discuss her observations at the host institution. In the third year, students would teach one or two sections of a course at the host institution and, in addition, would take the third common seminar and another course to strengthen the substantive preparation for teaching.

The program worked generally as was planned. Fifteen stu-dents were admitted into the program at the rate of five each year. The common seminars operated substantially as anticipated. How-ever, an attempt to have students read widely about higher education *per se* did not prove particularly worthwhile. As in the Rochester experiment, the students simply had too much other reading to attend to professional literature about college teaching. Work on the substantive courses also progressed according to plan. The balance between observation and teaching was somewhat asymmetrical. Some students in the second year gained teaching experience; several, even in the third year, spent more time observing than teaching. Placing students as interns or associate faculty members proved time-consuming and difficult. Most of the nearby institutions welcomed observation but were somewhat reluctant to accept people with less than a master's degree as teachers. The women selected for the program were able, and they experienced a tremendous sense of personal growth through the three years of the project. They felt that the combination of the common seminar, actual field work in colleges, and close relationships with an adviser helped them develop a sense of personal and professional identity. It is, of course, too early to tell whether these women will be placed in career positions as teachers, or if they will perform well; but, based on their seeming comprehension of the dynamics of teaching, their sense of personal growth, and their general attitudes toward teaching, the prognosis appears good.

University of Colorado. Although in each of the three previously mentioned experiments, seminars or colloquia dealing with higher education did not seem to work particularly well, institutions continue to experiment with seminars and probably should be encouraged to do so. It is just possible that out of such experimentation can come a format which would be adaptable. At the University of Colorado, the faculty of the department of biology attempted what it called a mini-institute prior to the beginning of the fall semester and then scheduled time throughout the academic year for other seminar activities. During the three-day mini-institute, nine topics were treated: philosophy of teaching biology at the University of Colorado; advances in biology teaching; preparation of learning objectives; the noninvestigative laboratory experience; investigative approach to the laboratory; role of the pre- and post-laboratory experiences; new advances in audio-visual media; criteria for writing laboratory investigations; and teaching for inquiry with films and slides.

During the semester the department conducted four full-day sessions at monthly intervals: (1) Systems analysis approach to improvement of undergraduate instruction: After discussion of the approach, the participants examined a lower division course and developed a program for systematic improvement. They then created the criteria for, and prepared, a model biology curriculum. (2) The audio-tutorial approach to teaching and assessment: This entailed an explanation of the Postlethwait System and its possible applications to all levels and types of courses. (3) Teaching biology to the nonmajor: Here each student prepared and evaluated a course outline for a model nonmajor course. (4) A critical analysis of evaluation devices and the preparation of effective test items: Graduate students were given experience in preparing test items and examining them for validity and reliability. These test items were designed to test for previously stipulated learning objectives.[7]

University of Iowa. At the University of Iowa a somewhat different approach was undertaken. There, the biology department organized a seminar which meets every other week and continues for as long as the sessions seem profitable. The seminars are conducted in a generally Socratic method, with graduate students bringing into the discussion their own early teaching experiences. The course outline is relatively straightforward: the rationale for inclusion of general biology as part of an undergraduate program, the role of biology in general education, and the purposes of undergraduate education. A discussion of how one actually uses a college course to achieve behavioral objectives opens up the matter on objectives and generally ends with criteria of excellence for courses, teachers, texts, laboratories, and examinations. Considerable stress is placed on outlining an elementary biology course, and each student is required to construct such an outline for group criticism. Being practically oriented, the seminar then demands that each student construct a single lecture to implement in part his proposed course outline. Similarly, he must create several laboratory exercises and develop, subject to group criticism, a final examination to test for achievement of the objectives earlier postulated.[8]

Other Approaches. To round off this sampling of experi-

[7] David O. Norris, "A Workshop to Train Graduate Students for College Teaching," in Dean, *Pre-Service Preparation of College Biology Teachers,* pp. 88–89.
[8] Norris, p. 90.

mental programs, the essence of several relatively satisfactory programs will be briefly indicated.

In a social science department, three levels of teaching are posited, and each student is expected to proceed through all three. Inexperienced teaching fellows attend lectures and instruct discussion sections under the supervision of third-level teaching fellows. At the second level, the fellow conducts some discussion sections and gives a number of lectures supervised by a faculty member. At the third level, he has full responsibility for a full lecture section and supervises some first-level fellows in their discussion sessions.

In a history department, each graduate student is limited to two one-hour sections of ten to fourteen undergraduates in order to allow greater time for preparation and to insure that he does not steal time from undergraduate teaching for his own studies. Two years of teaching are required of all Ph.D. candidates during the second and third years of a four-year graduate program. During the second year they teach discussion sections in the Western civilization course; during the third year, discussion sections in either Western civilization, Far Eastern history, or United States history, depending on their interests. The lecturer closely coordinates the discussion sections, but graduate students participate in course planning and selection of reading materials used in their sections. During the first year of graduate study, students must observe sections taught by faculty members, discussing their observations with those responsible for the course. General responsibility for supervising graduate student teachers rests with each lecturer in the course. However, each graduate student is assigned an adviser who must visit the student several times each year while he is teaching. The student receives academic credit for each semester of teaching and may elect teaching as one of the fields for the preliminary examination. At this institution, a good point is made that the graduate student is not a sub-junior faculty member, nor an underpriviliged citizen, but an apprentice who is acquiring the knowledge, skills, and credentials that are the prerequisites for faculty status.

Another history department, largely as an outgrowth of a regional work conference, adopted the requirement that all Ph.D. candidates teach at least one semester, preferably in the third year of residency, and that they take a course on the teaching of college history offered by the departmental chairman. During the year prior to teaching, the graduate student must observe the conduct of at least two classes and discuss his observations with the faculty member. All graduate student teachers are visited, and criticisms are conveyed to them in a conference. In addition, they must submit tests and examinations to their supervisor and provide a tape recording of at least one sample of their teaching.

A political science department conducts its teacher training by requiring each Ph.D. candidate to take a one-semester seminar on the problems of teaching political science prior to assignment as a tutor to undergraduate political science students. The graduate student tutor and the tutees meet several times during the semester, with the undergraduate student's term papers the focus of much of their discussion.

An economics department teaches a fairly straightforward organization of economics principles through a team consisting of a principal lecturer and graduate students. This team meets every two weeks to discuss the materials to be covered and ways they might be treated. Thereafter, the graduate student takes complete charge of his own discussion section and is rarely visited.

Finally, a mathematics department has developed quite a formal structure:

First year: Fall term—Four hours a week attending lectures in beginning calculus, finite mathematics (for students who have not assisted in the course before); three hours per week in problem sessions; assistance in grading three examinations. Winter term—One hour a week attending lectures (for students with previous experience assisting in the course); three hours a week in problem sessions; assistance in grading three examinations. Spring term—Repeat of fall and winter terms.

Second year: Fall term—Repeat of either fall or winter term of first year. Winter term—No teaching. Spring term— Four hours a week attending lectures in advanced undergraduate or beginning graduate course in material familiar to the student; one hour a week in problem session for the course and/or preparation of mimeograph lecture notes; homework in examination grading assistance.

Third year: No teaching.

Fourth year: Fall term—Teach one session of a multiple section sophomore or junior level course under supervision of course chairman. Winter term—Repeat of fall term or else teach, with more or less full responsibility, a junior or senior level course. Spring term—No teaching.[9]

Indications of Change

These and other examples of attempts to give graduate students better preparation for teaching are naturally of great interest and may possibly lead toward major reform. However, there is still ground for skepticism. The Presidential Advisory Committee on Undergraduate Instruction of the University of Toronto, for example, reported:

> We have consulted an extensive literature reporting many experiments in improving university and college teaching, chiefly in the United States, ranging from systems of teaching internships to systems of in-service seminars in university teaching methods. Most of these relied on professors of the various disciplines rather than professors of teaching methods, and most of them clearly had some merit. But we could not find any evidence that these pilot schemes could be followed up on a wide enough scale to do what needed to be done at any bearable cost of faculty time and energy. One of the pilot schemes that was thought to be most successful, which was conducted with lavish Foundation support, required one-fifth or two-fifths of the time of eight senior faculty members throughout an academic year to plan and operate an in-service seminar for twelve new junior members of the faculty. With or without Foundation support, nothing of this order can be thought to be feasible on the scale that would be needed to provide requisite help to all incoming junior faculty members in a large university.[10]

[9] Nowlis and others, *The Graduate Student as Teacher,* p. 47.
[10] *Undergraduate Instruction in Arts and Sciences* (Toronto: University of Toronto Press, 1967).

The logic of most attempts to prepare college teachers is relatively straightforward. Teaching experience is arranged in a definite sequence extending from observation of teaching by the graduate student to experience in conducting an upper division course. Supervision is provided with ample opportunity for consultation with an adviser or mentor professor. Also some exposure to the literature about college education and college teaching is provided, with opportunity for discussion of new ideas in a seminar or colloquium setting. Yet well-developed programs are still extremely rare. The question naturally arises as to why this is so. One reason is probably the dearth of persuasive evidence that these programs make a difference in how graduate students subsequently teach. Some techniques, according to anecdotal evidence, do bring about perceivable changes in how graduate students teach their sections. Thus the Michigan State University experiment, using videotape recordings of teaching assistants conducting classes, produced judgments on the part of both supervisors and participants that changes had indeed occurred; but those teaching assistants were not followed up to determine whether or not there had been any lasting results. This lack of evidence allows Berelson (and others of his persuasion) to contend that, while there are no objections to a systematic effort to improve the teaching skills of graduate students, there is no reason why teaching facility should not be allowed to develop during the early years of an official academic appointment.

Thus, at this point, it would appear that one of several alternatives will be followed in determining graduate programs in arts and sciences. First, public criticisms of the quality of college teaching may remain so clamorous that graduate schools will require teaching experience in order to indicate they are conscious of a problem and are attempting to do something about it. Second, and equally likely, such teacher-preparation programs may gradually be run down because of other demands on the time of students and faculty. Third, and seemingly quite unlikely, a few institutions (hopefully, prestige universities) may make a comprehensive study of the long-term effects of a supervised teaching curriculum organized for graduate student teachers. Models of how such studies could be conducted exist, but whether major graduate institutions will attempt them is highly conjectural.

Given the lack of evidence, the general professorial disinterest in the techniques of teaching looms as a substantial barrier to widespread acceptance of a system of teaching experience. Various questionnaire studies indicate that college professors do view teaching as an important activity from which they gain great personal satisfaction. Nevertheless, there seems to be a pervasive attitude that college teaching is a highly individualized activity which each must acquire through experience—unaided by others—or through study of specific techniques. Indeed, some professors regard teaching, even by teaching assistants, as such a private matter that it would be almost obscene for a senior faculty member to visit the classroom of an aspirant professor, much less to discuss practices with him. Until such intransigence is alleviated, systematic programs widely adopted by all departments in a graduate university are unlikely.

Even if long-held attitudes could be changed and persuasive evidence accumulated, an emphasis on preparation for teaching in a graduate program poses serious temporal and logistical problems. So intent seem graduate students on acquiring substantive knowledge in their specialty, and on developing the skills necessary to produce a satisfactory dissertation, that any infringement on their time is judged an imposition to be resisted. Faculty—similarly preoccupied with their own specialized interests, with normal departmental politics, and with administration—find the tedious hours required to supervise and consult with graduate teachers a luxury they simply cannot afford. This conflict over use of time epitomizes the central issue in graduate education. Is a graduate program designed to develop high substantive competencies, or is it designed to prepare individuals for a real-life vocation? In aggregate, the various changes discussed in the second part of this book, if generally accepted, would suggest a gradual resolution of the issue in favor of preparation for a profession, but the dead weight of inertia of a hundred years of existing practice remains a serious retardant.

Despite these negative comments, however, attempts on the part of graduate schools to add a teaching dimension to the programs of a substantial majority of graduate students seem worthwhile and should be encouraged. But several necessary conditions need to be realized to facilitate the effort. The first is an acceptance of greater structure to a total graduate program. So long as the length of a doctoral program is indeterminate, with graduate professors being able to add on course, seminar, or research requirements at will, a systematic inclusion of teaching experience will probably fail. Current interest in better definition of structure suggests that widespread integration of a teaching experience into the graduate program might occur.

Second, evidence repeatedly emerges that if departments are expected to assume responsibility for a teaching dimension, highly irregular patterns of practices will prevail. Therefore, in some way or other, graduate deans, aided and supported by presidents, should assume central responsibility for establishing the broad outlines and minimal practices of a program. This may suggest the necessity of providing an associate dean for instruction who would try to bring departmental practices into some kind of general alignment.

The last provision is of a different and much more profound order: that is for graduate schools and their departments to re-examine criteria used for admitting students into graduate study. Present criteria still emphasize intellectual power and interest in a subject. These traits have generally been assumed to be the essence of a successful college teacher. Yet there is room to ask, "But what if they're not?"

IX

Old and New Issues

Graduate education has always faced more unresolved issues than have other levels of education, probably because graduate education is a hybrid which combines elements of undergraduate and advanced professional education but with considerable uncertainty of purpose.

Unresolved Issues

Foreign Languages. Foreign language requirements have been justified throughout the history of graduate education on several grounds. First, it was presumed that knowledge of French and German were characteristics of the educated scholar and that no one achieving a graduate degree should be without those characteristics. Second, it was assumed that a scholar trained for comprehensive grasp of a discipline would need to read scholarly works in languages other than his own. And since it was assumed that the two most widely used languages in scholarship were French and German, these became the standard requirements. In spite of rather conclusive demonstrations that the language requirements were only hurdles hastily prepared for by students and not at all indicative of whether the language would or would not be used in scholarship, the requirements were maintained. But recently changes have been taking place, the most general of which is the transfer from the university to the departments of the responsibility for determining foreign language requirements. This development has taken place almost simultaneously with the rapid development of quantification as an essential tool for research and scholarship. Thus the argument is that there are a number of languages, verbal and quantifiable, and only those scholars directly and intimately involved in a field are in a position to know the appropriate languages for graduate students to cultivate.

Examinations. Universities are also beginning to examine the propriety of long sequences of rigorous examinations. Traditionally, a student admitted as a candidate for a degree has pursued all required course work, has taken an exhaustive and exhausting examination covering the entire field in which he has been studying, has completed a thesis, and then has taken an hours-long oral examination or an oral examination combined with a written examination. In a sense, this preoccupation with examinations has been a carry-over from attitudes toward education that were indigenous to undergraduate colleges: coercion and sanctions in the form of examinations were essential to motivate students. The recent relaxation of admission requirements and attempts to individualize educational programs have been accompanied by a substantial relaxation of examinations. Several alternatives to the traditional pattern have been attempted. One, to place the comprehensive written examination much earlier in the graduate program and to limit its scope, is designed to reveal whether a candidate has the ability to deal thoughtfully with some portion of the discipline in which he is working. A second variant is to substitute several long papers for the grueling comprehensive examination. Another has been to allow students several options to the oral examination by determining its nature: an examination of the entire field before starting to write a dissertation, an exposition of a thesis topic, or a final defense of a dissertation.

Theses. Much less pronounced are attempts to modify the

nature of thesis requirements. While theses as the completion of master's programs generally appear to be decreasing in frequency, the thesis as the proper culmination for a Ph.D. program seems almost as well entrenched as ever. However, when over three hundred graduate deans were asked to indicate what innovations were being attempted, fifty-three claimed consideration of elimination of the thesis requirement. There is inclination to accept the reality that a doctoral dissertation is not an original contribution to knowledge. A few institutions are exhibiting willingness to substitute scholarly essays in place of a dissertation requirement; but the number of institutions exploring this kind of change is still quite limited, except in connection with the Doctor of Arts program.

Supply and Demand. There are a number of other concerns that have emerged only since the late 1960s, whose resolution could affect the character of graduate education considerably. The first is the matter of overproduction of doctoral recipients. The conditions which necessitated the rapid expansion of graduate education during the late 1950s and 1960s—demands for highly trained professional and research people, and for additional college teachers for the anticipated marked increase of college students—have changed remarkably in a short period of time. While during the 1970s the number of positions requiring advanced degree holders will increase substantially, it will not increase as rapidly as the number of new degree holders. Universities will be able to educate many more doctoral candidates than can be employed in positions that have heretofore required that level of preparation. Unless institutions take corrective action, new doctorate holders of the 1980s will face an extremely bleak future.

Different studies projecting the number of advanced degree recipients by 1980 substantially agree on trends. The more cautious projections indicate between 350,000 and 400,000 doctor's degrees produced in the 1971–1980 period; the less cautious, about 500,000. All projections regarding demand on the basis of positions currently employing doctorates agree that the supply will be substantially greater than the demand. For example, during the 1960s, approximately 60 percent of the total output of new doctorates found their first positions in institutions of higher education; during the 1970s, only 25 percent can anticipate faculty positions, even though institutions are enlarging the proportion of faculty holding doctorates. Doctoral degree holders will therefore be forced, in larger numbers, into nonacademic work, and of that group substantial numbers will be forced into applied activities—administration and the like— rather than into research-oriented positions. Doctoral degree holders probably will not be without jobs because their high degree of education makes them too valuable. However, they will be forced into new sorts of occupations for which presumably their graduate work should have given them some preparation. "As the economy grows and changes, and as national priorities shift, a decade or more hence, there will be much use for persons who have academic training well beyond the master's level. Persons with such training, reasonably well adapted to actual job requirements, will have much to offer in a complex society and economy. The implications for the content of graduate education over the next decade have not been fully considered. Certainly, the traditional discipline- and research-oriented Ph.D. is not the sole means of preparing people for new roles. Graduate education which has thus far not been much shaken by the current agitation over the goals and methods of higher education may face a period of stressful readjustment as the labor market forces a reexamination of what graduate education is for."[1]

Institutional Involvement. How many institutions then should be engaged in graduate training, and at what levels of productivity? The federal government has already tried to exert a downward pressure on the output of doctorates through reduction in support for graduate students. In addition, several states are restraining the establishment of new doctoral programs or the expansion of existing ones (for example, the State University of New York). But overall a paradox has developed. Federal policies and individual decisions in some of the prestige private universities are restraining the growth of some of the best existing graduate departments. Yet, on the whole, the states have been unable to restrain the establishment of new graduate departments in institutions. Roose and Anderson[2] reached several relevant conclusions: They noted that developing institutions can create new graduate programs that achieve some degree of

[1] Dael Wolfle and Charles V. Kidd, "The Future Market for Ph.D.'s," *Science,* 1971, *123,* 7.
[2] Kenneth D. Roose and Charles T. Anderson, *A Rating of Graduate Programs* (Washington, D.C.: American Council on Education, 1970).

distinction relatively quickly. However, they questioned whether expansion of the number of programs in many institutions accomplishes more than could have been achieved through strengthening already strong graduate programs. They felt that, as a general rule, strong existing programs should be strengthened and that programs that fall below desired standards should be carefully examined and possibly eliminated.

Financial Aid. Graduate education is by far the most expensive form of education per student and appears likely to become more so. One estimate suggests that by 1980 the cost of graduate education could attain an annual rate of twenty billion dollars. A critical question is: Who or what agencies should pay what proportion of that amount? Prior to World War II, the amount of direct federal support of graduate students was negligible, as was extrainstitutional support from all sources. However, during the early 1960s the increased federal support of students played a significant part in expanding graduate enrollments. "In 1960, 5,500 Fellows and trainees were supported by the federal government at a cost of twenty-four million. This increased to 43,296 awards at two hundred and twenty-six million in 1968."[3] Then in the late 1960s came the substantial slowdown of support of graduate students, not only on the part of federal agencies but also on the part of private funds such as the Woodrow Wilson Fellowship Program. The question now arises as to what changes are likely in the future.

Recommendations of such groups as the Carnegie Commission on Higher Education or the Association of American Universities call for a restoration of federal support, albeit with some modification in detail. Thus the Carnegie Commission urges the establishment of specific programs by specific institutions to rectify known shortages, and an increase in educational opportunity grants. The Association of American Universities recommended "that the direct support of graduate students, requiring a substantial additional investment, should consist of fellowships and traineeship accompanied by cost-of-education supplements to institutions." In the same vein, another panel,[4] while not emphasizing crisis conditions,

[3] *Report on the Conference on Pre-doctoral Education in the United States,* p. 10.
[4] U.S. Department of Health, Education and Welfare, *Toward a Long-*

detailed a number of elements calling for increased federal support. It called for expansion of the NDEA Graduate Fellowships to support 30,000 students by 1975 to alleviate imbalances in the non-scientific fields and in support of part-time graduate students; for an increase in the education allowance for federal graduate fellowships to a level of perhaps $5000, with periodic adjustment of this figure if necessary as costs of graduate education rise; for expanded funding for existing NSF, NIH, and OE institutional grants to speed the development of new centers of excellence at the graduate level, and a similar program under the National Foundation on The Arts and Humanities; and for supplementation of existing research programs by maintaining grants equal to a percentage of federal research awards received by institutions of higher education. These recommendations are all based on the premise that there is little danger of producing an oversupply of highly qualified people, particularly if the orthodox, diversified Ph.D. program is modified to allow for alternate goals and courses of study. In addition, they are all based on the premise that society should be charged for the contribution graduate education makes to the nurturing of intellectual resources and leadership.

But, increasingly, the argument is advanced that the principal benefits from all of higher education, including graduate education, accrue to individuals, and that those profiting should pay in one way or another. A common theme that runs through much recent writing is that students do make educational decisions based on the economic returns anticipated, and that ways should be contrived to facilitate this kind of rational, economic decision-making. Richard B. Freeman, for example, has suggested two possible modifications of the current method of financing higher education: use of educational loans in place of direct subsidization of students, and the awarding of stipends for study in certain fields where there are real shortages. He feels there are at least three advantages in the use of loans. First, students obtaining loans will be encouraged to make more rational evaluations of costs and benefits. Second, tying repayment of loans to subsequent income, as was proposed by the 1967 President's

---

Range Plan for Federal Financial Support for Higher Education: A Report to the President (Washington: Government Printing Office, 1969).

Panel on Educational Innovation, minimizes risk of nonrepayment. And third, since some students who can afford full cost of their education will not opt for a loan, more funds will become available for economically marginal students. The second of his recommendations could lead to an increase in the responsiveness and efficiency of the labor market and could minimize overproduction in already saturated fields.[5]

Deans of graduate schools are beginning to think in these same terms. Sanford Elberg, Dean of the Graduate Division, at the University of California, Berkeley, has said that "students are being asked to assume a much greater percentage of their education. . . . The past system was not right. It was too affluent in certain respects. Now, with so many good students in need, priority will have to be given to need more than to merit." For the immediate future, Elberg favors low-interest loans and tuition awards; but in the long run, "the financing of higher education is up in the air—for the student and for the institutions. All institutions of higher learning may not be able to support a doctoral program—they may have to stop at the Master's. Perhaps there has to be a new Master Plan of the highest education." While the number of bright students who want the Ph.D. may continue to rise, "the number who recognize the fiscal facts of life may also rise. Students who see the employment possibilities may settle for the Master's degree to avoid the risk of being over-trained."[6] Thus, the current situation sees a clear perception of curtailed support for graduate students, considerable hope for restoration of support, yet an increasingly realistic recognition that during the 1970s new approaches will probably be necessary.

Developmental Needs of Students. The question of support of graduate education is at least widely recognized. In contrast, an emerging issue of potentially enormous significance has been given very little attention. This concerns the degree to which graduate education does or does not attend to the developmental needs of students in their late twenties. Part of the reform movement within professional fields seems to have been based on an awareness that

[5] Richard B. Freeman, *The Market for College-Trained Manpower* (Cambridge, Mass.: Harvard University Press, 1971).

[6] University of California, Berkeley, *House Bulletin,* Oct. 1971, 7 (1).

certain important developmental needs were being overlooked. Thus, placing clinical or field experience earlier in professional programs has been attempted in part to facilitate socialization into a profession. Attempts to infuse professional curricula with materials from the humanities have been made because of realization that graduate professional students were struggling with problems of ethics, social responsibility, and personal integrity. But with two exceptions—pleas for interdisciplinary programs, and a growing concern with the socialization of graduate students—little explicit attention has been given to the developmental needs of graduate students. Suggestive, however, of what might be considered in graduate programs, in response to imperatives to meet these needs, are several areas of teaching and learning elaborated by Joseph Katz and his associates.

First there is the academic-conceptual area, under which is included much of the traditional subject matter, descriptions, theories, hypotheses, and so on.

The next area is the esthetic-artistic one, the area of feelings, emotions, intuitions, sensitivity and sensibility. . . . This approach to reality requires its own sequence of training, and its own standards of performance which, though sometimes subject to a wider range of argument than standards in the more exact sciences, can obtain some degree of consensus among qualified people. . . .

Then there is the area of people-oriented activity. This area is in some sense akin to the esthetic, since it also involves the affective and feeling modes of response. For some people, working with others, understanding them and being of help to them, is a favorite mode of dealing with reality. . . . When we think of teaching this kind of "skill," we must bear in mind that its practitioners are often not as verbally facile as the ordinary academician. In this they resemble the artist whose teaching consists less in long lectures than in examples, in long looking or listening, and in the right words, sometimes quite few words, at the right time. . . . There are many students strongly oriented toward the political or administrative life. They might be taught, in the manner of some of the ancient Sophists, to master the arts of manipulation and exploitation. But to teach them the art of satisfying divergent interests without injury to one or several of the parties will require some pioneering efforts. . . .

The fifth area is that of inanimate man-made machines, computers, and the like. Some people find that they can deal with reality best by creating artificial replicas or artificial extensions of it. . . . Here we need two sorts of faculty: those who are particularly adept with students who have a primary orientation toward man-made objects—who need to have it brought into connections with other human activities—and those who are able to impart some of the pleasures and skills of these pursuits to those with some other orientation.

The sixth area is that of motoric expression. . . . given the fact that there is a large number of students whose favorite mode of relating to reality is via motoric expression, the problem of connecting their motoric responses with other parts of their personality deserves much greater attention.

Finally, we come to the art of sociability. Though it tends to be regarded as incidental, it actually occupies a major place in the informal learning that takes place during college, and spans the range from learning manners to developing the capacity for friendships and intimacy. Given the fact that informal learning of it brings only moderately satisfactory results, more attention to the factors that foster good human relations seems desirable.[7]

Katz reasons that if an educational program considered these elements, substantial programmatic change would come about.

Institutional Cases

When this monograph was being planned, it was hoped to include several detailed case studies of institutions which were considering major changes in graduate programs in arts and sciences. However, the typical response from graduate deans was that potential changes were likely to be of minor importance and were being made within departments rather than throughout a graduate school or graduate division. Nevertheless, discussion of possible

[7] Joseph Katz and others, *No Time for Youth* (San Francisco: Jossey-Bass, 1962), pp. 429–431.

changes by some institutions that have recently completed self-studies will reflect the problems and issues of graduate education and suggest possible directions for change: not that recommendations have necessarily been incorporated into actual practice—far from it. Dwight R. Ladd, after viewing a number of recent institutional self-studies, points out that relatively few recommendations in long, quite imaginative lists are actually translated into ongoing educational policy or practice.[8] But the recommendations are evidence of the general climate of opinion.

University of California, Berkeley. The earliest of these studies was conducted by a select faculty committee of the Academic Senate of the University of California, Berkeley, largely in response to the outbreak of student dissent in 1964. The report took pride in the achievements of its graduate program but noted the need to reconsider certain aspects of graduate education.[9] Many of the complaints which undergraduate students had made were echoed by graduates—excessively large courses, infrequent contact with faculty members, disappointment with the quality of instruction, and unchallenging educational programs. Many graduate students, in addition, were profoundly critical of shortages of study space and of a system where teaching assistants performing professional service were treated and regarded as marginal, menial laborers.

The report takes an unequivocal stand on the purpose of graduate education: "First and foremost [graduate education] is training and only as a by-product is it education. The graduate is viewed primarily as an initiate undergoing preparation for a defined vocation: historian, economist, or physicist. The task of the faculty is to insure that the student acquires the qualifications and special skills appropriate to the particular vocation. The justification for viewing graduate education as a form of specialized apprenticeship is that specialization is the pre-condition for the discovery of new knowledge or for making contribution to a given field." But this preoccupation with specialization may have been overdone, with resultant psychological damage to students. The time has arrived to

[8] Ladd, *Changes in Educational Policy.*
[9] The following recommendations are found in *Education at Berkeley* (University of California, Berkeley, Academic Senate, Mar. 1966).

reconsider the concept of specialization and to devise ways in which to serve better the growth of the individual graduate student as scholar, teacher, or human being.

Much of the unhealthy preoccupation with specialization comes from too rigid observance of departmental boundaries in required studies and from limitations of graduate programs. Too many departments, adhering to an obsolete concept of the Ph.D. as a master of all fields within a department, present students with the dilemma of either accumulating rapidly a great deal of superficial knowledge or of facing an endless academic program to insure complete mastery. The solution lies not in elimination of departments but in the recognition that departments cannot achieve their professed goals of developing comprehensive coverage. Rather, departments should prepare students to solve problems similar to those they will face in their subsequent careers. The emphasis should be on diverse ways of looking at problems, an awareness of what he must learn in order to deal with the problem and an understanding of the bodies of evidence, the concepts, and theories which are relevant to a particular problem. A principal barrier to such flexibility—to a focus on problems rather than a comprehensive grasp of knowledge —lies in the nature of comprehensive examinations given at the end of all course work, which imply the necessity of mastering all subject divisions. An important step would be to place the comprehensive examination very early in the student's training and to require only that he demonstrate an ability to work within the general field of his concentration. Thereafter, examinations would be a series of tasks, each independently performed as in the case of papers and minor research reports. The dissertation could then be more sensibly approached and could become a natural culmination of a period of progressively deep study.

The concept of students actively demonstrating skills rather than broad comprehension also implies a different attitude toward foreign language examinations. In a majority of cases, language requirements do not achieve the objective of providing an essential piece of intellectual equipment. The solution is not to discard language requirements but to seek ways of integrating language facility in actual work. Thus, the language requirement should be maintained only by those departments for which it is truly germane.

The concept of a comprehensive departmental curriculum has also contributed to excessively long programs for graduate students. While it would be unfortunate for a university-wide committee to dictate to any single department precise time limits for graduate programs (there are substantial differences in requirements of various fields), departments should be expected to conform to some generally recognized criteria. Thus the report recommends that "departments should make certain that capable full-time students having a sound preparation can earn the master's degree in three to five quarters and the Ph.D. in three to four years. The Graduate Council should periodically review all current graduate programs and report whether these norms are in effect."[10]

The report continues by outlining a paradox. Comprehensive departmental programs can be—and probably are—too inclusive and too limiting. Contemporary scholarship is increasingly interdisciplinary, yet graduate education continues to be almost exclusively limited to work within single departments. Faculties that require outside course work do so in a perfunctory manner and, as a general rule, do not assign the "outside field" any substantial weight in examining procedures. To rectify this serious deficiency a considerable array of interdisciplinary courses should be organized around specific problems. With a problems orientation, students are provided an intellectual reason for pursuing work in related fields. For such courses to be developed, departments must be willing to release faculty members to offer joint courses, and students must be encouraged by their advisors to experience these new sorts of curricular undertakings. Thus, departments are urged to allow graduate students, in close consultation with faculty advisors from several departments, to develop individual programs of advanced individualized study as a real and respected substitute for the major field typically covered in the comprehensive examinations.

A serious discrepancy in the graduate programs at Berkeley is the divorce between the graduate student's research on his dissertation and his teaching assistant experience. While many palliatives could be suggested, one important new direction would be enlarging the idea of research to include forms of inquiry intended to enable

[10] *Education at Berkeley,* p. 163.

the inquirer to communicate his findings to students. Departments should allow all graduate students to participate in undergraduate teaching appropriate to their skills, and should grant course credit to graduate students for work designed to relate the graduate curriculum to the problems of teaching.

The writers of the report also believe that the research paradigm has dominated graduate education at Berkeley to such an extent as to become a general cause for alarm. The actual number of true research scholars is probably only a fraction of the total number of successful doctoral candidates. In addition, large numbers of candidates complete all requirements for a Ph.D. except the dissertation and then fail to complete the dissertation for a variety of valid reasons. The time has come to question the whole system that makes the Ph.D. the only acceptable form of certification for college teaching. The university should take a stand on this issue and should consider the recommendation that the Graduate Council should frame necessary legislation creating a new degree of Doctor of Arts to require preparation equivalent to that normally required for advancement to candidacy for the Ph.D., but without requiring a dissertation.

The report recommends reversing the tendency to regard early graduate years as provisional. For example, a number of departments tailor the first graduate year to a master's degree and view it as a device for thinning out the graduate student body. The first year's work is thus meant to compensate for inadequate admissions procedures. This condition is aggravated by the nature of the preliminary examinations, which present still another hurdle and stress the conception of the provisional character of all work taken up to that point. The net effect is to harass students with endless examinations designed to settle the question of competence, a question which should have been settled at the point of entry. To alleviate this harassment and to provide graduate students with a greater sense of dedication to genuine scholarship, greater rigor should be exercised at point of admissions, with the collateral assumption that, once admitted, virtually all graduate students would be expected to complete the program in which they matriculated.

The report also devotes some attention to the rather less academic concerns of graduate students. During the last stage of a graduate student's career, his life is dominated by the thesis, and he has only limited contact with professors. Students who remain on campus discover that the only existing community consists of himself and his thesis, while others are forced by economic circumstances to find a job, which gives neither the time and facilities to finish the thesis nor the professional recognition due the late candidate and scholar. What seems to be needed to alleviate either of these two problems is a system of research institutes which could provide both supporting stipends and a definite sense of community. Such an institute could form a natural home for students in the last phase of their graduate careers.

Stanford University. Consistent with the overall viewpoint of the Berkeley recommendations was an analysis prepared at Stanford.[11] This analysis began with the caveat that the subject of graduate education had been studied much too superficially and that a commission should be created to study in greater detail Stanford's problems in graduate education.

A few years later, that recommendation was heeded when the Senate of the Academic Council commissioned a comprehensive study of graduate education on the campus. The senate set up a steering committee of faculty and students to give overall direction and supervision to the project. Under the guidance of the steering committee, separate committees of faculty and students studied in considerable depth such diverse topics as: the four-year Ph.D.; assessment and reporting of students' performance and prospects; the Ph.D. dissertation and alternative degrees; financial aid; and alternative programs. The study took more than a year to complete and included in-depth studies of each department carried out by departmental visiting teams. One of the more significant recommendations of the study, especially for long term growth and development, was the suggestion of the committee on graduate studies that the use of departmental visiting teams be continued in the future. These teams, composed of two or three faculty and two or three graduate students chosen from fields somewhat related to the department being visited, would make recommendations for program improvement and follow-up which could serve as a highly successful form of internal educational audit.

The committee on the four-year Ph.D. recommended that

[11] *The Study of Education at Stanford,* vol. 7, *Graduate Education.*

each department should present a clear timetable showing how the normal student could complete the Ph.D. in a total of four years. Departments whose program would regularly take longer than four years to complete would need to secure advance approval from the Committee on Graduate Studies. A reexamination of admission requirements was suggested; and departments were cautioned against allowing graduate students to devote much time to remedial work. Basic work in both foreign and computer languages should be completed before acceptance into graduate school. It was further advised that departments consider the advantages of offering delayed admission to those candidates who had persuasive reasons for postponing the beginning of graduate studies, as well as the conditional admission of otherwise well-qualified candidates who appeared to have a particular academic deficiency.

The committee on assessment and reporting submitted a long list of recommendations aimed at clarifying the status of each graduate student both in his own mind and in the minds of the department and departmental faculty. Taken as a unit, these recommendations provided for the orderly progress of each graduate student from his admission to the department to the reception of the Ph.D. or the termination of his graduate studies. There was a strong recommendation that each department establish procedures for qualifying students for the Ph.D. As a result of the qualification procedure, a student would either be qualified for the Ph.D.—and qualification should be considered synonymous with the recommendation for admission to candidacy—or be explicitly terminated. Admission to candidacy would imply that the student's position in his department was secure, subject only to continued satisfactory progress toward completion of the remaining degree requirements. This qualification procedure would occur at some point during the first two years of full-time doctoral study, and a student who had not yet been admitted to candidacy would not be allowed to register for the third year. First-year students not yet qualified for the Ph.D. would be subject to a diagnostic evaluation by the department, which would be intended to help them prepare for qualification the following year.

Other major recommendations of the committee on assessment and reporting concerned termination of students judged to be unqualified for the Ph.D. Departments were urged to be quite direct in terminating such students and to avoid using such indirect mechanisms as the denial or removal of financial aid. The committee also urged the senate to adopt a fairly intricate procedure calculated to insure due process for use by departments in determining who should be admitted to candidacy and who should be terminated:

(a) The responsible departmental committee shall review the student's academic record in the department and his performance during the qualification procedure and then vote. Minutes of the discussion and the vote shall be taken.

(b) If a committee has conducted this review, its decision must be approved by a majority vote of the departmental faculty present. Minutes of the departmental review shall be taken.

(c) In the event of a negative decision, the Director of Graduate Studies or the student's advisor shall, if possible, personally communicate the decision to the student and discuss it with him. The student shall also receive written notification of the department's decision, including the reasons for the denial of candidacy and the appeal procedure.

(d) A positive decision need be communicated to the student in writing only.

(e) The student shall be given the opportunity to examine his departmental file including the minutes of the faculty meetings and may request reconsideration by the responsible committee, giving his reasons for believing reconsideration is warranted.

(f) The committee may refuse to reconsider. The committee's response to the request for reconsideration shall be written and shall be included in the student's file.

(g) After a final negative decision at the departmental level, the student may appeal in writing to the Dean of Graduate Studies. The Dean shall review the petition, the student's departmental file, and the minutes of the faculty review. A decision by the Dean affirming the departmental refusal to grant candidacy shall be final.

The committee on the Ph.D. dissertation and alternative degrees made the laudable suggestion that graduate students should become increasingly involved with their research advisor from the very beginning of their graduate study. This type of contact was considered invaluable for developing and cultivating the student's research interests. Concerning the scope of the Ph.D. dissertation, the committee said: "It should be explicitly recognized that the fundamental goals of the dissertation project—i.e., to serve as the student's supervised apprenticeship in his chosen field, to allow him to demonstrate his mastery of the tools of the trade, and to give him a taste of scholarly accomplishment—can all be fulfilled even if the dissertation does not meet the traditional ideal of beginning a major contribution to knowledge based on independently designed and executed research. *The scope of the dissertation project should be compatible with an expectation of completion in a year or a year and a half of intense effort and in less time for the exceptionally lucky or talented student.*"

The committee on graduate student teaching recommended that the training of a student in a doctoral program should normally include teaching experience that would be supervised and evaluated by both a faculty member and the student in mutual consultation. Further recommendations provided for advertising available teaching positions and informing the officers of the central administration what the department was doing about providing teaching experience for graduate students.

University of Oklahoma. Presenting a somewhat different attitude regarding changes in graduate education is the report on the future of the University of Oklahoma.[12] The report assumes a steady growth of graduate enrollments and recommends that this growth be fostered to achieve several university goals: to provide the state with highly qualified young people entering the professions with a commitment to the future of Oklahoma; to recruit and keep a well-qualified graduate student body through the presence of a diverse, distinguished faculty; to enrich undergraduate education through such a faculty.

After noting the need to create more problem-centered programs of study, to facilitate easy interchange of graduate and under-

[12] Gordon A. Christianson, *The Future of the University* (Norman: University of Oklahoma Press, 1969).

graduate students within courses, and to limit the amount of teaching required of graduate professors, and the desirability of upgrading the conception of graduate students as younger scholars, the report makes a series of specific recommendations.

To support the general policy stressing growth in favor of graduate education, we recommend some actions applicable to all graduate and professional programs.

(1) Selective admissions standards and recruitment must be reviewed and changed consistent with our objectives, with care that recruiting programs are designed to attract a variety of students from all socio-economic backgrounds, and that recruitment is emphasized among minority and deprived groups.

(2) Procedures to unify and integrate all disciplines of programs should be established, such as: a course of instruction drawing on more than one academic unit; integrated budgetary, fiscal, and accounting practices; centralized, specialized research facility.

(3) Activities and contact with the various graduate professional schools should be related to community and student needs through: establishing active service programs as part of graduate instruction; stressing continuous adult graduate education to permit mobility from one social role to another; sending graduate and professional students and faculty to those parts of the world where their academic interests can be pursued, their talents and future challenges found; promoting faculty participation in community, urban, industrial, and professional activities to strengthen the relevance of graduate training.[13]

In elaboration of those principles, the report recommends that there should be no set progression from undergraduate to graduate work. Professional schools should include within their curricula work of a liberal nature, while at the same time the university should encourage highly specialized undergraduate courses of study. To prepare students to exploit more fully this seamless progression, a great deal more attention to orientation counseling of students would be proper, but it should also be recognized that early

[13] Christianson, pp. 65–66.

decisions are not necessarily binding. Hence, the graduate program should encourage greater versatility, and should allow more flexibility of changing from one program to another.

Considerably greater effort should be made in both the graduate professional fields and in graduate work in arts and sciences to relate academic training to on-the-job experience. "Intern programs should not be conducted at the expense of intellectual training. However, the graduate assistant should have on-the-job experience in instruction as well as training in the disciplines. . . . and consideration should be given to internships during the final year of medical education. Similarly, legal internships should be encouraged at an appropriate point in the senior year in Law School. For Engineering, Business, and other professions arrangements should be worked out with prospective employers for placement in a business organization to provide actual experience as part of the educational program prior to graduation."[14]

With respect to the problems of relevance and purpose, the report platitudinously noted: "The graduate and professional programs as expressed in the curricula should have relevance to the future lives of the students in the society. They should insure that questions of purpose, value, and meaning are posed in programs which offer the conceptual framework of thinking about these questions. To accomplish this end, there should be many programs offering different styles, each of which can adapt as the relevance of society shifts."[15]

Canadian Scene. Graduate work and research in Canadian universities began later than in the United States and developed much more slowly. However, during the 1960s, Canadian institutions in many respects followed the same lines of evolution detectable in the United States. Since the Canadian experience may suggest that some problems are simply endemic to graduate work regardless of where it is undertaken, it may be instructive to review some of the criticisms and suggestions for reform which were made in a comprehensive review of graduate education in Canada.[16]

[14] Christianson, p. 73.
[15] Christianson, p. 73.
[16] W. P. Thompson, *Graduate Education in the Sciences in Canadian Universities* (Toronto: University of Toronto Press, 1963).

Generally, administration of graduate schools has been lax and perfunctory. The graduate dean, as compared with deans of other schools, is in a relatively weak position since he has no authority over budgets, appointments, promotions, and the establishment of new positions; if reform is to come about, his role should be strengthened considerably. Graduate education in Canada has also suffered from inadequate financial backing, both for programs and for the support of graduate students. Apparently there was a tradition that graduate work was no more than a slight, inexpensive extension or adjunct of undergraduate education, hence did not require specific budgetary provision. Similarly, little attention had been given to the unique financial needs of graduate students with family responsibilities, and the need was recognized for more substantial graduate scholarships, with less expectation that students would take part-time work.

In Canada, as in the United States, the master's degree has lost prestige. If there is a real need for a master's degree, it should be strengthened, made quite distinctive, and not represent a deterioration in the research expectations of the Ph.D. degree.

Because enrollment growth of certain departments in Canadian universities has resulted in departmental prestige and political power, there has been a tendency to admit too many marginal students. Clearly, more sharply defined and higher admission standards would seem appropriate.

As a result of both the tradition of viewing graduate work as an extension of undergraduate work and the rapid increases in numbers, too many departments tend to require excessive course work. These classes take up such a large proportion of students' time that they are unable to devote adequate time to research. This tendency is related to a notable deterioration in research expectations, especially in regard to the thesis. A possible palliative might be to require that a thesis, in whole or in part, be published in a scientific journal before being accepted as satisfying degree requirements.

The Canadian study makes some definite recommendations which follow closely proposals being made in the United States. The minor requirement, which has deteriorated, ought to be strengthened to give a more interdisciplinary flavor to graduate programs. Similarly, there appears to have been a serious erosion of language requirements and performance levels on examinations. This erosion can be reversed by either eliminating the requirement or making it more demanding. The Canadian report suggests, as Berelson did earlier regarding the American situation, that the length of full-time graduate study is generally little more than meeting minimal requirements and is largely determined by the financial circumstances of graduate students.

The Canadian report devotes several pages to a matter that is only now beginning to receive attention in the United States: the tendency of developing institutions to enter graduate work. In Canada, too many small institutions were attempting to carry on graduate work for which they did not have the necessary personnel, facilities, or financial resources under the assumption that graduate instruction could be added onto the regular duties of undergraduate faculty. These smaller institutions apparently had not recognized that the essential ingredient for effective graduate programs is a first-class faculty of practicing scholars; or if they did recognize it, they lacked the resources to attract capable men. Several recommendations similar to those reforms suggested in the United States are offered. The National Conference of Canadian Universities and Colleges might undertake an accreditation mission by setting forth definite criteria and regulations for graduate education to which institutions offering graduate work should conform. Since accreditation recommendations are not binding, these would not limit creative institutional growth, but could exercise a healthy influence. Even without accreditation, institutions are urged to be more self-restraining. Institutions with limited resources, whatever their size, should restrict their graduate efforts to those fields in which they are specially qualified, should curb their ambitions to undertake graduate work in all or many disciplines, or in all major divisions of any one discipline, and should leave to others fields which other institutions are uniquely qualified to cultivate. Smaller institutions, which nonetheless wish to enter graduate work, could consider the possibility of coordination or the creation of consortia similar in form to the Washington Graduate Consortium. Out of such efforts could come real strengthening of the entire Canadian graduate effort.

A Developing Institution. Although the preceding cases present recommendations rather than actual changes, nonetheless the fact that changes are suggested places those institutions in a somewhat atypical position. Much more frequently institutions offering graduate work seem content to retain established procedures. The fully developed universities have gained recognition, power, and prestige from following orthodox modes of graduate education; and the aspiring developing institution sees those same orthodox modes as the route to academic excellence.

Illustrative of the lack of genuine attempts to bring about innovation is a large (14,000), developing (to become 20,000), publicly supported land-grant institution which sees its future in following the footsteps of a few nationally prominent land-grant institutions. Its graduate council and graduate dean have considerable power over program review and approval of graduate faculty, and they scrutinize syllabi for courses recommended for graduate status. The council, representing all of the schools, is composed of about half administrators and half faculty, with one graduate student representative. In a two-hour discussion of changes in graduate education, the council members revealed that not a great deal was happening. The institution was trying to create a new interdisciplinary program between computer science in the college of arts and sciences and engineering courses which maintained considerable strength in applied uses of the computer. Faculties from the schools of engineering and of arts and sciences had been meeting regularly, and neither faculty was willing to yield enough of its presumed perquisites and prerogatives to allow the interdisciplinary program to become viable. Faculty members from each school seemed so jealous of their discipline and presumed essential sequences of disciplinary courses that cooperation was almost judged contamination. Several members of the council were searching for ways to encourage faculty members of different fields to work together, but had found no good pattern of incentive for change. In part, this search was unproductive because, throughout the institution, departments were generally satisfied with orthodox modes of curriculum design and instruction. This satisfaction seemed reinforced by the attitude of some accrediting agencies (this in connection with such fields as engineering and chemistry) which placed strictures on how innovative programs could become. It was further strengthened by the institutional reward system which would not tolerate the long fallow period a professor would have to experience if he became genuinely involved in interdisciplinary work. In addition, an initial period of five to six years seemed essential before a new interdisciplinary complex would allow productive scholarship. Younger people were afraid to commit that much time, while older faculty were so well established and committed to other activities that they refused to spare the time.

The graduate council seemed aware that the institution was not likely to take even continuing criticism seriously except with regard to minor changes. The council hoped, therefore, to increase the selectivity of the graduate departments and, if time permitted, to assess the achievement of entering graduate students for better placement into programs. While course work might seem to some to be excessive, the fact that so many courses were required of graduate students was attributable to the heterogeneity of background of entering graduate students. Until more homogeneous preparation could be assured, courses would retain their importance, as would rather rigorous examinations and adherence to quite traditional theses. Except for teaching posts in junior colleges, there was little predisposition to emphasize training for teaching. Nor was there any real concern for the much publicized excessive length of time that graduate study required.

Some slight consideration was given to the excessively rigid departmental requirements for an undergraduate major on the part of graduate students. There was also some awareness that people within individual departments might be better off if they could talk across departmental lines and cooperate to some extent, but there was not much faith that this would happen. Some members of the council sensed that graduate students needed much more orientation to graduate work and quite early assessmment of individual strengths and weaknesses, but recognized that the time required for this careful guidance could not be accommodated within the institutional budgeting structure (which tied funding to full-time-equivalent students in specific courses). Overall, the graduate council seemed reasonably assured that the institution would ultimately achieve academic excellence and recognition in orthodox ways. But there was virtually no predisposition to overcome barriers which at least a few individuals recognized existed against innovation.

X

Guidelines for Change

Currently, American graduate education, although attempting to serve a multiplicity of purposes, uses only two basic program patterns: the education of individuals in research and the preparation of teachers for institutions of higher learning. The unresponsiveness of graduate schools to the needs for alternate designs condemns many people to a lifetime of second-rate status in powerful areas largely irrelevant to their training (for example, irrelevant to careers in government, industry and management, social work, and a number of vocations related to the health fields). Similarly, given the short half-life of a number of vocations requiring advanced training, and given the availability of current library resources and faculty members aware of frontier thinking, graduate schools have been almost completely unresponsive to the needs for reeducation and retraining of people in formal extension work.

Because of the organic ties between undergraduate and graduate education, American universities tend to treat graduate students as though they were undergraduates and to organize their learning along custodial or protective lines. Only the student protest of the 1960s began to dramatize that graduate students deserved forthright recognition as junior partners in professional work, rather than simply as older college students. This same linkage of graduate work to undergraduate work is responsible for an ineffective and inefficient funding of graduate education. The cost of graduate education has been centrally borne in most institutions by the budgets of undergraduate colleges supplemented by small internal and larger external grants, for the most part categorically related to research projects. Also, there is little hard information indicative of costs of graduate education. There is the general impression that graduate education is of necessity highly expensive; funds are properly devoted to it without relating those funds to the economically more profitable undergraduate effort. A reason for the lack of real success in upper division graduate institutions, although there is logical argument to support them, is this unhealthy linkage of undergraduate support to graduate education.

In a very real sense, graduate education is currently suffering from its successes in contributing to the growth of knowledge and to technological advance. These successes have given the public exaggerated expectations of the potential of graduate education. Fundamentally, "all graduate education can do is to make available bodies of knowledge and provide training and skills in the accumulation of knowledge and in methodologies appropriate to the resolution of problems. Ideally, it performs these functions in an environment conducive to intellectual growth and provides for periodic evaluations of this intellectual growth and competence."[1] When graduate students complain that their education does not impart values or provide immediate solutions for social problems, it indicates they have unreal expectations of what graduate education can accomplish.

But program changes are not enough. New options will succeed only if better methods are developed for identifying appropriate candidates, and graduate education has done very little with respect to this matter. Nor have graduate faculties come close to solving ways by which a greater number of minority group members

[1] Whaley, *Problems in Graduate Education*, p. 15.

can be admitted into graduate programs from which they could reasonably hope to emerge successfully some years later. "The graduate school should not attempt to control supply by admissions controls or quota systems but recognize instead that success on their part with new types of programs, aimed at providing highly trained manpower to resolve urgent problems of the present and the future, is the best assurance of maintaining proper balances between demand and supply. Graduate schools have obligations to assess as acurately as possible the opportunities existing for their different degree holders; but they also have responsibility for opening up new types of opportunities.[2]

Attempts to Change

Throughout the United States and Canada there is some evidence of hoped for, planned for, or attempted change, innovation, or reform in graduate education in the arts and sciences, but not as much as might be implied by the historic and continued criticisms of graduate education. Within the realm of curriculum and instruction, most institutions are attempting, in one way or another, at least to recognize the necessity for some interdisciplinary programs, and the various associations and learned societies make interdisciplinary work imperative. Similarly, the time students spend in obtaining graduate degrees, particularly the doctorate, is recognized as being excessive, and efforts should be made to compress a complete doctoral program into no more than four years beyond the bachelor's degree. But there is still either reluctance or inability on the part of institutions to impose the requisite constraints on departments to ensure that this norm is achieved.

In view of the alleged preoccupation of doctoral study with research, the attempts to strengthen research competence and to inject into doctoral programs specific and at the same time varied instruction concerning research tools and skills constitute a somewhat surprising cluster of recommendations. These attempts are especially characteristic of some of the humanistic fields such as history and English, while mathematical skills are deemed especially essential for social and behavioral scientists.

[2] Whaley, p. 21.

Research regarding admissions processes in graduate education provides reason for dissatisfaction with existing techniques. The slight positive relationships between previous academic performance or measures of academic aptitude and success in courses fail to account for most of the variance in graduate school performance. Graduate deans themselves and the reports of some of the disciplinary studies of graduate education also express dissatisfaction with the admissions procedure. However, there is no generally acceptable set of recommendations for change, only the aphorism that better admissions processes will mean better graduate students, hence better graduate schools. The entrance into graduate professional work of many minority group students and also many students who previously would not have sought graduate training is forcing thorough reconsideration of admissions policies. Minority group students have also forced graduate schools to examine programs of special relevance to somewhat specialized groups. Thus there is a substantial groundswell of interest in graduate programs in ethnic studies, in urban studies, and, to a somewhat lesser extent, in studies involving the concerns and life styles of women.

Perhaps the most widely discussed potential change in graduate education is the possibility of providing explicit instruction and experience in matters of pedagogy and curricular development. This concern may well have been forced first by serious student criticism of the nature of college teaching and second by the serious threat the highly recommended Doctor of Arts degree potentially poses to the Ph.D. degree. A substantial number of graduate schools thus are experimenting with models to provide training and experience in teaching, and these models typically consist of some seminar experience, some observation of teaching, and some reasonably supervised teaching experience. The sophisticated attempts provide graduate students with several different teaching experiences, each differing in complexity and longevity.

With respect to the organizational and structural component of graduate education, the overall thrust is to regularize practice and to make patterns symmetrical. Thus there is awareness that the present degree structure is highly irregular, with the meaning of such degrees as the Associate of Arts or the Master of Arts quite unclear. It would seem desirable, then, to clarify the significance of various degree levels and to regularize the time taken for completion of degree requirements. Attempts are also being made to regularize the substantial programs for postdoctoral students and to develop some ways to bring those programs into the central institutional registration process. Similarly, regional accreditation agencies are seeking devices by which to regularize and systematize minimal standards for institutional graduate performance, especially in view of the many developing institutions which aspire to full graduate status. Also, partly to control proliferating graduate programs and partly to regularize them, statewide boards of coordination or control are attempting to review and reject or approve recommended graduate programs.

Graduate faculties have finally begun to make some adjustments in matters long the objects of criticisms and complaint. Graduate schools or universities are tending to allow individual departments in matters long the objects of criticism and complaint. Grad-Institutions are likewise beginning to modify examining procedures, intending to place critical screening examinations much earlier in the candidate's career. They also seem disposed to consider elimination or reform of final oral examinations, which have too frequently degenerated into rituals or opportunities for professional sadism. A few institutions are attempting to remove or even modify the dissertation requirements.

Guidelines for the Future

These attempts to change or recommendations for change taken in the aggregate suggest some plausible overall directions but these are in themselves insufficient to assist planning for the future of graduate education. They do provide a basis from which can be derived, at least speculatively, guidelines and criteria for institutional consideration.

Alternative Tracks. Even though some professors believe that long and irregular periods of graduate study result in deepened scholarship, there is no evidence that this in fact results. Rather, graduate candidates who finish their degrees more quickly seem ultimately to be the more productive. Because people will use their graduate training in any of several different ways, there should be commonly based provisions for quite distinctly different options. The

provision of alternative tracks which can provide differential training seems preferable to the creation of new degrees such as the
Doctor of Arts or the Doctor of Engineering.

As a beginning, there should be at least three tracks: a research orientation; a teaching orientation; and an applied orientation. Assuming a four-year postbaccalaureate program, candidates
clearly destined for a research career would devote two years to
course and seminar work and two years to perfecting research
competency and gaining experience through reasonably sophisticated
research for their dissertations. The second track would relate to
those fields in which the only practical career paths lead to teaching,
or in which individuals can early detect whether teaching will be
appropriate for them. Students could spend the first two years in
course and seminar work and perhaps give specific attention to
the problems of teaching. A third year would include supervised
teaching, studying the problems of college students and colleges and
universities, and giving preliminary thought to a dissertation. The
last year would be the dissertation year, with a clear understanding
that the range of thesis topics would be much broader than for the
purely research degree. Thus a student aspiring to teach chemistry
could do a chemical dissertation, or a dissertation on how to teach
recent developments in chemistry, or even a dissertation involving
the administration of collegiate chemistry programs. The third
orientation quite clearly would be inappropriate for some fields.
Yet, as business, industry, and government expand the range of
positions requiring advanced training, the number of fields for
which an applied track would be appropriate is also likely to grow.
The division of time would be comparable to the division of time
for the teaching track: two years of basic graduate study, one year
of internship or work experience, and one year for the completion
of a dissertation that probably would be of an applied nature. Thus
an economics dissertation could deal with specific and applied policy
implications of economic decisions. Conceivably, and in many cases
hopefully, the internship would clearly relate to the subsequent dissertation. One could visualize a graduate student identifying an
applied problem early in his internship experience, elaborating the
means by which he would study it during the latter part of the

internship, and being prepared to move immediately to his research during the fourth year of graduate work.

Elements of Curriculum. Such an organization of the Ph.D. program into alternative tracks implies much more formal classification and organization of the graduate learning experience. It seems axiomatic that not all courses are designed to achieve the same sorts of objectives and that some means is necessary to distinguish between them. For this purpose, any of several sets of categories would be appropriate. One, which was originally designed to establish order within the undergraduate curriculum, appears to have distinct possibilities. It contains four elements, each of which would generally consume a fourth of a student's time, although the distribution of time is less important than the attempt to classify as a means of ultimately producing a more symmetrical graduate program. First, whether a field is disciplinary and lodged in an orthodox department or interdisciplinary and lodged in an institute or center, common substantive and procedural areas should be mastered by all graduate students. These areas, then, would define a set of common requirements taken by all students during the first two years of graduate study. At least part of these could be required for students seeking only a master's degree; all of them would be required for students anticipating a full doctoral program. The second element of the doctoral program is the special field of concentration, which very likely would consist of the dissertation and related work. The concentration on a dissertation should derive out of a context somewhat broader than the thesis study but considerably more specialized than the common requirements. The third element should involve the study of materials clearly viewed as context. Thus, an American Civil War dissertation would be undertaken from the context of course work dealing with that general period of American, European, or even Far Eastern history. A last element of the doctoral program would be aimed at broadening the entire intellectual base of graduate study. Students would use this time to elect widely both from within and without the department in which they concentrate. It might even be desirable to consider some provisions which would force students to undertake course work outside a department in fields that have direct relevance for the field of concentration.

Master's Program. Many of the points made in connection with doctoral work could with equal validity be made concerning master's programs. For example, a specified length of time to fulfill requirements should be determined, and courses to achieve different sorts of objectives should be designed. However, several additional recommendations pertaining exclusively to the master's degree can be made. First, there is no reason to warrant a research orientation in a master's degree program. If the degree is taken as part of a doctoral program, the research orientation will come afterward, and if the degree is a terminal one, its purpose should be primarily broadening or concerned with a technical application of a vocational or professional skill. Thus, the thesis has no legitimate part in the master's program. Second, the master's degree should be reestablished as a normal part of doctoral study. Hence, the first year should be quite clearly specified and so designed that it could equally serve as a termination of study or as a broad base for more specialized work at the doctoral level. However, there should be room in the master's program for a decided orientation toward problem-solving. Many people seek master's degrees so as to obtain some understanding and skills which can be applied to solving broad social problems. Probably, the master's degree in arts and sciences should be more or less equally divided between work in a prescribed core and work that could contribute greater depth of understanding as a basis for subsequent doctoral study. If the master's program is designed to develop certain competences needed for the terminal degree or for progression into doctoral work, then the design should allow for a final examination that would both signify the end of the master's program and serve as a qualifying exam for doctoral work.

Interdisciplinary Work. A curricular structure that makes explicit provision for broadening experiences for graduate students clearly implies great value placed on interdisciplinary work. Increasingly, graduate programs should make such provisions, both for students who need a broader foundation upon which to build a disciplinary concentration and for students concerned with an interdisciplinary problem. A number of devices can be recommended to facilitate interdisciplinary work. For departments to allow, or even to require, a certain proportion of graduate work to be taken outside a department is probably the simplest device. Clearly, if this is to function effectively, all departments must be willing to accept graduate students from other fields and to make appropriate modifications so that the students would not be penalized for having lacked any of the usual prerequisites. This is not an extreme posture, for increasingly the validity of specific prerequisites for most subjects can be challenged. But in addition to simply using the interdisciplinary capacity that exists in the full range of courses offered in a university, one major and several minor devices can be suggested. Centers and institutes are providing one form of interdisciplinary work, and institutions might seriously consider expanding their number. In a less formal way, special interdisciplinary committees can be created with relatively little difficulty to serve as advisors and managers of the programs of students who want a specially contrived interdisciplinary program.

Relevance. In many ways related to the preceding recommendations but of a different order is the recommendation that graduate faculties place greater emphasis on providing relevant experiences for graduate students. One gains the impression that graduate programs too frequently have been put together along the single dimension of intellectual experience in courses and seminars. This dimension is by no means invalid. One can argue strongly that students should have the experience of studying different courses with different professors. Indeed, greater variety along this dimension is probably in order, but greater attention to other dimensions of experience could conceivably result in a much richer graduate student career. To indicate some possibilities, it can be argued that every graduate student should have some field or clinical experience designed to establish more closely the relationships between academic work and reality, and to perfect skills of application. A well-contrived teaching experience is one example; an internship spent in an industrial context, another. In addition, each graduate student should have some experience working as a member of a group focusing on a specific problem. As originally conceived, the graduate seminar was intended to do this: the major professor blocked out a domain and each of the students contributed an element to its understanding. Some of the group research within the natural sciences also seems to provide this sort of group experience. Graduate student testimony suggests that for many graduate students the opportunity for a focused group effort is lacking, yet much subsequent professional work requires some expertise in functioning in a group of professionals. Thus, in instances in which group experience is not already available, appropriate situations should be contrived. There can, of course, be some serendipity. The graduate school of education at Stanford in 1971 found its faculty to be rather shorthanded owing to professors being on leave and unforeseen professional attrition. Graduate students themselves were asked to assume some responsibilities for advising entering graduate students and for maintaining a high graduate student *esprit de corps*. Thus, groups of students have come into existence by concentrating energies on commonly shared problems, with noticeable profit for the entire graduate program and for the development of group skills on the part of the graduate students themselves. This emphasis on the experiential may disturb some graduate faculties who assume responsibility only for the development in students of substantive knowledge. However, it should be stressed that graduate study should contribute to the total development of an individual and that such development does require specific provision of a variety of relevant activities.

Examinations. The great interest during the late 1960s on the part of students to change grading and examining patterns suggested that existing procedures were grossly inadequate. Comments of graduate students about the grading and examining they experienced suggests that malfunctioning is not exclusively an undergraduate phenomenon. There is considerable need for regularizing and improving examining procedures. Here it is argued that a graduate program in arts and sciences, like a program in one of the professional fields, should be designed to develop specific competences in students. These competences should be clearly specified so that graduate students understand what it is they are trying to develop. Examinations, then, should be so constructed as to test whether those competences have indeed been achieved. One obtains the distinct impression that questions in preliminary qualifying or candidacy examinations are intended to find out what students will do with the question. Thus, different students could go in quite different directions as they respond to the tasks set for them. Such openness possesses some intriguing elements, but can also contribute to unreliability in assessing student performance and can cause the student a great deal of anxiety as he tries to determine what precisely is expected of him. Several devices seem appropriate in this regard. First, every department offering graduate work should compile a graduate student manual which would indicate quite specifically at what points examinations would be conducted and what competences students would be expected to display. Then, if professors would make even slight efforts to construct examination questions designed to elicit these competences, the entire process might be made more rational. As a general rule, qualifying examinations have been placed unfortunately late in graduate students' programs, with a resultant dilemma. On the one hand, if a student successfully passes his courses, examining professors will be unwilling to allow that achievement to be sacrificed even if he does not perform well in the examination; on the other hand, the faculty is faced with the inconsistency of a student performing satisfactorily in courses yet judged incompetent on a reexamination of the competences those courses were intended to develop. It can be argued that the qualifying examination dealing with competences and areas clearly specified in advance should be placed at the end of the first year of graduate study. Having demonstrated such capacities, students should be relatively free from examinations and should prepare for the actual professional demands of research, teaching, or application.

Limiting the Curriculum. A prevailing characteristic of college and university curriculum, especially during the 1950s and 1960s, has been enormous proliferation of the number of courses offered. This is to be expected in view of the expanding areas of knowledge. However, courses all too frequently seem to have been added to college catalogs with no particular pattern or plan in mind save that of exposing a professor's own research interest or indicating an emerging parameter of a subject. This often results in impressive patterns of courses which on closer examination reveal major gaps in what should be basic preparation for graduate students. Departments, centers, or institutes should therefore ask themselves collectively what courses should be available if adequately prepared graduates are to be produced. Such group discussion of a departmental curriculum can quickly reveal serious gaps and can result in all the members of a department assuming a collective responsibility for the

curriculum rather than allowing it to represent primarily the idiosyncratic interests of individual faculty members. Departments would
thus assume a responsibility for graduate curricula similar to that
exercised by faculties with respect to general education requirements,
graduation requirements, and patterns of courses for undergraduate
students. In larger departments it is not asking too much for a curriculum committee to be charged with constant scrutiny of course
offerings and to be given some power to recommend substantial
changes. This process very likely would reduce significantly the overall number of courses being offered, and this, in turn, might ultimately
have implications for the economics of the institution.

Admissions. Admissions processes should be modified, but the
precise direction of change is still somewhat vague. Harvey's recently
summarized research of graduate admissions indicates a start:
"Some order and philosophy should be brought to the admitting of
students for graduate work. The impression exists that the admissions process on the graduate level is haphazard, if not indeed
capricious. It is doubtful that many departments are aware of the
limitations of grades or objective tests as predictors. Certainly, most
of the departments have not conducted validity studies of these
predictors at their institutions. Each graduate school should central-
ize enough of the admissions function so that (1) recruitment might
be improved; (2) limitations on the information in candidates'
folders realized; and (3) follow-up studies of admitted students
made. A better understanding of the relationship between admissions
criteria and graduate school success might be the result."[3]

From such a limited but still systematic base, problems of
how to identify potentiality among minority group members, how
to identify potential creativity, and how to identify differential aptitudes for teaching, research, or application would be possible. Larger
graduate institutions have considerable psychometric expertise in
departments of psychology, sociology, social psychology, and education. These, properly exploited, might help the entire graduate program improve admissions. Such a recommendation implies some
presumptuousness on the part of those expert in such matters, but
perhaps the time has come when graduate departments can no

[3] James Harvey, "Graduate School Admissions," *College and University Bulletin,* Nov. 15, 1971, pp. 4–5.

longer afford undue diffidence on the part of their own relevant expertise.

Improvement of Instruction. Student commentary suggests that much of the teaching they experience in seminars and graduate courses is far from effective and contributes little to their educational development. If this is so, it would seem reasonable that graduate faculties should give greater attention to the processes of instruction, guidance, advising, and supervision. Perhaps as a first step departments might begin to accumulate evidence concerning the teaching activities of professors as they are considered for promotion, reappointment, or tenure. Then, too, all professors might be encouraged to make greater use of student evaluation forms, which can be modified to be appropriate for styles of graduate teaching. Occasionally, members of a department might find it instructive and appropriate to engage in discussions of the nature of graduate teaching. If psychiatrists can discuss and change clinical procedures, if seasoned judges can participate in seminars on how to improve the judicial process, so should it be reasonable to expect departments of history, biology, or economics to ponder how the various acts of teaching can best be performed.

Departmentalism. It appears increasingly true that the powers and prerogatives of departments should in some ways be limited. One way that seems practicable is to strengthen the office of graduate dean by assigning him a definite role in the selection of faculty and a review authority for both the administrative details of a graduate program and the curricula developed by departments. If the principle could be accepted that the graduate dean could by right review course offerings in fields quite different from his own and could with propriety question departments concerning gaps or redundancies, this fact alone might produce substantial changes in the patterns of courses. Some institutions may achieve the same end (that is, maintain departments in the arts and sciences but still provide for greater responsiveness to broader institutional needs) by providing for divisional deans with considerable influence over appointments, control over budgets, and explicit responsibility for curricular matters. This last responsibility might be discharged through the use of associate deans, one for undergraduate studies and one for graduate studies. Still other institutions could deliberately foster expansion of the number of institutes and centers which through competition with departments might bring about greater concern for curricular and teaching matters. These suggestions, of course, run counter to the caveats contained in some of the case material describing changes in graduate schools. This suggestion, to assign greater power to administrative officers, is made deliberately and is based on the belief that departments, in essence seeking primarily to replicate their own members, do require stimulation and pressure from outside to be persuaded to modify additional practice.

Dissertations. While there will be variation according to field, as a general rule the nature of doctoral dissertations should be modified to allow a greater range of appropriate topics and methodology. An appropriate guideline to the range of dissertation effort would be a cataloging of the research and scholarly efforts of the graduate faculty itself. Thus, some professors are eminent bibliographers; others concentrate on theoretical model-building; others synthesize and interpret the work of others. Some professors devote their entire careers to producing isolated segments of new knowledge, while other professors deal constantly with broad issues and policy implications. If a given kind of scholarly activity can be judged as appropriate for a professor and become the basis on which he is rewarded, the same kind of activity should be judged appropriate as a dissertation for a graduate student. In the field of history, then, a detailed examination of a specific historical event, a broad, reflective essay on some historical trend, a biography, or even an historical novel should be appropriate. Similarly, in the biological sciences, a tightly controlled experimental study, an evaluative study of industrial uses of biological knowledge, a study on the history of science, or a study involving changed methods of teaching biological science should also be appropriate, for these all are indicative of the range of scholarly and research activities of practicing academicians.

Liberalizing the Program. Just as the professional schools are attempting to broaden the education of their students through incorporating materials from quite divergent subjects, so should graduate departments provide for broadening experiences at the Ph.D. level. If it is appropriate for a school of medicine or agriculture to introduce international dimensions to the curriculum, it would seem wise for doctoral programs in the arts and sciences to add elements of internationalism. If it is wise for a school of law to include more of the contemporary, the arts and sciences might also add contemporary materials. Assuming some validity to the concept of two or more separate cultures within the intellectual world, then there is reason for graduate departments to build bridges between cultures within the graduate experiences to introduce students to different cultures. Thus a graduate student in one of the natural sciences might be encouraged to take some work for graduate credit in the area of the humanities. Conceivably, work in the humanities could throw new and intensive light on perplexities within the science work itself.

Originally, graduate education was expected to prepare both scholars and broadly educated men and, later on, women also. Over the years that second mission has been lost sight of. It is still possible to restore some elements of that goal, but to do so will require substantial curricula revision. It is our belief that that revision should be undertaken.

Index

A

Accreditation: in Canada, 230; of graduate education, 172-174, 186, 237; of professional schools, 17

Administration education: continuing, 35; internationalization in, 63; internships in, 24; organizational patterns in, 33, 54-55; research in, 26; social and behavioral sciences in, 42

Admissions: to graduate education, 117-121, 236, 244-245; to professional education, 55-56

Agriculture education: balance in, 20; continuing, 35; internationalization in, 64

ALLEN, D. C., 103n

ALLEN, H. R., 69n

ALTMAN, R. A., 178-179

American Council on Education, 188, 189

American University, 175-176

Amherst College, 176-177

ANDERSON, C. J., 213-214

ANDERSON, G. L., 7n

Antioch College, 38, 39, 177, 183

Architecture education: balance in,

20; field work in, 58; flexibility in, 49; reforms of, 31-32, 40, 75-76, 180

ARROWSMITH, W., 188-189

Assembly on University Goals and Governance, 122

Association of American Colleges, 52

Association of American Universities, 214

ASTIN, H., 82n

Atlanta University, 137, 175, 176

B

Bard College, 177

BAYER, A. E., 82n

BECKER, H. S., 89

Behaviorism vs. humanism, 26-27, 104-106

BERDAHL, R., 170, 171-172

BERELSON, B., 83n, 84n, 97-100, 102, 107, 117, 121, 207, 230

BERG, I., 9

BIDWELL, P., 66

BLOOM, B. S., 76, 80

Boston College, 142-143

BOWEN, H. R., 114-115

BRODERICK, A., 45n

Index

253

29-76; relevance of, 86-87; socialization in, 16-17, 35, 66-68; specialization in, 5-6, 11; standards in, 5, 16; status of, 1-14; and technological revolution, 11-12; temporal readjustments in, 11, 24, 27, 31-32, 48-54, 71, 75; theory-and-skill conflict in, 5, 12-14, 17, 19-24, 87-88. *See also* specific professions
Professions, nature of, 1-3
Public health education, 65-66
PUSEY, N. M., 3, 50*n*, 70

R

Redlands, University of, 183
REICH, C., 97
REICHERT, K., 41*n*
Research, 25-26, 94-95
RICHARD, J. M., JR., 118-119
Rochester, University of, 196-198, 201-202
ROOSE, K. J., 213-214
ROSENSTEIN, A. B., 18-19, 25*n*
Rutgers University, 159

S

San Fernando Valley State College, 138
San Jose State College, 138
SANAGARO, P., 41
Sarah Lawrence College, 69, 200-202
SCHINDLER, J. S., 53*n*
SILK, L. S., 26*n*, 53*n*
SIZER, T. R., 41*n*
SMELSER, N. J., 119*n*
Smith College, 176-177
SNELL, J. L., 103*n*, 112-113
Social and behavioral sciences, 41-43, 74, 83-85
Social work education: balance in, 20, 79; calendar reform in, 52, 53-54; field experiences in, 34, 58; independent research in, 60; interdisciplinary work in, 41; manpower needs in, 16; organizational patterns in, 32; research in, 26; undergraduate work in, 31, 46

Southern Mississippi, University of, 159
SPURR, S. H., 56-57, 156-157, 159*n*, 163-164
Stanford University, 14, 17-18, 25-26, 30, 38, 39, 40, 43-44, 47, 101-102, 113, 122, 126-127, 130, 186, 223-226, 242
Stephens College, 38-39, 177
Stockton Junior College, 178
Students: developmental needs of, 216-218; financial aid to, 214-216; graduate education criticized by, 103-104; grouping of, 38, 111; and protests, 10-11; quality of, 3, 8-9; quantity of, 3, 5. *See also* Minority persons
Superboards, 167-172, 186-187, 237
Syracuse University, 102, 140, 163

T

TAYLOR, C. L., 3*n*, 50*n*, 70*n*
Teachers, college, preparation of, 93, 113, 188-209, 236, 238, 241; changes in, 189-195, 206-209; degrees for, 155, 159-164; experimental programs in, 195-206; principles of, 191-193; and supervised experience, 191-193, 226, 228
Teaching assistants, 192, 194-195, 198-200, 208
Teaching methods in professional education, 34-35, 37, 57-63
Theological education: applicants for, 3; balance in, 21-22; continuing, 70; field experiences in, 24, 34, 58; flexibility in, 49-50; interdisciplinary work in, 40; relevance of, 87; social and behavioral sciences in, 41-42; undergraduate work in, 30-31
Theses, 211-212, 246
THOMPSON, W. P., 228*n*
Toronto, University of, 206
TROW, M., 105-106
TUCKER, A., 103*n*
TYLER, R., 69, 76, 80-81